I0750529

Washington
and his
Masonic Compeers

WASHINGTON
AND HIS
MASONIC COMPEERS

SIDNEY HAYDEN

Athens ‡ Manchester

Washington and his Masonic Compeers

Old Book Publishing Ltd

Book Cover Design: Old Book Publishing Ltd

Title of original: Washington and his Masonic Compeers
Originally published in 1866

ISBN–10: 1-78107-072-5
ISBN–13: 978-1-78107-072-7

EDITOR'S NOTE

WASHINGTON

AND HIS

MASONIC COMPEERS.

BY

SIDNEY HAYDEN,

PAST MASTER OF RURAL AMITY LODGE, NO. 70, PENNSYLVANIA.

Illustrated with a copy of a Masonic Portrait of Washington,

PAINTED FROM LIFE, NEVER BEFORE PUBLISHED,

WITH NUMEROUS OTHER ENGRAVINGS.

"The memory of a brother is precious;
I will write it here."

FIFTH EDITION.

NEW YORK

MASONIC PUBLISHING AND MANUFACTURING CO.

432 BROOME STREET.

1866.

TO THE

HON. JOHN L. LEWIS,

PAST GRAND MASTER AND PAST GRAND HIGH PRIEST OF NEW YORK,
M. E. GENERAL GRAND HIGH PRIEST OF THE GENERAL GRAND CHAPTER OF
THE UNITED STATES, ETC.,

This Book

IS FRATERNALLY DEDICATED,

AS A SLIGHT TESTIMONIAL OF RESPECT FOR AN EMINENT MASON AND
DISTINGUISHED FELLOW-LABORER IN THE QUARRIES OF
AMERICAN MASONIC HISTORY,

BY HIS

SINCERE FRIEND AND MASONIC BROTHER,

THE AUTHOR.

PREFACE.

Biographies of Washington, and the most eminent of our countrymen who were contemporary with him, have been often written so far as relates to their public acts, and in many of them we have also a portraiture of their personal and domestic history. Such delineations, interwoven with their memoirs, give us a truer estimate of the character of the individual, and enable us to weigh with more exactness the impulses and influences that have impelled or retarded him in his public career.

Ancestry and kindred, domestic and social scenes in youth, mental, moral, and religious training, are the germs of character; and after stepping from the threshold of youth upon the platform of manhood, each foot-print in the onward path of life bears some impress of past and passing associations. These are therefore a part of every individual's true history, and his biography is imperfect without them. History is but a compound of these influences and actions, and each is a lamp to enlighten its pages. Extinguish it, and a shadow falls on some line of truth.

Our historians and biographers seldom mention a Fraternity which has existed in this country from its early colonial existence, and embraced in its membership a large number of our countrymen whose names are inscribed on our literary, civil, and military rolls of honor. Has this arisen from a prejudice against the institution of Masonry, or from a belief that its influences are unimportant?

The virtues which ennoble human character, are taught and cultivated in the lodge-room; and the mystic labors of the Master and his Craftsmen when convened, are such as fit men for the domestic relations of life and the highest duties of citizenship. WASHINGTON, with a full knowledge of the subject, wrote: "*Being persuaded that a just application of the principles on which the Masonic Fraternity is founded, must be promotive of virtue and public prosperity, I shall always be happy to advance the interest of the Society, and be considered by them a deserving brother.*"

As this part of WASHINGTON's history has been entirely omitted by his biographers, and studiously misrepresented by pamphleteers, the author of these sketches has made a diligent research in veritable records and documents of the last century for information on the subject. He has gratefully to acknowledge the assistance of many eminent Masons in this labor. Every Grand Master who was applied to, gave a cheering commendation and assent for a full examination of all records in his jurisdiction; and officers and members of lodges were ever ready to render all the aid in their power.

The brevity of many early Masonic records, and the entire loss of others, have left some parts of our work apparently unfinished in leading facts ; and time has silenced every tongue that a half century ago might have given interesting details of incidents, to which existing records sometimes barely allude. The unrecorded incidents in the Masonic life of WASHINGTON, which his compeers used to relate with so much satisfaction, are now, in the eye of history, among the uncertain traditions of the past, and we have given few of them a place in our sketch of his Masonic life. We have preferred the broken fragments of veritable records, to traditions, however pleasing, and apparently reliable.

WASHINGTON'S Masonic history might have been given by his contémporaries, in all its proportions, with fulness of detail. Now, it is like a beautiful column in ruins,—its parts broken, scattered, and moss-grown. We have labored industriously to collect these Parian fragments, and only wish some hand more skilful than our own, might have given each its due place and polish in the most beautiful pillar of the temple of American Masonry. We have faithfully used the gavel, the square, and the trowel in our work, and confidently submit to the Overseers all which pertains to their use. With the mallet and engraver's chisel we are less skilled, and the Masonic connoisseur will perhaps find in this part of our work little to admire. We have not presumed to engrave any lines of beauty of our own, but hope the eye will not look in vain for them in the memorial stones we present, which were wrought by the hands of WASHINGTON and his Masonic Compeers.

Of the Compeers, we have not written labored sketches. We have only given such Masonic facts as came under our observation in our researches in the Masonic history of WASHINGTON; but in each case, they are from veritable records. While they establish the Masonic brotherhood of the individual, we hope they may throw some light on his character, and make his memory more dear to our American brethren.

THE AUTHOR.

ATHENS,

Pennsylvania, April 10, 1866.

CONTENTS.

PART I.

PART II.

MAJOR HENRY PRICE.

PORTRAIT

SIR WILLIAM JOHNSON.

PORTRAIT.

SIR JOHN JOHNSON.

PEYTON RANDOLPH.

PORTRAIT.

ILLUSTRATIONS.

PART I.

WASHINGTON.

WASHINGTON.

CHAPTER I.

WASHINGTON's birth contemporaneous with introduction of Warranted Lodges in America.—Date of his birth from family record.—Emigration of his ancestors to America.—Death of his father.—His boyhood.—Paternal instruction.—Anecdote of his love of truth.—Faithfulness of his mother.—His early education.—His influence with his youthful associates.—Excels in athletic exercises.—His brother LAWRENCE an officer under Admiral VERNON.—Receives a commission as midshipman in the British navy.—Relinquishes it at the wish of his mother.—Engages as a land surveyor.—His commission as such.—An old log-hut in Clarke County.—Surveys for Lord FAIRFAX.—Illness of his brother.—WASHINGTON accompanies him to Barbadoes.—His death and will.—WASHINGTON becomes possessed of Mount Vernon.—Is appointed adjutant-general of Virginia militia.—Appearance and general character when he came to manhood.—A candidate for Masonry.

THE introduction of Freemasonry into America, and the birth of WASHINGTON, had nearly a contemporaneous date. The annals of the fraternity give no account of regularly organized lodges in this country until the third decade of the eighteenth century, and in its second year GEORGE WASHINGTON was born. For the record of his natal day, we are indebted to no heraldric college, no public register, but the old family Bible of his ancestors is still preserved, where, in the handwriting of his mother, as is supposed, the following record is found:

"GEORGE WASHINGTON, son to AUGUSTINE, and MARY, his wife, was born ye 11th day of February, 173½, about 10 in the morning, and was baptized the 3d of April following. Mr. BEVERLY WHITING and Capt. CHRISTOPHER BROOKS, godfathers, and Mrs. MILDRED GREGORY, godmother."

This date is according to the old style calendar then in use, and is equivalent to the 22d of February, 1732, new style.

The ancestors of GEORGE WASHINGTON emigrated to America from the north of England during the protectorate of OLIVER CROMWELL. His great-grandfather, JOHN WASHINGTON, is said to have inherited the blood of English nobility, both by paternal and maternal descent. He came to America and settled on the borders of the Potomac, Westmoreland County, Virginia, in 1657. From JOHN, first in the line of descent was LAWRENCE; second, AUGUSTINE; and third, GEORGE WASHINGTON, who was the third child of AUGUSTINE, and the first by his second marriage. His mother was a daughter of Colonel BALL, of Virginia.

His father removed, while he was a child, to the banks of the Rappahannock, opposite Fredericksburg, and died there when GEORGE was but eleven years old. We know but little of the paternal instruction he received in his boyhood, for his early orphanage, and the sparseness of detail relating to the domestic history of the yeomanry of Virginia at that period, leaves a blank in his youthful history, which his future greatness makes us wish were filled with all such incidents as became the germs of future character. It is said, however, by one of his early biographers, that his father instilled into his mind a noble and generous disposition; taught him to be kind and amiable to his playmates, and liberal in sharing with them any presents of fruits or cakes he might receive; telling him at the same time, that the great and good God delights above all things to see children love one another, and that He will assuredly reward all who act an amiable part.

The story of the cherry-tree and the hatchet has been often told, but the moral heroism of the tale is so characteristic of the man in after-life, and has so often swelled the breasts of youthful listeners to whom it has been related, with resolutions to bravely tell the truth under all circumstances, that we again repeat it, to inculcate that noblest masonic virtue, *the love of truth.*

"When George was about six years old, he was made the wealthy master of a *hatchet*, of which, like most boys, he was immoderately fond, and was constantly going about chopping every thing that came in his way. One day, in the garden, where he often amused himself hacking his mother's pea-bushes, he unluckily tried the edge of his hatchet on the body of a beautiful young English cherry-tree, which he barked so terribly, that the tree never got the better of it. The next morning, the old gentleman finding out what had befallen his tree, which, by the by, was a great favorite, came into the house, and with much warmth, asked for the mischievous author, declaring at the same time that he would not have taken five guineas for the tree. Nobody could tell him any thing about it.

Presently GEORGE and his hatchet made their appearance. 'GEORGE,' said his father, '*do you know who killed that beautiful little cherry-tree yonder in the garden?*' This was a *tough question*, and GEORGE staggered under it for a moment; but quickly recovered himself, and looking at his father, the sweet face of youth brightened with the inexpressible charm of all-conquering truth, and he bravely cried out, '*I can't* tell a *lie*, Pa; you know I *can't* tell a *lie. I cut it with my hatchet!*' '*Run to my arms*, you dearest boy,' cried his father in transports—'*run to my arms! Glad am I*, GEORGE, that you killed my tree, for you have paid me for it a *thousand times. Such an act of heroism in my son*, is worth more than a thousand trees, though blossomed with silver, and their fruits of purest gold.'"

To WASHINGTON'S mother has been also accorded, and is no doubt due, the credit of so directing the mental, moral, and religious character of his youth, as to give an exalted tone to every action of his after-life. Left, by her husband's death, with the weighty care of five children, she took upon herself the superintendence of their education, and the management of the complicated affairs of their estates, and so acquitted herself as to gain the proud satisfaction of seeing them all come forward into active life with fair prospects, and her first-born become the most beloved and exalted of American citizens. Though inheriting the name, the patrimony, and noble virtues of his father, history has paid its tribute to the faithfulness of his mother, by writing him a *widow's son.*

The schools of the colonies did not afford at that time great advantages for education, and WASHINGTON'S attainments were comprised within a knowledge of reading, writing, and arithmetic at first; but he afterwards studied surveying, geography, and history, in the first of which he became proficient. In such pursuits his early years were spent. Even during his boyhood he is said to have manifested a military taste, and to have exerted a commanding influence over his youthful associates, in all their amusements; and the well-remembered story of his casting a stone across the Rappahannock, a feat said never to have been accomplished by another, is proof that he excelled in athletic exercises. It was such scenes that afterwards fitted him to encounter perils, and take pleasure in adventures that needed strength of body, perseverance, and confidence in his own powers to insure success.

WASHINGTON's eldest brother, LAWRENCE, was an officer in the colonial troops, sent under Admiral VERNON, in the expedition against Carthagena, in South America; and through his influence, and in accordance with his own wishes, a commission as midshipman in a British ship of war, stationed off the coast of Virginia, was procured for him, when he was fifteen years of age; but in obedience to the wishes of his mother, he was induced to relinquish this commission, which his own desires and those of his brother made him anxious to retain. He engaged soon after as a land surveyor, and made such proficiency, that he soon became skilful in that profession. The records of Culpepper County state that on the 20th of July, 1749 (o. s.), "GEORGE WASHINGTON, Gent., produced a commission from the President and Master of William and Mary College, appointing him to be surveyor of this county; which was read, and thereupon he took the usual oaths to his majesty's person and government, and took and subscribed the abjuration oath and test, and then took the oath of surveyor according to law."

His employments as surveyor often called him into distant parts of the colony; and there was standing a few years ago, in Clarke County, an old log-hut, which well authenticated tradition states was occupied by him while surveying lands there for Lord FAIRFAX. It was about twelve feet square, and was divided into an upper and a lower room, the upper one of which was used to deposit his instruments. It was at least an interesting memorial of his humble life, before his merits called him to a more public sphere of action.

WASHINGTON was engaged as a surveyor for Lord FAIRFAX nearly three years, during which the open seasons were spent among the rich, uncultivated valleys and wild mountains of Virginia, and the winters with his mother at Fredericksburg, and his brother LAWRENCE at Mount Vernon. During the last year his brother becoming an invalid, went to the Barbadoes for his health, and WASHINGTON accompanied him. He returned in the spring of 1751, and soon after died, leaving his estate at Mount Vernon to his infant daughter, with a provision in his will, that if she died without issue, it should go to his brother GEORGE. She did so die in 1752, and WASHINGTON came into possession of the spot, whose fame has since become immortal,—not from its bearing the name of an English noble, but from its having been the cherished home and final resting-place of the greatest American citizen. WASHINGTON then was nineteen years of age, and held the position of adjutant-general in the Virginia militia, with the rank of major. He was said by his contemporaries at this period of his life to be grave, silent, and thoughtful, diligent and methodical in business, dignified in his appearance, strictly honorable in all his actions, and a stranger to dissipation and riot. Such was his early history and character when, in 1752, in the twenty-first year of his age, he offered himself to Fredericksburg Lodge as a candidate for the mysteries of Masonry.

CHAPTER II.

First introduction of Warranted Lodges in America.—First in Boston.—Philadelphia.—Charleston.—Origin of lodge in Fredericksburg.—Its officers in 1752.—WASHINGTON'S initiation.—Passing.—Raising.—The Bible and seal of Fredericksburg Lodge.—Brevity of early Masonic records.—WASHINGTON but twenty years old when initiated.—Time intervening between that and further degrees.—Sent by the governor of Virginia with message to French commander on Ohio.—Incidents of his journey.—His Indian name.—Commencement of French and Indian War.—WASHINGTON placed in command of Virginia forces.—His capitulation at Fort Necessity.—Joins General BRADDOCK'S expedition.—Performs the burial-service of that officer.—Unjust distinction towards colonial officers.—WASHINGTON visits Boston on the subject.—Becomes enamored with Miss PHILLIPSE.—Again takes command of the Virginia forces.—Participates in the capture of Duquesne.—Retires from military service.—Claims of some that he was made a Mason in a British military lodge without foundation.—Lodges held under different authorities at this time in America.—Lodge of Fredericksburg takes a new warrant from Scotland.—Washington Masonic Cave.—Elected member of House of Burgesses.—His first appearance in the assembly.—His marriage.—His domestic life previous to the Revolution.—Want of Masonic records in Virginia of this period.

ARRANTED Lodges had not been in existence in America twenty years, when WASHINGTON came to manhood; for we have no record of a regular lodge in this country held under authority of any recognized Grand Lodge previous to his birth. The first regular lodge, whose records exist, was established in Boston, in 1733, by HENRY PRICE, by virtue of a deputation from the Grand Master of the Grand Lodge of England, appointing him Provincial Grand Master of New England. In the following year, under an extension of his authority over all America, regular warrants were granted to lodges not only in New England, but in Philadelphia and Charleston, S. C.; so that while WASHINGTON was yet in his swaddling-clothes, the star of American Masonry, which arose in the East about the period of his birth, may be said to have rested over the place where the young child was.

Before WASHINGTON came to manhood, a lodge had been organized in Fredericksburg, under authority from THOMAS OXNARD, Provincial Grand Master at Boston, whose authority also extended over all the English colonies in America; and in 1752, when WASHINGTON sought admission in this lodge, its officers were, DANIEL CAMPBELL, Master; JOHN NEILSON, Senior Warden; and Dr. ROBERT HALKERSON, Junior Warden. The records of the few Masonic Lodges in America at that period are very concise, being limited in their details mostly to the election of officers, and the initiating, passing, and raising of members.

The records of Fredericksburg Lodge show the presence of WASHINGTON, for the first time in the lodge, on the fourth of November, 5752, leaving no doubt that he was initiated on that day, as on the 6th of November, the record continues, "Received of Mr. GEORGE WASHINGTON for his entrance £2:3."

"March 3d, 5753—GEORGE WASHINGTON passed Fellow Craft."

"August 4th, 5753—GEORGE WASHINGTON raised Master Mason."

The old record-book of the lodge is still preserved; also the Bible on which he was obligated, and the seal of the lodge. The Bible is a small quarto volume, and bears date, "Cambridge, printed by John Field, printer to the University, 1688." The seal is beautifully engraved, having for its principal device a shield crested with a castle, with castles also on each of its points, with compasses in its centre. Below the shield is the motto, "IN THE LORD IS ALL OUR TRUST"—the whole surrounded with "FREDERICKSBURGH LODGE," in a circle.

SEAL OF FREDERICKSBURGH LODGE.

Had the lodge at Fredericksburg known how deep an interest would be felt by succeeding generations in all that pertained to WASHINGTON, his Masonic record, even at that period, would probably have been made with more fulness of detail; and yet its very conciseness is confirmatory proof, if such were needed, of the verity of the facts there recorded. The lessons of history are progressive, and none could have known, as he passed through the mystic rites of Masonry in 1752, in presence of that chosen band of brethren in Fredericksburg Lodge, that the new-made brother then before them would win, in after-years, a nation's honor, gratitude, and love; and that when a century had passed, the anniversary of his initiation would be celebrated as a national Masonic jubilee.

WASHINGTON was initiated into Masonry a few months before he was twenty-one years of age. The lawful age at which a candidate may receive the mysteries is strictly conventional; while the *principle* upon which the requirement was founded is a landmark in Masonry. Different nations have established different periods during which the child shall remain under the pupilage and government of its parents. Masonry supposes each candidate admitted to her mysteries to have the absolute legal control of his own actions, and that the obligations he assumes are such as he can comply with without interference. For this reason alone, a slave, a prisoner, and common soldier in the army in some countries, are under legal restraints that disqualify them for being candidates for the mysteries of Masonry.

The custom of French lodges in admitting the sons of Masons at the age of eighteen years as candidates for Masonry, is based upon the supposition that the obligations they assume at that age (they being first approved of as *discreet*) they will fully comply with on account of the relation which the father bears to the lodge.

In WASHINGTON'S admission to the fraternity a few months before he became twenty-one years of age, if the conventional rule in this country and in other English lodges as then existing was not fully complied with, no Masonic principle was thereby violated. Without claiming for him a precocious manhood, we may safely assume from his early history, that at the age of twenty years, his physical, mental, and moral developments fitted him, not only for those active duties of citizenship which he had assumed under the civil laws of Virginia, but also as master of his own actions, for forming relations with a brotherhood that requires for the admission of its candidates, their free, voluntary, and unrestrained devotion to its duties.

Four months intervened, as the records show, after he was initiated before he became a Fellow Craft Mason; and still four more, before he became a Master Mason. He was soon after employed in important public duties by the governor of Virginia.) Political considerations then required that a messenger should be sent to some French military posts on the Ohio, to demand, in the name of the governor of Virginia, who was the British king's representative in the territory of which the French had taken possession, that they should at once depart and cease to intrude on the claimed English domain. It was late in autumn before such a commission was determined on by the governor, and the difficulties incident to the season, and the hazard of encountering, not only French, but Indian hostilities, were sufficient to try the fortitude of the boldest adventurer. WASHINGTON was solicited by the governor to undertake the commission. His reply was, "For my own part, I can answer that I have a constitution hardy enough to encounter and undergo the most severe toils, and, I flatter myself, resolution to face what any man dares." Nobly spoken! And yet it was but the reflection of a Masonic lesson he had learned on his admission into Masonry but one year before. What lesson learned in Masonry was ever by him forgotten or unheeded?

He left Williamsburg on the 30th of November, 1753, taking with him, on his way, a guide and a half-dozen backwoodsmen, and traversing a country little known, held conferences with Indian war-chiefs, and the French commandant, and returned after months of hardships and dangers, and made his report to the governor. History has told how, in this adventure, he encountered hunger, and cold, and weariness, how the French officer evaded a compliance with his demands, and how the wily Indian lurked around his path. History has told all this, and we need not repeat it here. His report and daily journal during this first public service were published soon after, both in this country and in Europe; and his prudence and his diplomacy met with general approbation. The Indians, during this interview with them, gave him the name of CANOTOCARIUS.

The refusal of the French to evacuate the posts on the Ohio, was followed by the contest which is known in history as the French and Indian War. Although no formal declaration of war was made between France and England until May, 1756, yet in 1754 hostilities commenced on the Anglo-American frontiers, and WASHINGTON was offered by the governor of Virginia the first command of troops raised in that colony for its defence. He declined the honor, as a charge too great for his youth and inexperience, but took rank second in command, as lieutenant-colonel. The death of his superior officer, Colonel FRY, however, soon placed him at the head of the Virginia troops; and his first lessons in active military life were in the school of experience, where he had few to counsel, none to direct him. His campaign was a short one, ending early in July by his capitulation to the French commander at Fort Necessity. It was the only time in his life in which he ever struck his flag to the foe.

In the following year, WASHINGTON joined General BRADDOCK as a voluntary aid in his unfortunate expedition against Fort Duquesne. History has told of the hardships and dangers of that campaign,—how, when BRADDOCK fell upon the battle-field, and most of his officers were wounded or slain, WASHINGTON skilfully conducted the little remnant of the army that remained from the fatal spot; and when his commander's grave was made, that he piously read by torchlight the prayers of the Church at his midnight burial.

From this time onward, WASHINGTON was the first colonial officer in Virginia during this war. He was, however, subordinate to officers of lower rank who held British commissions, his being only from the colonial government of Virginia. This unjust distinction was very distasteful to him, and in the winter of 1756 he visited Boston, to consult on this point with General SHIRLEY, who had been sent by the British government as the successor of BRADDOCK. He made his journey on horseback, and stopped some time in Philadelphia and New York. History has woven into its pages traditions of his becoming enamored while in New York with a Miss MARY PHILLIPSE, the sister of the wife of his host, Colonel BEVERLY ROBINSON. She is described as a lady of rare beauty and accomplishments, and it is said that WASHINGTON was so deeply interested in her charms, that when his military duties called him to Virginia, he intrusted the secret of his heart to a friend, who promised to keep him advised as to the prospect of any rival supplanting him in her esteem. His fears seem to have become a reality, for she soon after married Colonel MORRIS, who had been an associate with WASHINGTON in BRADDOCK'S army. Her husband and her family afterwards adhered to the British interests during the Revolution, and were all proscribed as traitors, and their property confiscated. It is said that many years later, when deprived of her extensive estates on the Hudson, an exile from her early home, a remark was made to one of her family, of the difference to her, between being the wife of an exile or of the hero of the Revolution and chief magistrate of his country; to which the reply was naively given, that "WASHINGTON would not, could not, have been a traitor with such a wife as Aunty MORRIS." With strong faith in woman's charms, we must still be permitted to doubt whether we owe to cupid's frowns the patriotism of WASHINGTON. Tradition has told, too, of an earlier charmer, a "lowland beauty" of Virginia, who had won the admiration of WASHINGTON in the days of his boyhood. It has been said that he then wrote sentimental verses to soothe his passion; and that in after-years, a son of this first flower that captivated his youthful heart became a favorite of his, in the person of General HENRY LEE.

Although the ostensible object of the war was the defence and occupancy of the territories on the Ohio, yet its chief aim and final result was to overthrow all French power in America. For this purpose, numerous independent expeditions were planned and executed by the various commanders against different and widely distant French posts, from Nova Scotia to the Ohio. WASHINGTON was connected with none of these, except such as protected the western border of Virginia, or were directed against Fort Duquesne. The capture of this post was his darling wish. In this he participated in November of 1758, and having secured its possession, he repaired with his troops to the spot where, three years before, so many of their friends and brethren had been slaughtered on BRADDOCK's ill-fated field, and gathering their whitened bones, buried them with funeral honors. It was a sad and solemn duty, and that burial-mound was watered with the tears of fathers, brothers, and sons. It was the scene in Roman history repeated, where the soldiers of GERMANICUS gathered up the bones of VARUS and his legions, that had lain in the forests for six years unburied, and paid the last offices of tenderness to their fallen countrymen. WASHINGTON now retired honorably from the army, and became a private citizen at Mount Vernon.

He had then been for six years a Mason, and the last five had been spent in military campaigns. His attendance on the meetings of his own lodge during this period could not have been frequent, and no local lodge existed nearer Mount Vernon. Our English brethren have claimed that WASHINGTON was made a Mason during the old French War, in a British military lodge, holding a warrant from the Grand Lodge of Ireland, granted in 1752. This lodge, called "The Lodge of Social and Military Virtues," was No. 227 on the registry of the Grand Lodge of Ireland, and was held in the forty-sixth British regiment. It still exists, we believe, as "Lodge of Antiquity" in Canada, and claims to have the Bible in its possession on which WASHINGTON was obligated as a Mason.

If WASHINGTON ever held any Masonic intercourse with that lodge, we believe it must have been during his visit to Philadelphia, New York, and Boston, in the winter of 1756. Previous to that time, only two British regiments were connected with the American service, and these were the forty-fourth and forty-eighth, which came over the year before with General BRADDOCK; but we know of no military lodge-warrant being held by either of these regiments. The forty-sixth regiment was sent to America soon after BRADDOCK'S defeat, and it served in the northern campaigns, and not in Virginia, where WASHINGTON held command. If WASHINGTON, therefore, had any connection with the lodge above alluded to, it must have been during his northern visit; and as he had been made a Mason, and received his first three degrees more than three years previous to that time, in an American lodge at Fredericksburg, held under authority from the Provincial Grand Master of Massachusetts, if he was obligated on the Bible of this British Military Lodge, it must have been an obligation given as a test oath to him as a visiting brother; or this lodge may have deemed the authority under which he had been made as insufficient, and have required him to be *healed* and re-obligated, to entitle him to the privilege of Masonic intercourse with a lodge held under a warrant from the Grand Lodge of Ireland.

All warranted American lodges, previous to the French War, had worked the rituals and acknowledged the authority of the Grand Lodge of England only (sometimes denominated the Grand Lodge of Moderns); but during this war, lodges holding warrants from the Grand Lodges of Scotland, Ireland, and the Ancients of London, were working in America. They probably owed their introduction to the military brethren. It is well known that little or no intercourse was held between these lodges and those working under the authority of the Grand Lodge of England; and it is a significant fact, that in 1758 WASHINGTON's own lodge in Fredericksburg relinquished its authority from the Provincial Grand Master of Massachusetts, and obtained a warrant from Scotland. These, and many other considerations, render it not improbable that WASHINGTON may, during his visit to the North in 1756, have met with this British Military Lodge, and in it, been re-made, or healed, and re-obligated, as was the custom of that day in admitting to Masonic intercourse Masons made under authority of Masonic bodies whose government and rituals varied from their own.

Traditions, which no Masonic records of that period now existing either verify or contradict, state that WASHINGTON and his Masonic brethren held military lodges during the old French War; and there is a cave near Charlestown in Virginia, a few miles from Winchester, where his headquarters for two years were held, which to this day is called "*Washington's Masonic Cave.*" It is divided into several apartments, one of which is called "*The Lodge Room.*" Tradition says that WASHINGTON and his Masonic brethren held lodges in this cavern. In the spring of 1844 the Masons of that vicinity held a celebration there to commemorate the event.

WASHINGTON's military services had not only gained the approbation of his countrymen, but had met with the applause of English officers in the army, so that

WASHINGTON'S MASONIC CAVE.

when he left the command of the Virginia provincials, he was the most popular American officer in the western military department. But in resigning his military command, he did not retire from the service of his native colony; for in 1758, while holding his commission as colonel, he was elected by the county of Frederick, of which Winchester was the county-seat, as its representative in the House of Burgesses in Virginia. As the election was a contested one, his expenses as a candidate for the office are thus given: "A hogshead and a barrel of punch, thirty-five gallons of wine, forty-three gallons of strong beer, cider, and dinner for his friends;" all amounting to "thirty-nine pounds and six shillings, Virginia currency." He was absent at that time at Fort Cumberland, and Colonel WARD, who sat on the bench and represented him as his friend that day, was carried round the town in the midst of general applause, all huzzaing for Colonel WASHINGTON. If this little episode in his life at the age of twenty-six is distasteful to the admirers of his staid dignity in after-years, they may remember that a century of changes has since passed over American society, but still leaving the popular heart bounding as wildly now at success in election contests, as in the settlements of Virginia, one hundred years ago.

When WASHINGTON made his first appearance in the Colonial Assembly, in January, 1759, the members of that body unanimously complimented him with a vote of thanks for his previous military services; and when the speaker communicated to him this vote in the most flattering terms, he rose from his seat to express his acknowledgment of the honor; and such was his extreme modesty and diffidence in his new situation, that he blushed and stammered, without being able to utter distinctly a word. The speaker relieved him from his embarrassing situation, by saying with a smile, "Sit down, Mr. WASHINGTON; your modesty is equal to your valor, and that surpasses the power of any language I possess."

The same month that WASHINGTON took his seat in the Colonial Assembly of Virginia, he married Mrs. MARTHA CUSTIS, a wealthy and accomplished widow, who had captivated his heart just at the close of his military services. She had been left about two years before, by the death of her former husband, Colonel DANIEL PARKE CUSTIS, with an ample fortune, and two lovely children, a son and a daughter. WASHINGTON met her by accident at the house of a friend in 1758, during a journey which his military duties called him to make to Williamsburg, and admiration, love, and the conquest of two willing hearts, soon succeeded. The nuptials are described as having been on the grandest scale, many gentlemen being present in gold-lace, but none "looking like the man himself." She, too, is said by her contemporaries to have been of rare beauty and loveliness; and it is not probable that WASHINGTON'S honey-moon was haunted by visions of either MARY PHILLIPSE, or his "lowland beauty." She was amiable and exemplary through life, and the virtues of both the mother and wife of WASHINGTON have long been enshrined in a nation's heart, and the dust of Virginia is sacred where they rest.

The succeeding fifteen years of WASHINGTON'S life were spent in domestic retirement, interrupted only by his public duties as member of the Colonial Assembly, in which body he continued his seat. His time was now devoted to agricultural and rural pursuits, but his ample fortune enabled him to maintain a style of living equal to Virginia gentlemen of the first rank in society; and his home, where all the domestic virtues clustered, became the unrivalled abode of refinement and hospitality. Williamsburg and Annapolis were the seats of colonial government of Virginia and Maryland, and during the winter, the *élite* of society in these colonies were accustomed to spend much of their time in those places, forming brilliant circles at the vice-regal courts of the royal governors. WASHINGTON and his family were stars of the first magnitude in these galaxies of intelligence and fashion.

We look in vain for the record of WASHINGTON'S Masonic life during this period, for few of the annals of Masonry in Virginia at that time now exist. Both records and traditions assert that her most noble sons were Masons, but the lapse of time and the devastations of war have left few memorials of their mystic labors. No general Grand East existed either in Virginia or Maryland, in which the brethren might convene; and the different lodges in these colonies, working under no common authority, and having little intercourse with their parent heads, were often remiss in the preservation of their records, leaving us now only the faint footprints of Masonry there from the old French War down to the Revolution. Colonial New England, New York, Pennsylvania, Carolina, and Georgia had at this period each their Provincial Grand Easts, whose master-workmen history has made her own; and when along the pathway of Masonry in colonial Virginia we see her noblest sons emerging from the obscurity of unrecorded Masonic fellowship, and with hand-grips strong and true greeting brethren from the North, the East, and the South, at the commencement of the Revolution, we deeply deplore the loss of records relating to the Mystic Art in that colony previous to that period. Enough yet remains to inspire the poet's pen, and a gifted brother has written:

"Brave old Virginia—proud you well may be,
When you retrace that glorious dynasty
Of intellectual giants, who were known
As much the nation's children as your own—

Your brilliant jewels, aye, you gave them all,
Like Sparta's mother, at your country's call!
The Senate knew their eloquence and power,
And the red battle in its wildest hour.
No matter whence—to glory or the grave—
They shone conspicuous, bravest of the brave.
One o'er the bravest and the best bore sway—
Bright is his memory in our hearts to-day!
His bosom burned with patriotic fire—
Virginia's son became his country's sire;
And in those lofty claims we proudly vie,
He was our brother of the Mystic Tie!"

CHAPTER III.

Commencement of the Revolution.—State of Masonry in the colony at that time.—First Congress at Philadelphia.—PEYTON RANDOLPH, its president, a Mason.—WASHINGTON a member.—Second Congress.—Death of Mr. RANDOLPH.—WASHINGTON appointed commander-in-chief of the army.—Death of General WARREN.—WASHINGTON takes command of the army.—Mrs. WASHINGTON visits the headquarters.—Formation of American Union Military Lodge.—Seal of this lodge.—Origin of its design.—St. John's Regimental Lodge.—Removal of American Union Lodge to New York.—Its disasters at the battle of Long Island.—WASHINGTON evacuates New York.—Crosses New Jersey, and after the battles of Trenton and Princeton, goes into winter-quarters at Morristown.—State of Masonry in America at this period.—WASHINGTON selected as Grand Master by lodges in Virginia.—Campaign of 1777, and winter-quarters at Valley Forge.—WASHINGTON at prayer.—Statue of him at Lancaster, Pennsylvania.—Campaign of 1778.—WASHINGTON present at Masonic celebration in Philadelphia.—Dr. SMITH's sermon.—Published, with dedication to WASHINGTON.—Colonel PARK's Masonic Ode.—"WASHINGTON," a Masonic toast.—Campaign of 1779.—Masonic celebration near West Point.—Washington Military Lodge formed.—WASHINGTON's visits to this lodge.

HE commencement of the American Revolution was a new era in the Masonic as well as political history of our country. As the biographer of WASHINGTON's public history is obliged to trace it along the pathway of current public events, so also his Masonic life, when fully given, must be blended with the Masonic history of the times in which he lived. From the first introduction of warranted lodges into America in 1733, until the commencement of the Revolution, Masonry had been in a state of progress in this country, so that in 1774 there were warranted lodges in each of the thirteen colonies, and in seven of them Provincial Grand Lodges. Massachusetts and Pennsylvania had then each two grand bodies of this class, making nine supervising Masonic powers in the colonies ; and when we add to these the Grand Lodges of Scotland, Ireland, and the two of England, which each exercised Masonic authority in this country, we find the sources of Masonic power in the colonies then to be *thirteen.* The number of their subordinate lodges is lost to history, and the roll of the workmen who wrought upon the first temple of American Masonry has passed into the archives of the Grand Lodge above. The foundations of that temple still remain but

> "Its walls are dust, its trowels rust—
> Its builders with the saints, we trust."

In 1774, when the clouds of political adversity were gathering thick above our country, and seemed ready to burst upon it with all their complicated gloom, a congress of delegates from the different colonies was convened at Philadelphia, and WASHINGTON was a member from Virginia. There were assembled in that council-chamber men who had never met before. From New England, from the banks of the Hudson, the Delaware, the Susquehanna, and the Potomac, and from far down in the sunny South they came, and all looked kindly on each other then; for common dangers and a common weakness bespoke the necessity of a unity of action. Many brothers of the mystic tie were members of that body, and over its deliberations PEYTON RANDOLPH, the Provincial Grand Master of Virginia, was selected from the bright roll of master workmen, to preside. Mr. ADAMS said it was a collection of the greatest men upon this continent, in point of abilities, virtues, and fortunes. WASHINGTON'S position in it may be seen from a remark made by PATRICK HENRY, who was also a member, to one who asked him whom he considered the greatest man in that body. "If you speak of eloquence," said he, "Mr. RUTLEDGE of South Carolina is by far the greatest orator; but if you speak of solid information and sound judgment, Colonel WASHINGTON is unquestionably the greatest man on that floor."

A second session of which WASHINGTON was also a member, assembled the following year in Philadelphia, and Mr. RANDOLPH was again called to preside over its councils. His health, however, failing, JOHN HANCOCK was elected his successor as president; and before the session closed, Mr. RANDOLPH died, and his remains were taken to Virginia and buried with Masonic honors. The contest at arms between the colonies and the mother country had already begun at Concord and Lexington, and WASHINGTON was elected commander-in-chief of the American army. He was at this time forty-three years of age. He had left his home at Mount Vernon but a few weeks before, expecting soon to return; but the duties of his appointment admitted of no delay, and after giving a few written directions for his domestic business, and executing a will, which he inclosed in an affectionate letter to his wife, he repaired to Cambridge, where the army was then stationed.

The British troops then held possession of Boston; and the very day that WASHINGTON received his commission, the battle of Bunker Hill was fought, and in it fell General JOSEPH WARREN, Grand Master of the Massachusetts Grand Lodge. It was the first grand offering of American Masonry at the altar of liberty, and the ground-floor of her temple was blood-stained at its eastern gate. The second Grand Master who fell at the post of duty, was PEYTON RANDOLPH, in the following October, whose death has been already noticed. One fell on the battle-field, and the other in the council-chamber of our country. Both their graves were wet with a nation's tears, and their Masonic brethren placed on each the green acacia.

WASHINGTON reached Cambridge on the 2d of July, and on the following day took command of the army. There were gathered around him a stern band of determined men, who had left their peaceful avocations and taken arms to defend their hearth-stones. Of uniform they had little, and their arms were such as were found in possession of men unused to war. Some of their officers had before held command in the old French and Indian War, and some had never held a sword before. To maintain his numbers, provide for their necessities, and reduce them to discipline, was WASHINGTON'S first care. But the year closed dark and gloomy upon the prospects of the army. Mrs. WASHINGTON left Mount Vernon late in the fall to spend the winter months at headquarters, and many of the officers were also joined by their wives; but the other officers and soldiers had few pleasures in their winter-quarters to make them forget the homes they had left.

During the previous French and Indian War, military lodge warrants had been granted by the Grand Lodge of Massachusetts to brethren in the army; and at the close of wearisome marches, and in their cheerless camps, the Masonic lodge-room became a bivouac in the tired soldier's life, where his toils and privations were forgotten, and the finest feelings of his heart cultivated. While the Connecticut line of the army was encamped during this winter at Roxbury, near Boston, a movement was made by the brethren in it, early in February, to establish a Masonic lodge in their camp. For this purpose they applied to the Grand Officers of the Grand Lodge of Massachusetts, of which JOHN ROWE was Grand Master, and Colonel RICHARD GRIDLEY his Deputy, for the necessary authority. The petition was signed by Colonel SAMUEL H. PARSONS, Colonel SAMUEL WYLLYS, Colonel JOEL CLARK, Major JOHN PARK, Major THOMAS CHASE, Captain EZEKIEL SCOTT, and sundry other brethren, praying that they might be formed into a regular lodge.

By appointment from Colonel RICHARD GRIDLEY, the Deputy Grand Master, a meeting of the brethren was held in the Roxbury camp, on the 13th of February, 1776. At this meeting, it was agreed that Colonel CLARK be recommended as Master, Major PARK as Senior Warden, Major CHASE as Junior Warden, Colonel PARSONS as Treasurer, and Ensign JONATHAN HART as Secretary. The foregoing proceedings having been presented to the Deputy Grand Master, who was not present at the meeting, upon the 15th of the same month he issued to them a warrant or dispensation to hold a lodge in their camp at Roxbury, or wherever their body should remove on the continent of America, provided it was where no other Grand Master held authority.

It was called American Union Lodge, and both its name and the device on its seal were significant of the aid lent by Masonry in the hour of our country's need. Both were expressive of the great sentiment which then pervaded the American heart. If Liberty was its key-note, Union was its watchword. The union of the Anglo-American colonies for mutual defence had been proposed in 1741, by DANIEL COXE of New Jersey, the first Provincial Grand Master in America. It had again been advocated in 1754 by Dr. FRANKLIN, Provincial Grand Master of Pennsylvania, who also symbolized the idea at the close of an essay, which he published on this subject, by a wood-cut representing a snake divided into parts, with the initial letter of each colony on a separate part, underneath which he placed the motto, "JOIN OR DIE."

The purposes for which both COXE and FRANKLIN had unsuccessfully advocated a federal union of the colonies, had been to protect them against the French. When the Revolution commenced, and the union of the colonies against British aggression was urged, many of the newspapers adopted FRANKLIN'S device and motto. When the Union had taken place, the device was changed as a newspaper heading, and a coiled rattlesnake, with its head erect to strike, was substituted, with the motto, "DON'T TREAD ON ME." Both these devices and mottoes were inscribed on flags and other ensigns of war of the provincial troops at the commencement of the Revolution. This device, as a colonial emblem, was soon after changed to a circle consisting of a chain with thirteen links, containing in each an initial letter of one of the thirteen colonies. It was also placed upon some of the currency of the colonies as early as 1776.

SEAL OF AMERICAN UNION LODGE.

The seal of American Union Lodge bore the same popular American idea in its symbolism, having as its principal device a chain of thirteen circular links, around a central part, on which was the square and compasses, with the sun, moon, and a star above, and three burning tapers beneath them, the extremities of the chain being united by two clasped hands. For the leading idea of the symbolism of the chain representing the union of the colonies, the brethren were probably indebted to Dr. Franklin, who visited the American camp in 1776, as one of a committee from Congress to confer with Washington on the affairs of the war; and the seal is supposed to have been engraved by Paul Revere, a distinguished Mason and patriot of Massachusetts, who was often employed at that period to engrave such designs.

Although a Military Lodge warrant had been granted by the Masonic authorities of New York on the 24th of July, 1775, for a lodge in the provincial troops of that colony, which was called St. John's Regimental

Lodge, yet the American Union Lodge was the first organized in the *Continental* army, and may be justly regarded as the eldest Masonic daughter of the American Union. It was organized in troops of which WASHINGTON had command, and though his military duties did not admit of his attendance on its meetings during the time the army was encamped around Boston, he subsequently often joined his Masonic brethren within its walls, and ever inculcated among its members, both by precept and example, a love of Masonry. This lodge went with his army, when it removed to New York, and held its meetings there while the city remained in his possession. Its last meeting there was on the 15th of August, 1776, a few days before the disastrous battle on Long Island. The next subsequent record of this lodge states:

"The British troops having landed with a large body on Long Island, the attention of the American army was necessary to repel them. On the ever memorable 27th of August, the Right Worshipful JOEL CLARK, ELISHA HOPKINS, OZIAS BISSELL, JOSEPH JEWETT, NATHANIEL GORE, being taken prisoners; and on the 13th of September, Brother JAMES CHAPMAN, MICAJAH GLEASON, killed; WILLIAM CLEAVLAND and JOHN P. WYLLYS taken prisoners, and Brother OTHO H. WILLIAMS taken prisoner at Fort Washington, by which misfortunes the lodge was deprived of its Master, and some most worthy members, and many other brethren were called to act in separate departments, wherefore the lodge stood closed without day.

"(Signed) JONATHAN HART, Secretary."

No further meetings of this lodge were held until

March, 1777; and in the mean time, JOEL CLARK, its Master, died in captivity.

After the disastrous battle of Long Island, WASHINGTON found it impossible for the safety of his army to retain possession of New York, and he evacuated the city about the middle of September, after having his headquarters there five months. From this time until the close of 1776, he did not long enjoy a resting-place for his troops. His strongholds upon the Hudson were lost, and he retreated from river to river in New Jersey, till he had crossed the Delaware, and encamped on its Pennsylvania side. There he turned upon his pursuers, and on the 25th of December recrossed the river amidst floods of ice, surprised a portion of the British army while engaged in their Christmas revels at Trenton, and gained a decided victory. This at once turned the tide of war, and after further successes at Princeton, his army went into winter-quarters at Morristown.

The close of 1776 was the darkest period in the history of American Masonry. Every Grand East on the American continent was shrouded in darkness. Massachusetts and Virginia had each lost a Grand Master since the commencement of the war; the old Grand Lodge of New York was dissolved, by its Grand Master, Sir JOHN JOHNSON, fleeing from his home, and becoming an officer in the British army; the labors of the Grand Lodge of Pennsylvania were suspended, and their hall was soon after made a prison-room for citizens who were disaffected to the American cause. In the spring of 1777 a ray of light first arose in the East. The members remaining of Dr. WARREN'S Grand

Lodge were convened, and they resolved, that as the political head of this country had destroyed all connection between the States and the country from which that Grand Lodge derived its commissioned authority, it was their privilege to assume an elective supremacy, and they accordingly elected JOSEPH WEBB their Grand Master. Virginia, too, a few months later, called a convention of its lodges, which recommended to its constituents GEORGE WASHINGTON as the most proper person to be elected the first independent Grand Master of Virginia. WASHINGTON at that time had held no official position in Masonry, and he modestly declined the intended honor, when informed of the wish of his Virginia brethren, for two reasons: first, he did not consider it masonically legal, that one who had never been installed as Master or Warden of a lodge, should be elected Grand Master; and second, his country claimed at the time all his services in the tented field. JOHN BLAIR, therefore, the Master of Williamsburg Lodge, who was an eminent citizen of Virginia, was elected in his stead.

The military campaign of 1777 gave to history, in quick succession, the battles of Brandywine and Germantown, the evacuation of Philadelphia by Congress, and its occupation by British troops, and closed by the retirement of the American army into winter-quarters at Valley Forge. Here, as the shoeless army marched to their cheerless encampment, hundreds of bare feet left footprints of blood in their frozen path. WASHINGTON was moved to tears at the sight, and his touching exclamation of "*poor fellows,*" was responded to by a "God bless your Excellency, your poor soldiers' friend," by the suffering soldiers. Masonic traditions state that military lodges were held in the camp at Valley Forge, which WASHINGTON often attended, but the loss of their records prevents us from verifying the statement. His headquarters that winter were at the house of a Quaker preacher; and tradition has told us how the man of peace surprised him one day in a retired place, praying audibly and fervently for the success of the American arms, and that he thereupon assured his family that America would finally triumph, for such prayers would surely be answered.

"Oh! who shall know the *might*
Of the words he utter'd there?
The fate of nations then was turn'd
By the fervor of that prayer.

"But wouldst thou know his *words*,
Who wander'd there alone?
Go, read enroll'd in heaven's archives
The prayer of WASHINGTON!"

There is an interesting Masonic memorial of WASHINGTON at this period, which has long been in possession of Lodge No. 43, at Lancaster, Pennsylvania. While Congress held its sessions in York, during the time the British occupied Philadelphia, WASHINGTON visited that borough, and his striking and majestic appearance so impressed a young man of that vicinity, that he carved a life-size statue of him from a single block of wood, which was afterwards presented to Lodge No. 43, and is still in its possession. The name of the young self-taught artist who carved it has long been forgotten, but the outlines and expression of the statue are said to bear a striking resemblance to WASHINGTON at that period.

During the following year the British troops evacuated Philadelphia, and the campaign of 1778 closed with the contending armies in nearly the same position as they were in the summer of 1776. In the latter part of December, WASHINGTON visited Philadelphia, where Congress was in session; and while there, the Grand Lodge of Pennsylvania celebrated the festival of St. John the Evangelist. WASHINGTON was present on the occasion, and was honored with the chief place in the procession, being supported on his right by the Grand Master, and on his left by the Deputy Grand Master. More than three hundred brethren joined in this procession. They met at nine o'clock, at the college, and being properly clothed, the officers in the jewels of their office, and other badges of their dignity, the procession moved at eleven o'clock, and proceeded to Christ Church, where a Masonic sermon, for the benefit of the poor, was preached by the Rev. Bro. WILLIAM SMITH, D. D., Grand Secretary of the Grand Lodge of Pennsylvania. In it he beautifully alluded to WASHINGTON, who was present, as the Cincinnatus of America; saying also, "Such, too, if we divine aright, will future ages pronounce the character of a **********; but you all anticipate me in a name, which delicacy forbids me on this occasion to mention. Honored with his presence as a Brother, you will seek to derive virtue from his example." Great poverty and distress had been occasioned in Philadelphia by the British troops during their occupancy of the city, and in accordance with Masonic custom, a call was made on the fraternity in this sermon for the relief of those in distress. Having eloquently presented the duty of charity, the Rev. Brother closed his discourse by saying: "But I will detain you no longer, brethren! you all pant to have a foretaste of the joy of angels, by calling into exercise this heavenly virtue of charity, whereby you will give glory to the Thrice Blessed Three, Father, Son, and Holy Ghost, one God over all!" At the word "glory," the brethren rose together; and in reverential posture, on pronouncing the names of the Triune God, accompanied the same by a corresponding repetition of the ancient sign or symbol of Divine homage and obeisance, concluding with the following response, "Amen! So let it ever be!" More than four hundred pounds were immediately collected for the relief of the poor, and the Grand Lodge of Pennsylvania was made on the occasion the almoner of WASHINGTON'S bounty. This sermon of Dr. SMITH was published soon after, by direction of the Grand Lodge, and the profits arising from its sale were also given to the poor. The pamphlet was prefaced with the following dedication to WASHINGTON:

"To his Excellency, GEORGE WASHINGTON, Esq., general and commander-in-chief of the armies of the United States of North America—the friend of his country and mankind, ambitious of no higher title, if higher were possible—the following sermon, honored with his presence when delivered, is dedicated in testimony of the sincerest brotherly affection and esteem of his merit.

"By order of the Brethren,

"JOHN COATS,

"Grand Secretary, *pro tem*."

No earlier production, either literary or Masonic, had been dedicated to WASHINGTON. We regret the want of Masonic records to give the names of other visiting brethren who were present at this festival. An ode commemorative of WASHINGTON's participating in the ceremonies, and the position he occupied, was written a few months after by Colonel JOHN PARK, a distinguished member of American Union Lodge, addressed to Colonel PROCTOR, of Pennsylvania, bearing date, February 7, 1779, in which he says:

"See WASHINGTON, he leads the train,
'Tis he commands the grateful strain;
See, every crafted son obeys,
And to the godlike brother homage pays.
* * * * * * * *
Let fame resound him through the land,
And echo, '*Tis our Master Grand!*
* * * * * * * *
'Tis he our ancient craft shall sway,
Whilst we, with *three times three, obey.*"

We have no doubt, from this time onward it was the desire of many of the brethren, especially those in the army, to see WASHINGTON placed at the head of American Masonry. At a public festival of American Union Lodge, held at Reading, in Connecticut, on the 25th of March, 1779, the first toast given was, "GENERAL WASHINGTON;" which was followed by one to "*The memory of* WARREN, MONTGOMERY, *and* WOOSTER," three distinguished Masons who had fallen on the battle-fields of the Revolution. From this time onward the name of WASHINGTON became a Masonic toast, and the first in order at all Masonic festivals.

On the 23d of June, WASHINGTON established his headquarters at New Windsor, on the Hudson, near Newburg. The following day American Union Lodge met at Nelson's Point, and proceeded from thence to West Point to celebrate the festival of St. John the Baptist. Being joined by a number of Masonic brethren from the brigades there, and on Constitution Island, they proceeded from General PATTERSON'S quarters, on the opposite side of the river, to the Robinson House, where they retired to a bower in front of the house, and were joined by General WASHINGTON and his family. Here addresses were delivered by Rev. Dr. HITCHCOCK and Major WILLIAM HULL (afterwards General HULL of the war of 1812). Dinner, music, toasts, and songs closed the entertainment. WASHINGTON then returned to his barge, attended by the wardens and secretary of the lodge, amidst a crowd of brethren, the music playing "GOD save America;" and as he and his family embarked to recross the river to New Windsor, his departure was announced by three cheers from the shore, which were answered by three from the barge, the music beating the "Grenadiers' March." Many distinguished officers of the army, who were Masons, were present at this festival; and the brethren in the Massachusetts line soon after petitioned the Massachusetts Grand Lodge for a warrant to hold a travelling lodge in their camp. The petition was granted on the 6th of October, 1779, constituting General JOHN PATTERSON, Master, and Colonel BENJAMIN TUPPER and Major WILLIAM HULL, Wardens. The lodge was called "WASHINGTON LODGE." Captain MOSES GREENLEAF of the Eleventh Massachusetts Regiment afterwards became Master of this lodge. His son, SIMON GREENLEAF, late Past Grand Master of Maine, said he had often heard his father mention WASHINGTON'S visits to this lodge while commander-in-chief, and the high gratification they gave to the officers and members, especially as he went without ceremony, as a private brother.

CHAPTER IV.

WASHINGTON's headquarters again at Morristown.—Attends Masonic celebration there, December 27, 1779.—Masonic army convention proposed.—Its meeting and proceedings.—Its address to American Grand Masters.—Existing Grand Lodges at this time.—Grand Lodge of Pennsylvania propose a General Grand Lodge, and choose WASHINGTON as General Grand Master.—Sends notification of these proceedings to other Grand Lodges.—Letter to JOSEPH WEBB.—His reply.—Second letter to Mr. WEBB.—Grand Lodge of Massachusetts submits proposition from Grand Lodge of Pennsylvania to subordinate lodges.—Resolutions of Warren Lodge at Machias, Maine, in favor of WASHINGTON as General Grand Master.—Final action of Grand Lodge of Massachusetts in the matter.—Pennsylvania ever after opposes a General Grand Lodge.—WASHINGTON afterwards considered as General Grand Master.—Receives letters as such from Cape François.—His Masonic medal.—Pennsylvania Ahiman Rezon dedicated to him.—Copy presented to him.—Military Lodges of the Revolution.—Lodges in the British army.—Anecdotes of.—Action of King David's Lodge at Newport.—Capture of CORNWALLIS.—News of in Philadelphia.—Death of JOHN PARKE CUSTIS.—WASHINGTON visits his mother.

AT the close of 1779, WASHINGTON's headquarters were again at Morristown, New Jersey, where they had been during the winter of 1776–77. Here the American Union Lodge was again at work, and also various other military lodges, which had been organized in the American army. On the 27th of December, the American Union Lodge met to celebrate the festival of St. John the Evangelist. Besides the regular members of the lodge present, the record shows the names of sixty-eight visiting brethren, one of whom was WASHINGTON. At a previous meeting of this lodge, held on the 15th of December, its records show that its Master, Major JONATHAN HART, was appointed one of a joint committee from the various military lodges in the army "to take into consideration some matters for the good of Masonry." At the festival meeting on the 27th, "a petition was read, representing the present state of Free-Masonry to the several Deputy Grand Masters in the United States of America, desiring them to adopt some measures for appointing a Grand Master over said States." It was ordered that this petition be circulated through the different lines of the army; and also "that a committee be appointed from the different lodges in the army, from each line, and from the staff of the army, to convene on the first Monday of February next, at Morristown, to take the foregoing petition into consideration." This committee accordingly met at Morristown, on the 7th day of February, 1780, and the following is a copy of its proceedings:

"At a committee of Ancient Free and Accepted Masons, met this 7th day of the second month in the year of Salvation, 1780, according to the recommendation of a Convention Lodge, held at the celebration of St. John the Evangelist.

"Present, Brother JOHN PIERCE, M. M., delegated to represent the Masons in the military line of the State of Massachusetts Bay, and Washington Lodge, No. 10; Brother JONATHAN HART, M. M., delegated to represent the Masons in the military line of the State of Connecticut, and American Union Lodge; Brother CHARLES GRAHAM, F. C., delegated to represent the Masons in the military line of the State of

New York; Brother JOHN SANFORD, M. M., delegated to represent the Masons in the military line of the State of New Jersey; Brother GEORGE TUDOR, M. M., delegated to represent the Masons in the military line of the State of Pennsylvania; Brother OTHO HOLLAND WILLIAMS, M. M., delegated to represent the Masons in the military line of the State of Delaware; Brother MORDECAI GIST, P. W. M., delegated to represent the Masons in the military line of the State of Maryland; Brother PRENTICE BROWN, M. M., delegated to represent St. John's Regimental Lodge; Brother JOHN LAWRENCE, P. W. M., delegated to represent the brothers in the staff of the American army; Brother THOMAS MACHIN, M. M., delegated to represent the Masons in the corps of artillery."

The brothers present proceeded to elect a president and secretary, whereupon Brother MORDECAI GIST was unanimously chosen president, and Brother OTHO HOLLAND WILLIAMS unanimously chosen secretary of this committee.

The committee proceeded to take into consideration an address to be preferred to the Right Worshipful Grand Masters in the respective United States, whereupon Brother WILLIAMS presented the following address:

"TO THE RIGHT WORSHIPFUL,

THE GRAND MASTERS OF THE SEVERAL LODGES IN THE RESPECTIVE UNITED STATES OF AMERICA.

UNION. FORCE. LOVE.

"The subscribers, Ancient Free and Accepted Masons in convention, to you, as the patrons and protectors of the craft upon this continent, prefer their humble address.

"Unhappily, the distinctions of interest, the political views, and national disputes subsisting between Great Britain and these United States have involved us, not only in the general calamities that disturb the tranquillity which used to prevail in this once happy country, but in a peculiar manner affects our society, by separating us from the Grand Mother Lodge in Europe, by disturbing our connection with each other, impeding the progress, and preventing the perfection of Masonry in America.

"We deplore the miseries of our countrymen, and particularly lament the distresses which many of our poor brethren must suffer, as well from the want of temporal relief, as for want of a source of *light* to govern their pursuits and illuminate the path of happiness. And we ardently desire to restore, if possible, that fountain of charity, from which, to the unspeakable benefit of mankind, flows benevolence and love: considering with anxiety these disputes, and the many irregularities and improprieties committed by weak or wicked brethren, which too manifestly show the present dissipated and almost abandoned condition of our lodges in general, as well as the relaxation of virtue amongst individuals.

"We think it our duty, Right Worshipful Brothers and Seniors in the Craft, to solicit your immediate interposition to save us from the impending dangers of schisms and apostasy. To obtain security from those fatal evils, with affectionate humility, we beg leave to recommend the adopting and pursuing the most necessary measures for establishing one Grand Lodge in America, to preside over and govern all other lodges of whatsoever degree or denomination, licensed or to be licensed upon the continent; that the ancient principles and discipline of Masonry being restored, we may mutually and universally enjoy the advantages arising from frequent communion and social intercourse. To accomplish this beneficial and essential work, permit us to propose that you, the Right Worshipful Grand Masters, or a majority of your number, may nominate as Most Worshipful Grand Master of said lodge, a brother whose merit and capacity may be adequate to a station so important and elevated, and transmitting the name and nomination of such brother, together with the name of the lodge to be established, to our Grand Mother Lodge in Europe for approbation and confirmation, and that you may adopt and execute any other ways or means most eligible for preventing impositions, correcting abuses, and for establishing the general principles of Masonry; that the influence of the same in propagating morality and virtue may be far extended, and that the lives and conversation of all true Free and Accepted Masons may not only be the admiration of men on earth, but may receive the final approbation of the Grand Architect of the Universe, in the world wherein the elect enjoy eternal light and love.

"Signed in convention, at Morristown, Morris County, this 7th day of the second month, in the year of our Saviour 1780, Anno Mundi, 5780. Which being read, was unanimously agreed to sign, and ordered to be forwarded with an extra copy of their proceedings, signed by the president and secretary, to the respective Provincial Grand Masters; and the committee adjourned without day."

There were Grand Lodges in active existence in but three of the States at this time—viz., Massachusetts, Pennsylvania, and Virginia; and although the name of WASHINGTON for General Grand Master does not appear in the foregoing petition from the Masonic convention in the army, yet it was formally signified to these Grand Lodges that he was their choice. The events of the period we are now sketching are of great interest, not only in the Masonic history of WASHINGTON, but also in the Masonic history of our country. Our records show that the action of the brethren in the army was the prelude to the great changes that were soon wrought in the polity of American Masonry, and that he was first in the hearts of Masons, as well as first in the hearts of his countrymen. Previous to the reception of the address of the Army Convention by the Grand Lodge of Pennsylvania, but while these proceedings were in progress, an emergent meeting of that grand body was convened at Philadelphia, on the 13th of January, 1780, to consider the propriety of appointing a General Grand Master over all the Grand Lodges formed or to be formed in the United States; and its records show, that

"The ballot was put upon the question whether it be for the benefit of Masonry, that a GRAND MASTER OF MASONS throughout the United States shall now be nominated on the part of this Grand Lodge; and it was unanimously determined in the affirmative.

"Sundry respectable brethren being put in nomination, it was moved that the ballot be put for them separately, and his Excellency, GEORGE WASHINGTON, Esq., general and commander-in-chief of the army of the United States, being first in nomination, he was balloted for as Grand Master, and elected by the unanimous vote of the whole lodge.

"Ordered, that the minutes of this election and appointment be transmitted to the different Grand Lodges in the United States, and their concurrence therein be requested, in order that application be made to his excellency in due form, praying that he will do the brethren and Craft the honor of accepting their appointment."

A committee was chosen to expedite the business, and to inform themselves of the number of Grand

Lodges in America, and the names of their officers, and prepare a circular letter to be sent them. So little was known, at this time, by the Provincial Grand Lodges in this country of their sister Grand Bodies in other States, that months elapsed before the necessary information came before the Grand Lodge of Pennsylvania, on which to act in carrying out the resolution of January 13th, relative to a correspondence in relation to the appointment of a General Grand Master. On the 27th of the following July, having learned that there was a Grand Lodge in Virginia, of which JOHN BLAIR was Grand Master, the Grand Secretary was directed to write to Mr. BLAIR and request the concurrence of that Grand Lodge (*if Ancient Masons*) in the appointment of General WASHINGTON as Grand Master General of Masons in America. A similar letter was also directed to be written to Colonel WILLIAM MALCOLM, of Fishkill, New York; and as they had learned that there was a Grand Lodge at work in Boston, of which Colonel WILLIAM PALFREY was a member, Colonel PROCTOR, of Philadelphia, was directed to confer with him. Having made these preliminary inquiries, the Grand Secretary of the Grand Lodge of Pennsylvania addressed the following letter to JOSEPH WEBB, Grand Master of the Massachusetts Grand Lodge:

"PHILADELPHIA, August 19, 1780.

"JOSEPH WEBB, Esq.:

"SIR—I do myself the honor to address you, by orders from the Grand Lodge of Ancient York Masons, regularly constituted in the city of Philadelphia. This Grand Lodge has under its jurisdiction, in Pennsylvania and the States adjacent, thirty-one different regular lodges, containing in the whole more than one thousand brethren. Inclosed, you have a printed abstract of some of our late proceedings; and by that of January 13th last, you will observe that we have, so far as depends on us, done that honor which we think due to our illustrious brother, General WASHINGTON—viz., electing him Grand Master over all the Grand Lodges formed, or to be formed, in these United States; not doubting of the concurrence of all the Grand Lodges in America to make this election effectual.

"We have been informed by Colonel PALFREY that there is a Grand Lodge of Ancient York Masons in the State of Massachusetts, and that you are Grand Master thereof. As such, I am, therefore, to request that you will lay our proceedings before your Grand Lodge, and request their concurrent voice in the appointment of General WASHINGTON, as set forth in the minutes of January 13th, which, as far as we have been able to learn, is a measure highly approved by all the brethren, and that will do honor to the Craft.

"WILLIAM SMITH,
"*Grand Secretary.*"

To this, Mr. WEBB returned the following answer:

"BOSTON, September 4, 1780.

"SIR—Your agreeable favor of the 19th ult. I duly received on the 31st, covering a printed abstract of the proceedings of your Grand Lodge. I had received one near three months before, from the Master of a travelling lodge of the Connecticut line; but the evening after I received yours, it being Grand Lodge, I laid it before them, and had some debate on it. Whereupon it was agreed to adjourn the lodge for three weeks, to the 22d inst.: likewise, to write to all the lodges in this jurisdiction to attend themselves, if convenient, by their Masters and Wardens; and if not, to give instruction to their proxies here concerning their acquiescence in the proposal.

"I am well assured that no one can have any objection to so illustrious a person as General WASHINGTON to preside as Grand Master of the United States; but at the same tim it will be necessary to know from you his prerogatives as such; whether he is to appoint Sub-Grand or Provincial Grand Masters of each State. If so, I am confident that the Grand Lodge of this State will never give up their right of electing their own Grand Masters and other officers annually. This induces me to write to you now, before the result of the Grand Lodge takes place; and I must beg an answer by the first opportunity, that I may be enabled to lay the same before them. I have not heard of any States, except this and yours, that have proceeded as yet, since the independence, to elect their officers, but I have been hoping they would. I do not remember of more Grand Masters being appointed when we were under the British government, than in South Carolina, North Carolina, Pennsylvania, New York, and Massachusetts; but now it may be necessary.

"I have granted a dispensation to New Hampshire, till they shall appoint a Grand Master of their own, which I suppose will not be very soon, as there is but one lodge in that State. Inclosed, I send you a list of the officers of our Grand Lodge, and have the honor to be,

"With great respect and esteem,
"Your affectionate brother and
"Humble servant,
"JOS. WEBB, G. M."

This communication was laid before the Grand Lodge of Pennsylvania, at a special Grand Communication, on the 16th of October; and a committee, consisting of Colonel PALFREY and the Grand Secretary, Dr. WILLIAM SMITH, was appointed to prepare an answer; and they laid the same before the Grand Body on the following evening, to which it adjourned. The following is a copy:

"PHILADELPHIA, October 17, 1780.

"JOSEPH WEBB, Esq.:

"RESPECTED SIR, AND RIGHT WORSHIPFUL BROTHER—Your kind and interesting letters of the 4th and 19th ult., by some delay in the Post-Office, came both to my hands together, and that not before the 10th inst. They were both read and maturely considered at a very full Grand Lodge last evening; and I have it in charge to thank you, and all the worthy members of the Grand Lodge of Massachusetts, for the brotherly notice they were pleased to take of the proposition communicated to you from the Grand Lodge of this State.

"We are happy to find that you agree with us in the necessity of having one complete Masonic jurisdiction under some one Grand Head throughout the United States. It has been a measure long wished for among the brethren, especially in the army; and from them the request came originally to us, that we might improve the opportunity, which our central situation gave us, of setting the measure on foot. From these considerations, joined to an earnest desire of advancing and doing honor to Masonry, and not from any affected superiority, or of dictating to any of our brethren, we put in nomination for Grand Master over all these States (and elected so far as depended on us) one of the most illustrious of our brethren, whose character does honor to the whole Fraternity, and who, we are therefore persuaded, would be wholly unexceptionable. When our proposition and nomination should be communicated to other Grand Lodges, and ratified by their concurrence, then, and not before, it was proposed to define the powers of such a Grand Master General, and to fix articles of Masonic union among the Grand Lodges, by means of a convention of committees from the different Grand Lodges, to be held at such time and place as might be agreed upon. Such convention may also have powers to notify the Grand Master General of his election, present him with his diploma, badges of office, and install with due form and ceremony.

"To you who are so well learned in the Masonic Art, and acquainted with its history, it needs not to be observed that one Grand Master General over many Grand Lodges, having each their own Grand Master, is no novel institution: even if the peculiar circumstances of the Grand Lodges in America, now separated from the jurisdiction from whence they originated, did not render it necessary. We have also a very recent magnificent example of the same thing in Europe, which may serve, in respect to the ceremonies of installation, as a model for us. I will copy the paragraph as dated, at Stockholm, in Sweden, the 21st of March last, as you may not have seen it.

"'The 19th of this month (March, 1780) will always be a remarkable day to the Free Masons established in this Kingdom, for on that day the Duke of Sundermania was installed Grand Master of all the lodges throughout this Kingdom, as well as those in St. Petersburg, Copenhagen, Brunswick, Hamburg, etc. The lodge at St. Petersburg had sent a deputy for this purpose, and others had intrusted the diploma of instalment to Baron Leganbrepud, who had been last year to Copenhagen and Germany on this negotiation.

"'The instalment was attended with great pomp. The assembly was composed of more than four hundred members, and was honored with the presence of the king, who was pleased to grant a charter to the lodge, taking it under his royal direction, at the same time investing the new Grand Master with an ermine cloak; after which he was placed upon a throne, clothed with the marks of his new dignity, and there received the compliments of all the members, who, according to their rank, were admitted to kiss the hand, sceptre, and cloak of the new Grand Master, and had delivered to them a silver medal, struck to perpetuate the memory of this solemnity, which passed in Exchange Hall. It is said that the king will grant revenues for the commanders, and that this Royal Lodge will receive each year an annual tribute. This solemnity hath raised the order of Free Masons from a kind of oblivion into which they were sunk.'

"What the particular authorities of the Grand Master of the United States were to be, we had not taken upon us to describe, but, as before hinted, had left them to be settled by a convention of Grand Lodges or their deputies. But this is certain, that we never intended the different Provincial or State Grand Lodges, should be deprived of the election of their own Grand Officers, or any of their just Masonic rights and authorities over the different lodges within the bounds of their jurisdiction.

"But when new lodges are to be created beyond the bounds of any legal Grand Lodge now existing, such lodges are to have their warrants from the Grand Master General. And when such lodges become a number sufficient to be formed into a Grand Lodge, the bounds of such Grand

Lodge are to be described, and the warrants be granted by the General Grand Master aforesaid; who may also call and preside in a convention of Grand Lodges, when any matter of great or general importance to the whole United Fraternity of these United States may require it. What other powers may be given to the Grand Master General, and how such powers are to be drawn up and expressed, will be the business of the convention proposed.

"For want of some general Masonic authority over all these United States, the Grand Lodge of Pennsylvania, *ex necessitate*, have granted warrants beyond its bounds, to Delaware and Maryland States; and you have found it expedient to do the same in New Hampshire: but we know that necessity alone can be the plea for this.

"By what has been said above, you will see that our idea is to have a General Grand Master over all the United States, and each lodge under him to preserve its own rights, jurisdiction, etc., as formerly under the Grand Lodge of Great Britain, from whence the Grand Lodges of America had derived their Warrants, and to have this new Masonic Constitution, and the powers of the General Grand Master, fixed by a convention aforesaid.

"Others, we are told, have proposed that there be one Grand Master over all the States, and that the other Masters of Grand Lodges, whether nominated by him, or chosen by their own Grand Lodges, should be considered as his deputies. But we have the same objection to this that you have, and never had any idea of establishing such a plan, as has been suggested before.

"This letter is now swelled to a great length. We have, therefore, only to submit two things to your deliberation: 1st. Either, whether it would be best to make your election of a General Grand Master immediately, and then propose to us a time and place where a committee from your body could meet a committee from ours to fix his powers and proceed to instalment; or, 2d. Whether you will first appoint a place of meeting, and the powers of the proposed Grand Master; then return home and proceed to the election, and afterwards meet anew for instalment. This last mode would seem to require too much time, and would not be so agreeable to our worthy brethren in the army, who are anxious to have this matter completed.

"As you will probably choose the first mode, could not the place of meeting be at, or near, the headquarters of the army, at, or soon after, St. John's-day next? At any rate, you will not fix a place far northward, on account of some brethren from Virginia who will attend. For we propose to advertise the business, and the time and place of meeting, in the public papers, that any regular Grand Lodges which we may not have heard of, may have an opportunity of sending representatives. Your answer, as soon as possible, is requested, under cover to Peter Baynter, Postmaster of Philadelphia.

"I am, etc., by order,

"William Smith,

"*Grand Secretary.*"

The Grand Lodge of Massachusetts having submitted the consideration of the matter to her subordinates, one of her lodges at Machias, in Maine, passed the following resolutions, as shown by this record.

"At a meeting of Warren Lodge, held at Machias, Maine, October 31, 1780, the subject of appointing a General Grand Master of all the United States was proposed, and the following resolutions were adopted:

"*First*, That it will be for the advancement of Masonry, that a Grand Master of Masons be appointed throughout the United States of America.

"*Second*, That the said Grand Master be chosen annually on the feast of St. John the Baptist, by a majority of the Grand Lodges throughout the United States of America, or at such other time as they shall judge necessary.

"*Third*, That the said Grand Master shall have no power but what shall, from time to time, be delegated to him by a majority of the Grand Lodges throughout the United States of America.

"*Fourth*, That the said Grand Master call a convention of all the Grand Lodges in the United States, within three months after his election, at such place as he shall judge most conducive to the good of the Craft; such convention to consist of one person chosen from each Grand Lodge.

"*Fifth*, That the Grand Master sit as president of the convention, to examine into any abuses that may have crept into Masonry, and rectify the same, examine the Book of Constitutions, abrogate, make, or alter laws, if they shall judge necessary, and lay their proceedings before the Grand Lodges for their approbation.

"*Sixth*, That his Excellency General GEORGE WASHINGTON be General Grand Master of Masons throughont the United States of America.

"The Right Worshipful Master and Wardens are directed to write to our representatives in the Grand Lodge, informing them of our resolutions."

The Grand Lodge of Massachusetts, however, having more fully considered the subject, thought the election of a General Grand Master of the United States, at that time, premature and inexpedient, and ordered the following resolution of their Grand Body to be sent to the Grand Lodge of Pennsylvania.

"Boston, January 9, 1781.

"As the Grand Lodge have not been acquainted with the opinions of the various Grand Lodges in the United States, respecting the choice of a Grand Master General, and the circumstances of our public affairs making it impossible we should at present obtain their sentiments upon it, therefore, voted, That no determination upon the subject could, with the propriety and justice due to the Craft at large, be made by this Grand Lodge, until a general peace shall happily take place throughout the continent.

"From the Grand Lodge records,

"Wm. Haskins, *Secretary.*"

This correspondence with the Grand Lodge of Massachusetts was the last effort made by the Grand Lodge of Pennsylvania to establish a General American Head over all the lodges in this country; and in later times, when the project has been advocated by other Grand Bodies, her voice has been invariably against it. From her action in 1780 arose, undoubtedly, the wide-spread appellation of the title of General Grand Master to Washington,—an historical error, which has not yet been eradicated in the minds of all Masons. There is no doubt that in the minds of all his Masonic compeers, after the independence of this country was attained, he was justly regarded as the Great Patron of the Fraternity in America, which led many to believe, at the time of his death, and long after, that he had held official rank as General Grand Master.

Nor was WASHINGTON's fame as a Mason, or the belief that he was General Grand Master, confined to this country; for, in 1786, two letters in French were addressed to him, from Cape François, as "*Grand Master of America*," soliciting a lodge-warrant for brethren on that island; which letters WASHINGTON caused to be laid before the Grand Lodge of Pennsylvania, and they accordingly granted the warrant. A venerable brother in Virginia also informs us that his father, who was a Mason in Scotland, emigrated to this country soon after the close of the Revolutionary War; and that he had often heard him say, that his Masonic brethren in Scotland congratulated him, when he left, on the advantages and protection he would enjoy from Masonry in this country, as General WASHINGTON they said was Grand Master of Masons here. This illusion

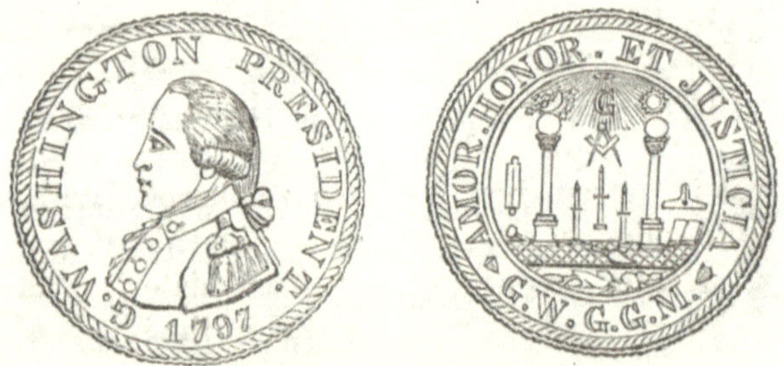

WASHINGTON MASONIC MEDAL, 1797.

was also perpetuated by a Masonic medal, which was struck in 1797, having on its obverse side the bust of WASHINGTON in military dress, with its legend, "G. WASHINGTON, PRESIDENT, 1797;" and on its reverse side, the emblems of Masonry, surrounded by the inscription,

"AMOR, HONOR, ET JUSTICIA," and the initials, "G. W., G. G. M."

Although the Grand Lodge of Pennsylvania did not succeed in creating a General Grand Mastership, and elevating WASHINGTON to that office, as was her desire, and also that of the Military Lodges of the army, from whom the proposition first sprang, yet that Grand Body still continued to regard him as first among

ARMS OF THE FREEMASONS.

American Masons. At her first meeting for reorganization, after the British troops evacuated Philadelphia, she had appointed a committee, of which the Rev. Dr. WM. SMITH was chairman, to prepare a new Book of Constitutions. Dr. SMITH accordingly digested and abridged the English Book of Constitutions used by the Ancient York Masons; and on the 22d of November, 1781, submitted to the Grand Lodge the result of his labors, which was a Book of Constitutions, &c., which has since been known as "SMITH'S Ahiman

Rezon." It was approved and unanimously adopted at that meeting, and ordered to be printed, with the Masons' coat of arms as a frontispiece; and the Grand Lodge further resolved, "In case our beloved and illustrious brother General WASHINGTON permit it to

be dedicated to him, that his Excellency's arms be prefixed to the dedication." At a meeting of the Grand Lodge, in December, 1782, it was further resolved that Dr. SMITH'S Masonic sermon and prayer, which had been delivered in presence of WASHINGTON, on the 28th of December, 1778, should also be published in the work. The book was printed in 1783, with the following dedication, but WASHINGTON'S coat of arms was not inserted:

"TO HIS EXCELLENCY GEORGE WASHINGTON, ESQ.,

"*General and Commander-in-Chief of the Armies of the United States of America:*

"In testimony, as well of his exalted services to his country, as of that noble philanthropy which distinguishes him among Masons, the following Constitutions of the most ancient and honorable fraternity of Free and Accepted Masons, by order and in behalf of the Grand Lodge of Pennsylvania, etc., is dedicated, by his Excellency's most humble servant and faithful brother,

"WILLIAM SMITH, *G. Secretary.*

"*June* 24, 1782."

At a meeting of the Grand Lodge, held on the 10th of June, 1787, it was ordered that the Right Worshipful Grand Master and Deputy Grand Master present to General WASHINGTON a copy of this Book of Constitutions; and in an inventory of his library, made by the appraisers of his estate after his death, this book appears in the schedule.

The Military Lodges of the Revolution should not be forgotten, in a just tribute to the memory of WASHING-

TON. There were ten of these instituted in the American army, in the following order, and by the following authorities:

1st. St. John's Regimental Lodge, in the United States Battalion, July 24, 1775, by the old Provincial Grand Lodge of New York (Moderns).

2d. American Union Lodge, in the Connecticut line, February 15, 1776, by the Grand Lodge of Massachusetts (Moderns).

3d. No. 19, on the Pennsylvania Grand Lodge Registry, in the first regiment of Pennsylvania artillery, May 18, 1779, by the Grand Lodge of Pennsylvania (Ancients).

4th. Washington Lodge, in the Massachusetts line, October 6, 1779, by the Massachusetts Grand Lodge (Ancients).

5th. No. 20, on the Pennsylvania Grand Lodge Registry, in a North Carolina regiment, —— 1779, by the Grand Lodge of Pennsylvania (Ancients).

6th. No. 27, on the Pennsylvania Grand Lodge Registry, in the Maryland line, April 4, 1780, by the Grand Lodge of Pennsylvania (Ancients).

7th. No. 28, on the Pennsylvania Grand Lodge Registry, in the Pennsylvania line, —— 1780, by the Grand Lodge of Pennsylvania (Ancients).

8th. No. 29, on the Pennsylvania Grand Lodge Registry, in the Pennsylvania line, July 27, 1780, by the Grand Lodge of Pennsylvania (Ancients).

9th. No. 31, on the Pennsylvania Grand Lodge Registry, in the New Jersey line, March 26, 1781, by the Grand Lodge of Pennsylvania (Ancients).

10th. No. 36, on the Pennsylvania Grand Lodge Registry, in the New Jersey line, September 2, 1782, by the Grand Lodge of Pennsylvania (Ancients).

Masonic records, and the concurrent testimony of WASHINGTON's compeers, both show that while commander-in-chief of the American revolutionary army he countenanced the establishment and encouraged the labors of these Military Lodges, wisely considering them as schools of urbanity, well calculated to disseminate those mild virtues of the heart, so ornamental to human character, and particularly useful to correct the ferocity of soldiers, and alleviate the miseries of war. The cares of his high office engrossed too much of his time to admit of his engaging in the duties of the chair; yet he found frequent opportunities to visit these lodges, and thought it no degradation to his dignity to stand there on a level with his brethren.*

There were many Masonic Lodges also connected with the British army during this period, and on several occasions the warrant and other property of such lodges were captured by American troops, but in each case they were promptly returned. One of these lodges was No. 227, on the registry of the Grand Lodge of Ireland, which has claimed that WASHINGTON was made a Mason in it during the old French War. The "*London Freemasons' Magazine*" states, "during the Revolution, its lodge-chest fell into the hands of the Americans; they reported the circumstance to General WASHINGTON, who embraced the opportunity of testifying his estimation of Masonry in the most marked and gratifying manner, by directing a guard of honor, un-

* See BIGELOW's address on the death of WASHINGTON.

der a distinguished officer, should take charge of the chest, with many articles of value, and return them to the regiment. The surprise, the feeling of both officers and men, may be imagined, when they perceived the flag of truce that announced this elegant compliment from their noble opponent, but still more noble brother. The guard of honor, with their flutes playing a sacred march, the chest containing the constitution and implements of the craft, borne aloft, like another Ark of the Covenant, equally by Englishmen and Americans, who, lately engaged in the strife of war, now marched through the enfiladed ranks of the gallant regiment, that with presented arms and colors hailed the glorious act by cheers, which the sentiment rendered sacred as the hallelujahs of an angel's song."

On another occasion, "during the war of the Revolution, while the army was encamped in New Jersey, a party of American troops was sent out on a foraging expedition, and on their way fell in with a number of British soldiers, who had been placed as a guard over some baggage which was being removed to a distant place. A skirmish ensued, they were taken prisoners, and with their baggage removed to the American army. On an examination of the baggage, a Templar's sash and Master's apron were found, which excited some surprise among the soldiers, and were immediately carried to the tent of the commander-in-chief. As soon as his eye fell upon them, he gave instructions that the baggage should be carefully protected from all injury, that inquiries should be made after the owner of these articles, and if found, that he be requested to repair immediately to his tent.

"He soon made his appearance. Kind words and friendly greetings attended his reception. He was treated with the utmost care while a prisoner, and was soon after sent home to England on parole, attended by all the comforts and conveniences which it was possible to bestow upon him in those times of trouble. This person was Sergeant KELLY of the British army, who, after his arrival home, lived to a good old age, and preserved that sash and apron with the greatest care. On his dying bed, surrounded by his kindred—and among the number was an old and tried friend, who was a brother Mason—he ordered the sash and apron to be produced, and calling his old friend and brother to his side, exacted from him a promise, to forward, after his death, the same to Montgomery Lodge, in the city of New York, with an accompanying letter, stating it to be a memento to the fraternity, of the kindness and fraternal regard of GEORGE WASHINGTON towards an humble brother and a stranger; and as a testimonial that 'the memory of the just is blessed, and shall live and flourish like the green bay-tree.' These relics were presented to Montgomery Lodge in 1838, where they now remain, and are preserved with care." *

A military alliance with France had been formed in 1778, by which auxiliary French troops were sent to America; and early in 1781, WASHINGTON visited Rhode Island to confer with the French commander on the approaching campaign. A lodge existed there, known as King David's Lodge, whose warrant had been granted by GEORGE HARRISON, Provincial Grand Master of New York, to MOSES M. HAYS, a Jewish citi-

* See FOLGER's address, November 4, 1852, before Benevolent Lodge, New York.

zen of New York city, bearing date February 17, 1769, empowering him to hold a lodge in that city. This warrant he had taken to Rhode Island in 1780, and was then holding a lodge under it in Newport. Having learned that Washington was daily expected there, this lodge, upon the 7th of February, 1781, appointed a committee, consisting of Mr. Hays and others, for the purpose of preparing an address, in behalf of the lodge, to present to him. At a meeting of the lodge, held at the request of the Master, February 14th, this committee reported, "That, on inquiry, they find General Washington not to be a Grand Master of North America, as was supposed, nor even Master of any particular lodge; they are therefore of opinion, that this lodge would not choose to address him as a private brother, and at the same time they think it would not be agreeable to our worthy brother to be addressed as such." The lodge therefore voted that the address be entirely laid aside for the present.

The campaign of this year is ever memorable for the capture of Cornwallis at Yorktown. "In that village," says the Honorable Robert G. Scott, of Virginia, "was Lodge No. 9, where, after the siege had ended, Washington, La Fayette, Marshall, and Nelson came together, and by their union bore abiding testimony to the beautiful tenets of Masonry."*

The surrender of Cornwallis was a day of jubilee in the American army, and Washington ordered all offenders in the camp who were under arrest, to be par-

* See Brother Scott's address at laying the corner-stone of the Washington Monument at Richmond. This statement we have been unable to verify.

doned and set at liberty. He also acknowledged an overruling Providence in their success, by directing that divine services should be held in the army, and public acknowledgments rendered to GOD for his signal interposition in their behalf. But it was not the army alone that gave way to joy and thanksgiving on this occasion, for the whole country was jubilant. "The news of the surrender," says a writer of that day, "reached Philadelphia between one and two o'clock *at night*. The watchman in those days were in the habit of calling the hour. They were all Germans, and the welkin resounded—'*Oh, bast two o'clock; und* CORNWALLIS *is taken!*' Windows were thrown up by ladies in night-caps to catch the sound, and forthwith every house was illuminated." Congress also appointed a day of national thanksgiving, and voted thanks and other testimonials to WASHINGTON and his officers.

But while the heart of America beat wildly with joy on this occasion, that of WASHINGTON was smitten with grief by a deep domestic affliction; for he was compelled to hasten from the field of his recent triumph to Eltham, a few miles distant, to attend the deathbed of his stepson, JOHN PARKE CUSTIS, the only remaining one of the two children of his wife at the time of his marriage. WASHINGTON, who had never had children of his own, had loved these with all a parent's fondness. The daughter had died just before the war, and his grief on that occasion was equalled only by that of Mrs. WASHINGTON. She had then just grown to womanhood, and was called *the dark-eyed lady of Mount Vernon.*

The loss of JOHN PARKE CUSTIS, who had served as one of his aid-de-camps during a part of the war, and who had contracted his death-fever at Yorktown, was keenly felt by WASHINGTON, and he at once adopted his two youngest children as his own, and they became *the children of Mount Vernon* of after-years. These, too, were a boy and girl, whose names as "GEORGE WASHINGTON PARKE CUSTIS" and "NELLY CUSTIS," were long interwoven with the associations of Mount Vernon.

We may be permitted to give one other scene in WASHINGTON'S domestic relations at this time, and carry the reader with us to the home of his mother at Fredericksburg, which he visited soon after the battle of Yorktown. No pageantry of war, no sounding trumpets, no waving banners announced his coming. She was alone, and her aged hands were diligently employed in domestic industry, as WASHINGTON approached her threshold. A smile of recognition, a warm embrace, and the endearing name of GEORGE, uttered with trembling lips, were a mother's greeting. As she inquired concerning his health, she marked the lines of care and toil that seven years had traced on his manly brow, and then spoke of old friends and associations, but of his present fame and glory not a word. WASHINGTON had been accompanied to Fredericksburg by many distinguished officers of the French and American armies, and the citizens of Virginia for many miles around gathered there to welcome the conquerors of CORNWALLIS. In the evening a splendid entertainment was provided, to which the mother of WASHINGTON was specially invited. She remarked that her dancing days were past, but that she should feel happy in contributing to the festivities of the occasion, and consented to attend. When the elegant circle, composed of French and American chivalry, graced with the beauty of the smiling daughters of Virginia, was formed, WASHINGTON entered the room with his mother leaning on his arm, dressed in the plain but becoming garb of the Virginia lady of the olden time. To the attentions and greetings she received from the companions in arms of her son, the renowned warriors of two continents, her words were dignified and courteous, although her manners were reserved. No complimentary attentions that were shown to her produced haughtiness in her demeanor; and at an early hour, wishing the company much pleasure in their entertainment, she remarked it was "high time for old folks to be in bed," and retired, leaning as before on the arm of her son. Those foreign officers who had seen the pageantry and pride of the artificial distinctions of society in the Old World, looked with wonder and admiration on the Spartan plainness of the mother of WASHINGTON; and remarked, that a country which produced such mothers, might well boast of illustrious sons.

CHAPTER V.

LA FAYETTE returns to France.—He is a Mason.—WASHINGTON receives letter from WATSON & CASSOUL with Masonic regalia.—His reply.—This regalia now in Lodge No. 22, at Alexandria.—WASHINGTON at Newburg.—Military Lodges there.—Masonic "Temple."—Its dedication.—Lodge meetings in it.—Celebration at West Point.—WASHINGTON present at celebration of Solomon's Lodge at Poughkeepsie.—Address to him.—Closing scenes of the Revolution.—The "Newburg letters."—WASHINGTON calls a council in the Lodge-room.—Origin of the Society of the Cincinnati.—WASHINGTON its first president.—An earlier proposed "Order of American Knighthood."—WASHINGTON proposed as its Grand Master.—Object of the Society of the Cincinnati.—Opposition to it.—Its Masonic features.—Army disbanded at Newburg.—WASHINGTON's farewell to his officers at New York.—Resigns his commission to Congress at Annapolis.—Extract from his address.—Extract from President Mifflin's address.

AT the close of the campaign of 1781, LA FAYETTE, believing the war virtually closed, returned to France. He had enlisted in our cause during the darkest period of the Revolution, and had been an angel of hope to WASHINGTON, when despondence was written on the brow of many an American soldier. Of all the names on the bright roll of our country's history during the Revolution, that of LA FAYETTE stands next to WASHINGTON.

LA FAYETTE is supposed to have been made a Mason in one of the Military Lodges of this country, but the record of it is lost. Traditions which we shall consider in their proper place, state that it was at Morristown—at Newburg—at Albany—and perhaps at other places that he received his degrees, and even that WASHINGTON presided as Master on some of those occasions. While we are unable to verify these, we entertain no doubt that the Masonic tie existed between them at this time, and was strongly felt.

WASHINGTON was well known in France as a Mason at this period; and a Franco-American mercantile firm there, composed of Messrs. WATSON & CASSOUL, both of whom were Masons, wishing to send some testimony of respect to him, procured some nuns in a convent at Nantes to manufacture a Masonic sash and apron of the finest satin, wrought with gold and silver tissue, on which the French and American flags were combined with various Masonic emblems beautifully delineated. They were executed in a superior and expensive style, and forwarded from France to WASHINGTON, accompanied by the following letter. Mr. WATSON had known General WASHINGTON in America. He was the youthful officer who had charge of the convoy of powder from Providence to the American camp, when they were so destitute of that article before Boston.

"TO HIS EXCELLENCY GENERAL WASHINGTON, *America:*

"MOST ILLUSTRIOUS AND RESPECTED BROTHER — In the moment when all Europe admire and feel the effects of your glorious efforts in support of American liberty, we hasten to offer for your acceptance a small pledge of our homage Zealous lovers of liberty and its institutions, we have experienced the most refined joy in seeing our chief and brother stand forth in its defence, and in defence of a new-born nation of republicans.

"Your glorious career will not be confined to the protection of American liberty, but its ultimate effect will extend to the whole human family, since Providence has evidently selected you as an instrument in His hands to fulfil His eternal decrees.

"It is to you, therefore, the glorious orb of America, we presume to offer Masonic ornaments as an emblem of your virtues. May the Grand Architect of the universe be the guardian of your precious days, for the glory of the western hemisphere and the entire universe. Such are the vows of those who have the favor to be, by all the known numbers,

"Your affectionate brothers,

"WATSON & CASSOUL.

"EAST OF NANTES, 23d 1st month, 5782."

WASHINGTON replied to this letter as follows, from his headquarters at Newburg:

"STATE OF NEW YORK, August 10, 1782.

"GENTLEMEN—The Masonic ornaments which accompanied your brotherly address of the 23d of January last, though elegant in themselves, were rendered more valuable by the flattering sentiments and affectionate manner in which they were presented.

"If my endeavors to avert the evil with which the country was threatened by a deliberate plan of tyranny, should be crowned with the success that is wished, the praise is due to the GRAND ARCHITECT of the universe, who did not see fit to suffer His superstructure of justice to be subjected to the ambition of the princes of this world, or to the rod of oppression in the hands of any power upon earth.

"For your affectionate vows, permit me to be grateful, and offer mine for true brothers in all parts of the world, and to assure you of the sincerity with which I am,

"Yours,

"G°. Washington.

"Messrs. Watson & Cassoul, East of Nantes."

This letter is still in the hands of the family of Mr. Watson, at Port Kent, New York. It is the earliest Masonic correspondence of Washington that is known to be extant. The sash and apron to which it relates were often worn by Washington, and were after his death presented by his legatees to Washington Lodge, No. 22, at Alexandria, where they are still preserved.

Our sketch now leads us again to the banks of the Hudson, near Newburg, where the principal northern forces under Washington were stationed. Here, in 1782–3, in rude huts erected to shelter them, they awaited the progress of events which might close their military labors, and secure to them the boon for which they had endured years of toil, privations, and peril; or which might require them to again renew their weary marches, and bare their breasts in deadly conflicts.

Many Military Lodges existed in the army at this period, but the records of most of them are lost. So well established had these camp-lodges become, and so beneficial to the brethren, that in providing the necessary conveniences for the troops in their quarters on the Hudson at this time, an Assembly-room, or Hall was built, one of the purposes of which was to serve as a Lodge-room for the Military Lodges. Wash-

INGTON himself ordered the erection of the building. It was a rude wooden structure, forming an *oblong square*, forty by sixty feet, was one story in height, and had but a single door. Its windows were square unglazed openings, elevated so high as to prevent the prying gaze of the cowan. Its timbers were hewed, squared, and numbered for their places; and when the building was finished, it was joyously dedicated, and called "*The Temple of Virtue.*"

This *Temple*, or "Assembly-room," as it was sometimes called, was not appropriated exclusively to Masonic purposes; but on the Sabbath it was used as a chapel for religious services, and at other times for meetings of the officers of the army, and also for dancing and other festive amusements. The American Union Lodge met in this room on the 24th of June, 1782, preparatory to celebrating the festival of St. John the Baptist, and proceeded from thence to West Point, where they were joined by Washington Lodge, when a procession was formed at the house of General PATTERSON, its first master; and both lodges proceeded from thence to the "Colonnade," where a dinner was provided, and an oration delivered by Colonel JOHN BROOKS, Master of Washington Lodge, and afterwards governor of Massachusetts. American Union Lodge then returned to their room at the temple, and closed in good time. We have no record of WASHINGTON'S being present on this occasion; but at a celebration of the festival of St. John the Evangelist, on the 27th of December of the same year by King Solomon's Lodge at Poughkeepsie, WASHINGTON was present as a visitor. The imperfect records of that lodge state, that "after dinner the following address was presented to his excellency, Brother WASHINGTON:"

"We, the Master, and Wardens, and Brethren of Solomon's Lodge, No. 1, are highly sensible of the honor done to Masonry in general by the countenance shown to it by the most dignified character ——."

We have given the language of this address as it stands recorded on the minute-book of the lodge; but it has the appearance of being the commencement of an address to WASHINGTON which the secretary neglected fully to record. We regret that he did not give us the full address, and WASHINGTON'S reply. It was the first instance we have met with of a formal Masonic address by any lodge to WASHINGTON.

The drama of the Revolution had been virtually closed at Yorktown, in October, 1781, by the capture of CORNWALLIS, and the operations of the armies in the two succeeding years partook more of the nature of an armistice than of military campaigns. The principal British force remaining in America was still in possession of the city of New York, and WASHINGTON'S headquarters were still at Newburg. The scenes which occurred at Newburg during the cantonment of the troops there from the autumn of 1781 to the final disbanding of the army in November, 1783, are not without interest in the Masonic history of WASHINGTON.

It was during this transition period from war to peace, when inaction had given the officers and soldiers of the army time to reflect on their past and present sufferings, and the future that was before them, that a spirit of discontent arose almost to mutiny and rebellion.

Earnest but respectful solicitations had been made to Congress for relief from their embarrassments, by an adjustment of their meritorious claims; but the tardy action of that body so increased the discontent of the army, that a call was made, from a then unknown source, for a grand convention of the officers to meet and demand of Congress in unequivocal terms immediate redress. Two anonymous letters, artfully written, appealing to the passions of the army, and denouncing as a traitor to its interests any one who should venture to recommend moderation and delay, were at the same time put in circulation.

WASHINGTON saw that a crisis had come when the integrity of the army and the authority of Congress must be maintained, or all the toil, privation, and blood of the past eight years, and all the glorious hopes of the future, would be at once lost. He therefore ordered a council of his tried and trusty officers to meet at the lodge-room in the "Temple," and by his own wise counsels in it, obtained another proof of the devotion of the army, and the attachment of the officers to him as their commander.

No historian can ever determine the influence of that mystic tie that bound so many of the officers of that suffering patriot army in bonds of Masonic brotherhood to WASHINGTON, in the happy termination of this incipient treason. He had often joined with them in the same room in Masonic labors; and while, by the constitutions of Masonry, neither the civil or military concerns of the country could have been discussed in the lodge, yet who will say that the lessons taught and learned there were not instrumental, in the hands of WASHINGTON, in directing and controlling the minds of his associate officers at this critical period. But the veil which then covered the hand that so cunningly penned those anonymous letters, which sought to draw even WASHINGTON himself from his devotion to the civil authorities, still rests on the strength of that mystic tie that bound so many of that patriot band to him, and through him to our country.

We have already noted in our sketch the strong desire of the Masonic brethren in the army that WASHINGTON should be constituted the head of Masons in this country. But as the time for the disbanding of the army drew near, and no definite action of the whole Fraternity in America had been taken, an affectionate regard of the officers for their commander, and for each other, led them to form an association among themselves, having the social features of the Masonic institution as its leading principle, and designed, by inculcating benevolence and mutual relief, to perpetuate their friendships, and incite in their minds the most exalted patriotism. The idea of such a society is said to have originated with General KNOX, who communicated his plan to Baron STEUBEN; and at a general meeting of the officers, on the 13th of May, 1783, with the approbation of WASHINGTON, they instituted the "Society of the Cincinnati," and he became its first president, and continued to hold the office until his death.

In a sermon delivered on the 4th of July, 1790, before the State Society of the Cincinnati of Pennsylvania, by the Rev. WILLIAM SMITH, D. D., and provost of the college at Philadelphia, he claims that the *name* of CINCINNATI for this society was adopted from a suggestion of his, in a Masonic sermon preached before the Grand Lodge of Pennsylvania in presence of WASHINGTON, on the festival of the Evangelist in 1778, in which he alludes to him as the "Cincinnatus of the age."

The newspapers of that period give an account of an earlier proposed association, or "New Order of American Knighthood," as it was called. As early as March 25, 1783, the Philadelphia papers stated that,

"On the next anniversary of Independence, the 4th of July, a new Order of Knighthood, called the *Order of Freedom*, will be established, and the installation take place in the city of Philadelphia.

"Patron of the Order;—ST. LOUIS.

"Chief of the Order;—President of Congress for the time being.

"Grand Master;—General WASHINGTON.

"Chancellor;—Dr. FRANKLIN.

"Prelate;—Dr. WITHERSPOON.

"Genealogist;—Mr. PAYNE.

"Gentleman Usher;—Mr. THOMPSON.

"Register and Secretary;—Mr. DIGGS.

"Herald;—Mr. HUTCHINGS.

"Twenty-four knight companions, consisting of the governor of each State for the time being, which they reckon nineteen.

"General LINCOLN;—General GREENE;—General WAYNE;—Colonel LEE.

"The robe is to be scarlet and blue, with ermine,—the ribbon a broad satin, with thirteen alternate stripes of red and white; to which will be suspended an embossed medal of gold and enamel, on the front of which will be represented Virtue, the genius of the United States, dressed like an Amazon, resting on a spear with one hand, and holding a sword with the other, and treading on Tyranny, represented by a man prostrate, a crown fallen from his head, a broken chain in his left hand, and a scourge in his right; in the exergue, *Sic semper tyrannis.* On the reverse is a group: Liberty with her wand and Pileus; on one side of her, Ceres with a cornucopia in one hand, and an ear of wheat in the other; on the other side, Eternity, with the globe and Phœnix. In the exergue, *Deus nobis hoc otia fecit.* The loop of the medal is to be formed by the figure of a rattlesnake with the tail in its mouth, as an emblem of eternity. An erect staff of liberty, terminated by a cap at top, will be fixed to the body of the snake, and under it the motto of *In recto decus.*"

This we believe to have been the earliest attempt in the United States to form a social institution modelled after civic distinctions of society in Europe. Who its projectors were, who its advocates, and who its opposers, we have not learned. Although such a society never went into existence, yet as it contemplated for General WASHINGTON the distinguished honor of being its Grand Master, and as a curious prelude to the formation of the Society of the Cincinnati, we have given it a place in this sketch.

The Society of the Cincinnati was designed as an association of the officers of the army after its disbanding, and of their eldest male descendants, to whom the privilege of membership was to be hereditary. It provided for a golden medal or "Order," as a badge of distinction to its members, and made provision also for funds from the attainment of membership and voluntary contribution, for the relief of its indigent members.

The Society of the Cincinnati thus became an organized body, without any known opposition either in the army or from citizens in civil life. Its associations were pleasing to its members, and they doubtless looked forward to its future meetings as social reunions, without any idea of personal aggrandizement to themselves. But a strong feeling of jealousy and opposition to the society soon sprang up in different States; and, as it was claimed by many that it created a new order of hereditary nobility, the public mind became strongly opposed to it in many of them. Pennsylvania, Massachusetts, and Connecticut officially declared the institution unjustifiable, and Rhode Island proceeded so far as to annul the civil privileges of all her citizens who should be members of it, and declare them incapable of holding any office under her government. While this opposition to the society in America arose from a belief that it was dangerous to the liberties of the country, it is a curious commentary on the fallibility of opinions, and the strength of prejudice, that Gustavus the Third, king of Sweden, forbade the Swedish officers who had served in the French army during the American war, to wear the badges of the Cincinnati, on the ground that the institution had a *republican* tendency, and was not suited to his government.

WASHINGTON saw, that though the institution was innocent in itself and laudable in its real objects, yet, that the prejudices of the people were too deeply disturbed by it; and by his recommendation its constitution was changed at its next annual meeting, by withdrawing all claims of its members to hereditary distinctions, disclaiming all interference with political subjects, and placing their funds under the immediate cognizance of State legislatures, retaining only their right to indulge their own private feelings of friendship, and the acts of benevolence which it was their intention should flow from them.

The social and benevolent features of this society were strikingly similar to the same features in Masonry, from which, doubtless, the leading idea was drawn. Many of its members were Masons, and as such, well understood the social influence of a union that embraced in its objects, not only the welfare and happiness of its members while living, but of their widows and orphans after them. From this institution, Masonry may also a few years later have drawn some of its principles of government in the higher bodies of the Ancient York Rite.

The autumnal months of 1783 were the last in the military life of WASHINGTON. His army had been disbanded at Newburg, and he had seen each corps of his remaining soldiers file by him for the last time, and pass onward to their homes. He then hastened to New York, where his final adieu was to be taken of his officers. The British troops had evacuated the city on the 25th of November; and on the 4th of December, at meridian, WASHINGTON's principal officers assembled at FRAUNCES' tavern, to take a final leave of their commander.

The scene was affecting beyond comparison. There

were gathered there those who for eight long years had been his faithful associates in privations and dangers; who had followed him in many weary marches, and fought by his side in many an unequal battle. Many were there who had sat with him in the war-councils of the camp, and mingled with him in the mystic labors of the Masonic lodge-room. And now they were met to bid him, as their loved commander, a last farewell!

As WASHINGTON entered the room, and stood for the last time before them, he could not conceal his emotions. Filling a glass with wine, he raised it, and said: "With a heart full of love and gratitude, I now take leave of you; and most devoutly do I wish that your latter days may be as prosperous and happy as your former ones have been glorious and honorable." He tasted the wine, and, with voice trembling with emotion, said: "I cannot come to each of you, to take my leave; but shall be obliged to you, if each of you will come and take me by the hand." General KNOX stood nearest to him. WASHINGTON grasped his proffered hand, and, incapable of utterance, drew him to his bosom with a tender embrace. Each officer in his turn received the same silent affectionate farewell. Every eye was filled with tears, every heart throbbed with emotion, but no tongue interrupted the tenderness of the scene. To those who had known him only as the stern commander, it was like JOSEPH's making himself known to his brethren; but to those who had met him as a brother in the lodge-room, it was but the renewal of the mystic grasp, and the well-remembered silent embrace they had each known before.

"Weeping through that sad group he pass'd,
Turned once, and gazed, and then was gone—
It was his tenderest, and his last."

A corps of infantry received him at the door, and as he passed through their ranks, they saw his broad bosom heave with emotions to them unseen before; and the sobs of sorrow, and the tears that fell fast on their cheeks, told how well they loved him. WASHINGTON hastened on board a barge upon the Hudson that was ready to receive him, and as the dipping oar sped him from them, he raised his hat above his head, and bade all whom he left behind a silent adieu.

But there was still another link to be severed in the chain that bound him, as commander-in-chief, to our country, and he hastened to Annapolis, where Congress was then in session, to return to their hands the commission he had received from them eight years before, and lay before them a sword unstained with dishonor. He arrived at Annapolis on the 19th day of December, and immediately signified to Congress his purpose to resign into their hands his commission, and desired their pleasure as to the time and manner of its reception. That body, desirous of giving dignity to the spectacle, and honor to him who was its chief actor, appointed the following Tuesday, at meridian, to honor him with a public audience, and receive from his own hand the high commission he bore.

Upon the 23d of December, at the hour appointed, the closing scene in the drama of the Revolution took place. The chosen representatives of the States were each in their seats, and a few distinguished foreigners and Americans were admitted to their floor, while the gallery was crowded with citizens. As WASHINGTON entered, every spectator arose and stood uncovered, while the members of Congress, representing the supreme majesty of the people, remained covered in their seats. Nine years before he had been a member of that same body, as an honored delegate from Virginia, and had been elected from his seat, by their own wise choice, to receive a commission he now held in his hand to return again to them. But to whom was he to return it? As representing the sovereignty of the people, the body was indeed the same; but, alas! many familiar faces were not there. The first president of that body, PEYTON RANDOLPH, was not there. Loving hands had, years before, borne him to his last resting-place in the green fields of Virginia, and his Masonic brethren had planted the acacia over his grave.

As WASHINGTON advanced to offer his commission to General MIFFLIN, then president of the body, amidst a deep and solemn silence, he addressed him in words of felicitation on the happy termination of the war, commended the interests of our country to the protection of Almighty God, and closed by saying:

> "Having now finished the work assigned me, I retire from the great theatre of action; and bidding an affectionate farewell to this august body, under whose orders I have so long acted, I here offer my commission, and take my leave of the employments of public life."

President MIFFLIN received his commission with words of gratitude and tenderness, and closed by saying:

"We join you in commending the interests of our dearest country to the protection of Almighty God, beseeching him to dispose the hearts and minds of its citizens to improve the opportunity afforded them of becoming a happy and respectable nation; and for you, we address to him our earnest prayers, that a life so beloved may be fostered with all his care; that your latter days may be as happy as they have been illustrious, and that he will finally give you that reward which this world cannot give."

5

CHAPTER VI.

WASHINGTON arrives at Mount Vernon.—Receives a letter from lodge at Alexandria.—His reply.—He resumes domestic employments.—His feelings on the occasion.—Calls upon his time and attention burdensome to him.—Employs Mr. LEAR as secretary.—A visit from Mr. WATSON.—Receives invitation to attend celebration of St. John the Baptist by Lodge at Alexandria.—His reply.—He attends the celebration.—Is elected an honorary member of the Lodge.—LA FAYETTE visits America.—Presents WASHINGTON Masonic sash and apron.—Apron afterwards presented to Grand Lodge of Pennsylvania.—Distinction between WATSON & CASSOUL apron and LA FAYETTE apron.—Laying of the cornerstone of the Academy at Alexandria.—Grand Lodge of New York dedicates its first book of constitutions to WASHINGTON.—Such dedications to him usual during his lifetime.—Grand Lodge of Pennsylvania becomes an independent body, and requires her lodges to renew their warrants.—WASHINGTON president of convention to form Federal constitution.—Lodge at Alexandria takes a new warrant from the Grand Lodge of Virginia, and chooses WASHINGTON as Master.—Interesting records and correspondence at that time on the subject.—WASHINGTON elected President under the Federal constitution.—Masonic incidents relating to this election in Philadelphia.—Holland Lodge in New York elects WASHINGTON an honorary member.—Copy of its letter and certificate to him.—Old "Washington Chapter" of New-York.—WASHINGTON's last visit to his mother.—Her death and grave.

WASHINGTON proceeded to Mount Vernon immediately after resigning his commission at Annapolis, and arrived there on the following evening. It was the 24th of December, three days before the anniversary of St. John the Evangelist. A lodge of Freemasons had been formed in Alexandria, a few miles from his home, in the preceding February. It was working under a warrant from the Grand Lodge of Pennsylvania, and numbered, 39. Robert Adam was its Master, and many of Washington's old friends and neighbors, in and about Alexandria, were its members. This lodge was preparing to celebrate the coming festival of St. John the Evangelist, on the 27th; and the following letter, signed by the officers of the lodge, was addressed to General Washington:

"Alexandria, 26th December, 1783.

"Sir—Whilst all denominations of people bless the happy occasion of your excellency's return to enjoy private and domestic felicity, permit us, sir, the members of Lodge No. 39, lately established in Alexandria, to assure your excellency, that we, as a mystical body, rejoice in having a brother so near us, whose pre-eminent benevolence has secured the happiness of millions; and that we shall esteem ourselves highly honored at all times your excellency shall be pleased to join us in the needful business.

"We have the honor to be, in the name and behalf of No. 39, your excellency's

Devoted friends and brothers,

Robert Adam, M.,
E. C. Dick, S. W.,
J. Allison, J. W.,
Wm. Ramsey, Treas.

"His Excellency General Washington."

Washington had but two days before returned to the quiet of his own loved home, after years of toil and dangers in the camp and in the battle-field, and he might well have said to them:

"Now give me rest; my years demand
 A holiday, companions dear:
My days are drawing to an end,
 And I would for that end prepare.

"Now give me rest; but when ye meet,
 Brothers, in that beloved spot,
My name with loving lips repeat,
 And never let it be forgot."

WASHINGTON was unable to attend this festival, but he sent to the lodge the following reply:

"MOUNT VERNON, 28th December, 1783.

"GENTLEMEN—With a pleasing sensibility, I received your favor of the 26th; and beg leave to offer my sincere thanks for the favorable sentiments with which it abounds.

"I shall always feel pleasure when it may be in my power to render service to Lodge No. 39, and in every act of brotherly kindness to the members of it, being with great truth,

"Your affectionate brother
and obedient servant,
"G°. WASHINGTON.

"ROBERT ADAM, Esq., Master,
Wardens and Treasurer of Lodge No. 39."

WASHINGTON'S feelings and employments on returning to private life may be best seen from his own correspondence; and from various letters of his written at that period, the following extracts are given:

"The scene is at last closed. * * * * On the eve of Christmas I entered these doors, an older man by nine years than when I left them. * * * * I am just beginning to experience that ease and freedom from public cares, which, however desirable, takes some time to realize. It was not till lately I could get the better of my usual custom of ruminating, as soon as I waked in the morning, on the business of the ensuing day; and of my surprise at finding, after revolving many things in my mind, that I was no longer a public man, nor had any thing to do with public transactions. * * * * * I hope to spend the remainder of my days in cultivating the affections of good men, and in the practice of the domestic virtues. * * * * * The life of the husbandman, of all others, is the most delightful. It is honorable, it is amusing, and with judicious management, it is profitable. * * * * * I have not only retired from all public employments, but I am retiring within myself, and shall be able to view the solitary walk, and tread the paths of private life with a heartfelt satisfaction. Envious of none, I am determined to be pleased with all; and this, my dear friend, being the order of my march, I will move gently down the stream of life, until I sleep with my fathers."

Such sentiments are so perfectly in accordance with the precepts of Masonry, that they are worthy of a place in WASHINGTON's Masonic history. But in his retirement to Mount Vernon he was not lost to the world, nor forgotten by his countrymen. With Virginian hospitality, his doors were ever open, and all who had a claim on his friendship or his kindness were ever received with welcome; and he was ready, too, to respond to letters written to him from people of every condition, and upon every subject. But the anxiety of those who travelled abroad was so great to carry some testimonial from him, and of those who remained at home to possess some memorial of his kindness, that the labor of replying to the numerous letters addressed to him became a burden. To an intimate friend he wrote

"It is not, my dear sir, the letters of my friends which give me trouble, or add aught to my perplexity. I receive them with pleasure, and pay as much attention to them as my avocations will permit. It is in reference to old matters with which I have nothing to do; applications which oftentimes cannot be complied with; inquiries, to satisfy which would employ the pen of an historian; letters of compliment, as unmeaning, perhaps, as they are troublesome, but which must be attended to; and commonplace business, which employ my pen and my time, often disagreeably. Indeed, these, with company, deprive me of exercise; and unless I can obtain relief, must be productive of disagreeable consequences. Already I begin to feel their effects. Heavy and painful oppressions of the head, and other disagreeable sensations often trouble me. I am, therefore, determined to employ some person who shall ease me of the *drudgery* of this business. * * * * * * To correspond with those I love is among my highest gratifications. Letters of friendship require no study; the communications they contain flow with ease, and allowances are expected and made. But this is not the case with those which require research, consideration, and recollection."

WASHINGTON was compelled to employ a young gentleman of talents and education to relieve himself of these irksome labors, and to his care such correspondence was afterwards committed. This was TOBIAS LEAR, who remained his private secretary until his death. Many personal narratives have come down to us of the kind reception WASHINGTON gave his guests at Mount Vernon, and among them is one from the pen of the late Hon. ELKANAH WATSON, who visited him in the winter of 1785. He had been the senior partner of WATSON & CASSOUL in France during the war, and has been already referred to in this sketch as having corresponded with WASHINGTON at that time, and sent him a box of Masonic regalia.

"The first evening," says he, "I spent under the wing of WASHINGTON'S hospitality, we sat a full hour at table by ourselves without the least interruption, after the family had retired. I was extremely oppressed by a severe cold and excessive coughing, contracted by the exposure of a harsh winter journey. He pressed me to take some remedies, but I declined doing so. As usual after retiring, my coughing increased. When some time had elapsed, the door of my room was gently opened, and on drawing my bed-curtains, to my utter astonishment I beheld WASHINGTON himself standing at my bedside, with a bowl of hot tea in his hand. I was mortified and distressed beyond expression. This little incident occurring in common life with an ordinary man, would not have been noticed; but as a trait of the benevolence and private virtue of WASHINGTON, deserves to be recorded."

As WASHINGTON had been unable to attend the festival of the Evangelist in December, his Masonic brethren in Alexandria resolved to give an entertainment for him in the following February, and the lodge directed its secretary to write to him to know when it would be convenient for him to favor them with his company. At a subsequent meeting of the lodge, held on the 20th of February, the Worshipful Master,

Mr. ADAM, informed the brethren that it had been intimated to him that it would be inconvenient for WASHINGTON to attend at present, and the invitation was postponed.

On the approach of the festival of St. John the Baptist in June, the lodge addressed WASHINGTON an invitation to join them, to which he sent the following reply:

"MOUNT VERNON, June 19, 1784.

"DEAR SIR—With pleasure, I received the invitation of the master and members of Lodge No. 39, to dine with them on the approaching anniversary of St. John the Baptist. If nothing unforeseen at present interferes, I will have the honor of doing it. For the polite and flattering terms in which you have expressed their wishes, you will please accept my thanks.

"With esteem and respect,

"I am, dear sir,

"Your most ob't serv't,

"G°. WASHINGTON.

"WM. HERBERT, Esquire."

The records of the lodge, which are still extant, accordingly show that WASHINGTON attended as a Mason this festival; and that its Master, ROBERT ADAM, read to the lodge a most instructive lecture on the rise, progress, and advantages of Masonry, and concluded with a prayer suitable to the occasion. The Master and brethren then proceeded to Mr. WEISE's tavern, where they dined; and after spending the afternoon in Masonic festivity, returned again to the lodge-room, where, as the record states, "The Worshipful Master, with the unanimous consent of the brethren, was pleased to admit his Excellency General Washington, as an honorary member of Lodge No. 39. Lodge closed in perfect harmony at six o'clock."

In the autumn of 1784, La Fayette came to America, and visited Washington at Mount Vernon. Of all the generals of the Revolution he had been the most beloved by Washington; and both to him and to his wife in France had the hospitalities of Mount Vernon been often tendered by Mr. and Mrs. WASHINGTON. Madame LA FAYETTE had wrought with her own hands in France a beautiful Masonic apron of white satin groundwork, with the emblems of Masonry delicately delineated with needle-work of colored silk; and this, with some other Masonic ornaments, was placed in a highly finished rose-wood box, also beautified with Masonic emblems, and brought to WASHINGTON on this occasion as a present by LA FAYETTE. It was a compliment to WASHINGTON and to Masonry delicately paid, and remained among the treasures of Mount Vernon till long after its recipient's death, when the apron was presented by his legatees to the Washington Benevolent Society, and by them to the Grand Lodge of Pennsylvania, in whose possession the apron now is, while the box that contained it is in possession of the lodge at Alexandria. The apron presented to WASHINGTON by Messrs. WATSON & CASSOUL two years before, and which is still in possession of Lodge No. 22 at Alexandria, has been often mistaken for this; but the two aprons may be easily identified, by the WATSON & CASSOUL apron being wrought with gold and silver tissue, with the American and French flags combined upon it, while the LA FAYETTE apron is wrought with silk, and has for its design on the frontlet the Mark Master's circle, and mystic letters, with a *beehive* as its *mark* in the centre. The same device is beautifully inlaid on the lid of the box in which it was originally presented to WASHINGTON; and as this box is also in possession of Lodge No. 22 at Alexandria, and kept with the WATSON & CASSOUL apron, it has by many been supposed that this was the apron presented in 1784 by LA FAYETTE. This mistake has also, perhaps, been perpetuated by a statement, that when LA FAYETTE visited this lodge during his visit to America in 1824, he was furnished with the apron now in possession of Lodge No. 22, and in the box in which he had in 1784 presented one to WASHINGTON, to wear on the occasion; and that he there alluded to it as the one he had in former years presented to his distinguished American brother. Even were this statement true, a lapse of forty years might have misled him in the identity of the apron, particularly as it was handed to him for the occasion in the well-remembered box in which he had, in his early Masonic life, presented one to WASHINGTON. The historic descriptions of the aprons leave no doubt as to the identity of each, and both are among the valued memorials of WASHINGTON'S Masonic history. The WATSON & CASSOUL sash and apron, and also the Masonic box in which the LA FAYETTE apron was presented to WASHINGTON, were presented to Lodge No. 22, at Alexandria, June 3, 1812, by Major LAWRENCE LEWIS, a nephew of WASHINGTON, in behalf of his son, Master LORENZO LEWIS.

During the interval between the close of the Revolution and the first presidency of WASHINGTON, although engrossed with a multitude of cares, he was ever mindful of the interest of society around him, and became the benefactor of the churches and schools. The citizens of Alexandria in 1785 engaged in the erection of an academy in that town, and its corner-stone was laid with Masonic ceremonies on the 7th of September of that year, by ROBERT ADAM, Master of Lodge No. 39 of Alexandria, assisted by the brethren of that lodge. Upon this stone was deposited a plate with the following inscription.

"The foundation of the Alexandria Academy was laid on the 7th of September, 1785, in the ninth year of the independence of the United States of North America. ROBERT ADAM, Esquire, Master of Lodge No. 39, Ancient York Masons, attended by the brethren, and as a monument of the generosity of the inhabitants, stands dedicated to them, and all lovers of literature."

The master then made a present, in the name of the lodge, of five dollars to the workmen, as was the custom on such occasions at that period. General WASHINGTON was one of the trustees and patrons of this academy; and in the following December he endowed it with one thousand pounds, the interest of which he directed should annually be appropriated for the education of orphans and indigent children. The number who were the yearly recipients of this endowment was twenty; and hundreds have thus been since aided by this fund in fitting themselves for useful and honorable stations in life. The building still stands on the foundation-stone which ROBERT ADAM and his Masonic brethren laid in 1785; and the lapse of time and the devastations of war have neither laid it waste nor diverted it from its original purpose.

Masonry was at that time fast assuming in this country an independent American polity; and in 1785 the Grand Lodge of the State of New York, which had been chartered as a Provincial Grand Body while the British troops held possession of its commercial city, virtually renounced its fealty to its parent head in

London; and under ROBERT R. LIVINGSTON, a Grand Master of its own election, it formed for itself a new Book of Constitutions, which was dedicated to WASHINGTON as follows:

"To HIS EXCELLENCY GEORGE WASHINGTON, ESQ.—In testimony, as well of his exalted services to his country, as of his distinguished character as a Mason, the following Book of Constitutions of the ancient and honorable Fraternity of Free and Accepted Masons, by order, and in behalf of the Grand Lodge of the State of New York, is dedicated.

"By his most humble servant,

"JAMES GILES, Grand Secretary.

"A. L., 1785."

The honor of receiving the dedication of Masonic publications had not been conferred on any American Mason previous to WASHINGTON; and this was the third time this distinction was shown him. It is worthy of note in this sketch, that to him such honors were generally given in this country during his lifetime, and they were multiplied until the period of his death, both by Grand Lodges and individual Masons; and when the acacia had fallen on his coffin-lid, some Masonic funeral eulogies were dedicated to Mrs. WASHINGTON.

The Grand Lodge of Pennsylvania terminated its provincial existence in 1786, and became an independent Grand Body. It therefore required its former subordinates to take out new warrants under its new organization. No. 39 at Alexandria had for three years been working under the provincial authority of this Grand Lodge, although at the same time a Grand Lodge of rightful jurisdiction existed in Virginia.

The American Masonic rule, of conceding to each State Grand Lodge Masonic supremacy in its own civil limits, was not universal under the provincial system; and it was no doubt WASHINGTON'S frequent intercourse with the brethren of Philadelphia which had led the Masons of Alexandria to seek their first warrant from the Grand Lodge of Pennsylvania. The lodge at Alexandria did not renew their warrant when the Grand Lodge of Pennsylvania first became independent, but continued until 1788 to work under their first authority.

During this period the Convention which formed the Federal Constitution met in Philadelphia. WASHINGTON was its president, and many distinguished Masons were its members, among whom was EDMUND RANDOLPH, Grand Master of Virginia. As Philadelphia was at that time the most important Grand East in America, there can be no doubt but that the state of Masonry in the new relations of the country was often discussed there; and that from circumstances there considered, the lodge in Alexandria was induced soon after to change its fealty from the Grand Lodge of Pennsylvania to that of Virginia. Its records are of interest at this period, and are as follows:

"*May* 29, 1788.—The lodge proceeded to the appointment of Master and Deputy Master to be recommended to the Grand Lodge of Virginia, when GEORGE WASHINGTON Esq., was unanimously chosen Master; ROBERT McCREA, Deputy Master; WM. HUNTER, Jun., Senior Warden; JNO. ALLISON, Junior Warden.

"*Ordered*, That Brothers McCREA, HUNTER, ALLISON, and

Powell wait on General Washington, and inquire of him whether it will be agreeable to him to be named in the charter.

"*Ordered*, That Brothers Hunter, Jun., and Allison apply to the Grand Lodge at Richmond for a charter for this lodge, and that they be repaid the expenses attending the procuring of it."

"*October* 25, 1788.—Motion made by Brother Hunter, and seconded by Brother Simms, that a committee be appointed to draw up a letter to the Grand Lodge at Richmond, agreeable to the former order of this lodge, requesting a new charter from that honorable body, and that Brother Hunter apply for the same at the expense of this lodge. It is also further ordered, that Brothers McCrea and Simms be appointed to write to the Grand Lodge at Richmond accordingly."

The records of the lodge, under date of November 22, 1788, contain the following copy of the letter written on the occasion:

"The brethren of Lodge No. 39, Ancient York Masons, were congregated, and have hitherto wrought under a warrant from the Grand Lodge of Pennsylvania, who having since the Revolution declared themselves independent of any foreign jurisdiction, and also notified us that it was necessary that we should renew our warrant under the new established Grand Lodge; the brethren comprising this lodge, taking the same under consideration, and having found it inconvenient to attend the different communications of that honorable society in Philadelphia, and as a Grand Lodge is established in our own State at Richmond agreeably to the ancient landmarks, whose communications we can with more ease and convenience attend, have at sundry preceding meetings resolved to ask your honorable society for a new warrant, which has already been communicated to you by letter, and also by our Brother HUNTER personally, who hath obtained an entry of this lodge on your minutes. We have now to observe that at a meeting of this lodge, on the 25th instant, it was unanimously resolved, that an application should be immediately made by this lodge to your honorable society for a charter, which we now do, and pray that it may be granted to us.

"It is also the earnest desire of the members of this lodge that our Brother GEORGE WASHINGTON, Esq., should be named in the charter as Master of the lodge. The names of the other necessary officers of the lodge will be mentioned to you by our Brother HUNTER."

The Grand Lodge of Virginia, in accordance with this request, granted a new warrant to the lodge at Alexandria, constituting Bro. GEORGE WASHINGTON its first Master under its new warrant; and its registry number was changed from No. 39 of Pennsylvania, to No. 22 of Virginia. The following is a verbatum copy of its Virginia warrant:

"EDMUND RANDOLPH, G. M.,

"To all and every to whose knowledge these presents shall come, GREETING:

"Whereas it has been duly represented to us, that in the county of Fairfax and borough of Alexandria in the Commonwealth of Virginia, there reside a number of the brethren of the Society of Freemasons, who have assembled as a lodge agreeably to the regulations of Masonry by the title of the Alexandria Lodge; and it appearing to be for the good and increase of the Fraternity that the said brethren should be encouraged to proceed and work, as heretofore they have done in a regular lodge.

"Know Ye, that we EDMUND RANDOLPH, Esquire, governor of the Commonwealth aforesaid and Grand Master of the Most Ancient and Honorable Society of Freemasons, within the same, by and with the consent of the Grand Lodge of Virginia, do hereby constitute and appoint our illustrious and well-beloved Brother GEORGE WASHINGTON, Esquire, late general and commander-in-chief of the forces of the United States of America, and our worthy brethren ROBERT McCREA, WILLIAM HUNTER, Jr., and JOHN ALLISON, Esqrs., together with all such other brethren as may be admitted to associate with them, to be a just, true and regular lodge of Freemasons, by the name, title, and designation of the Alexandria Lodge No. 22.

"And further do hereby appoint and ordain, all regular lodges to hold and acknowledge, and respect them as such; hereby granting and committing to them and their successors full power and authority to assemble and convene as a regular lodge, to enter and receive Apprentices, pass Fellow Crafts and raise Master Masons according to the known and established customs of Ancient Masonry and NO otherwise; and also to elect and choose Masters, Wardens, and all other officers annually, at such time or times as to them shall seem meet and convenient; and to exact from their members such COMPOSITION as they shall judge necessary for the support of their lodge, the relief of their brethren in distress and contribution towards the Grand Charity and agreeably to the Book of Constitutions and the laws of the Grand Lodge of Virginia; and recommending to the brethren aforesaid to receive and obey their superiors in all things lawful and honest as becomes the honor and harmony of Masons; and to record in their books this present charter with their own regulations and bye-laws, and their whole acts and proceedings from time to time as they occur, and by no means to desert their said lodge hereby constituted, or form themselves into separate meetings, without the consent and approbation of their Master and Wardens for the time being. All which by acceptance hereof they are holden and engaged to observe; and the brethren aforesaid are to acknowledge and recognize the Grand Master and Grand Lodge of Virginia as their superiors, and shall pay due regard and obedience to all such instructions as they have received or hereafter shall receive from thence. And lastly, they are requested to correspond with the Grand Lodge, and to attend the meetings thereof by their Master and Wardens, or their proxies being Master Masons and members of their said lodge.

"Given under the Seal of the Grand Lodge at Richmond in the State of Virginia, the 28th day of April A. L. 5788, A. D. 1788.

"By the GRAND MASTER'S COMMAND.

"WILLIAM WADDILL,
"Grand Secretary.

"*Witness.*
"WM. WADDILL, G. S." [SEAL.]

After the death of WASHINGTON, this lodge, while Colonel GEORGE DENEALE was its Master, desired to change its name from *Alexandria Lodge No.* 22, to *Washington Alexandria Lodge No.* 22. Its records therefore show, under date of October 11, 1804, the following resolution:

"*Resolved,* That the Worshipful Master of this lodge apply

to the Grand Master of the Grand Lodge of Virginia for permission to alter the designation of this lodge from that of the *Alexandria Lodge No.* 22, to that of the *Alexandria Washington Lodge No.* 22."

The following extract from the records of the Grand Lodge of Virginia shows its compliance with the request; and the memory of WASHINGTON as a Mason, and the first Master of this lodge under its Virginia charter has been perpetuated in this name.

"At a Grand Annual Communication of the Grand Lodge of Virginia, begun and held in the Masons' Hall, in the city of Richmond, on the 9th day of December, Anno Lucis 5805, Anno Domini 1805.

"Whereas, at the last Grand Annual Communication a request was made by the Alexandria Lodge No. 22 for permission to change the name of the said Lodge to that of the Alexandria Washington Lodge, No. 22, which request was acceded and a new charter ordered to be issued; and whereas this order did not meet the wishes of the Brethren of the said Lodge, who having had our illustrious Brother General GEORGE WASHINGTON for their first Master, whose name is inserted as such in their original charter, they then were and still are desirous of preserving their said charter, as an honorable testimony of his regard for them and only wish to be permitted by the Grand Lodge to assume the name of the Alexandria Washington Lodge, No. 22, without changing their said charter therefor.

"*Resolved*, That the said lodge be permitted to assume the said name, and that it be henceforth denominated the Alexandria Washington Lodge, No. 22; and that an authenticated copy of this resolution be attached to their said charter.

"Duly copied by me from the records of the Grand Lodge of Virginia, as witness my hand and the seal of the said Grand Lodge, this 17th day of December, A.L. 5805, A.D. 1805.

"WM. H. FITZWHYLSONN, [SEAL.]
" Grand Secretary."

The foregoing records conclusively show, not only WASHINGTON'S connection with this lodge while under its Pennsylvania warrant, but also that by the choice of his brethren, and by the terms of its Virginia warrant, he became its first Master under it. If further evidence were wanting, it is found in the records of this lodge under date of December 20, 1788, which state:

"His Excellency, General WASHINGTON, unanimously elected Master; ROBERT MCCREA, Senior Warden; WM. HUNTER, Jun., Junior Warden; WM. HODGSON, Treasurer; JOSEPH GREENWAY, Secretary; Dr. FREDERICK SPANBERGEN, Senior Deacon; GEORGE RICHARDS, Junior Deacon;"——

At this meeting it was also resolved, that the brethren of the lodge dine together on the 27th, and "that his Excellency General WASHINGTON be invited." The imperfect records of the lodge, however, leave us no account of the festivities on that occasion.

From these interesting, but humble records of WASHINGTON'S Masonic life, we turn for a moment to the annals of his public history, and find that at the same time he was directing the tide of the mighty events that were affecting the welfare of our infant republic. When the constitution of 1787 was submitted to the people of the several States for their ratification, he anxiously watched its fate, believing, as he said, that if it was not adopted, *the next one would be written in blood*. When this corner-stone of the Federal Union was accepted, and a master builder was to be chosen to preside over the rising temple of a republican government, he looked with a calm, but not wishful eye, on the position he might be called to fill, and in the early months of 1789 again obeyed his country's mandate, and exchanged the domestic quiet of Mount Vernon for the supreme magistracy of the Union. We look through the vista of near fourscore years, and contemplate WASHINGTON as the unanimous choice of the citizens of each State for President. He was indeed the unanimous choice of the States, but not of all the citizens in them; and when the dust of three-quarters of a century is brushed from the record-book of the oldest lodge in the city of Philadelphia, we find by the report of a committee of that lodge, made a few years ago upon its history, that—

"In the winter of 1788–9, discord and dissension were so rife as to cause serious disturbances among the brethren, arising from the political questions of the day, when the government was first organized upon its present basis, and Brother GEORGE WASHINGTON was elected the first President of the United States. It appears the members were pretty equally divided on the question of his election, and scenes any thing but harmonious took place at the meetings held that winter.

"Contention and strife obtained such a foothold in the lodge, that at the first Grand Quarterly Communication of 1789, the lodge surrendered its warrant to the Grand Lodge.

"Brother WASHINGTON was elected President in March 1789, and those brethren who had advocated his election, united in a petition to the Grand Lodge for a return of the warrant; and this was granted at the second Grand Quarterly Communication held in June of the same year. Union and harmony now prevailed, and the lodge prospered in its labors."

How strangely an institution divine in its teachings, thus reveals the human passions of its members!

But while such dissensions were disturbing the harmony of the oldest lodge in Philadelphia, the Masonic brethren in New York were rejoicing on the elevation of so distinguished a brother to the presidency, and preparing to welcome his advent to their city, which was then the Federal capital. Holland Lodge of New York, therefore, whose membership embraced a distinguished class of citizens, elected him an honorary member, and transmitted to Mount Vernon a certificate of the same, as shown by the following extracts from their records:

"HOLLAND LODGE, March 6, 5789.

"*Resolved*, That the Worshipful MASTER VANDEN BROECK, Senior Warden STAGG, Junior Warden WILCOCKS, Brothers BARON STEUBEN and EDWARD LIVINGSTON, be a committee to communicate to his Excellency, in any mode they may deem most proper, this proceeding of the lodge."

This committee, therefore, addressed to WASHINGTON

the following letter, inclosing a certificate of honorary membership:

"HOLLAND LODGE,
"NEW YORK, March 7, 5789.

"SIR—As a committee appointed for that purpose, we have the honor of transmitting to your Excellency the inclosed certificate from the Holland Lodge.

"We are directed, sir, to express a hope that the earnest wishes of our constituents on this subject may not be disappointed; that the name of WASHINGTON may adorn as well the archives of our lodge as the annals of our country; and that we may salute as a Masonic Brother, him whom we honor as the political father of our country.

"We have the honor, etc.,

"R. J. VANDEN BROECK, Master,
"JOHN STAGG, Jun., Senior Warden,
"WILLIAM WILCOCKS, Junior Warden,
"FRED. DE STEUBEN, } Members,
"EDWARD LIVINGSTON, }
of Holland Lodge.

"His Excellency, GEO. WASHINGTON, Esq."

For the benefit of the curious Masonic reader, we give a copy of this certificate.

"In the East the place of Light, } { And the Darkness
Where Peace and Silence reign, } { Comprehended it not.

"To all men enlightened and spread abroad on the face of the Earth, *Greeting:*

"We, the Master, Wardens, and Brethren of Holland Lodge, Ancient Masons, held in the city and State of New York, in North America, do hereby certify that in consideration of the Masonic virtues which distinguish our worthy

Brother GEORGE WASHINGTON, he was unanimously elected an Honorary Member of our lodge.

L. S. "In testimony whereof, we, the Master and Wardens, have hereunto set our hands, and caused the seal of the lodge to be affixed, this 6th day of March, A. D. 1789, and A. M. 5789.

"R. J. VANDEN BROECK, Master.
"JOHN STAGG, Jun., Senior Warden.
"WILLIAM WILCOCKS, Junior Warden.

"*Attest.*
"—— ——, Secretary."

This was the second honorary membership conferred by Masonic lodges on WASHINGTON; the first having been conferred by his own lodge, at Alexandria, previous to his becoming its Master. Another honor was about the same time shown to him by Masons of New York, by calling the second Chapter of Royal Arch Masons in that city WASHINGTON CHAPTER. This Chapter was instituted before Grand Chapters had existence; and while the immemorial usage of Masonry sanctioned those members of any lodge who had a legal warrant to meet and work as Master Masons, if they had also a knowledge of higher Masonic degrees, and suitable members to work in them, to congregate as Chapters under the same warrant, and thus extend a knowledge of the Royal Art. The old Washington Chapter of New York city was closely associated with Holland Lodge, and perhaps was organized under the sanction of its warrant. It, however, during the last decade of the past century granted charters for Chapters in Rhode Island and Connecticut, and assumed prerogatives which have since been conceded to Grand Chapters. It is not known that WASHINGTON was further connected with this Chapter than its bearing his honored name; nor has it ever been shown from any record that he was a Royal Arch Mason. The Royal Arch, however, and various intermediate degrees being at that day conferred under Masters' Warrants, with little or no record kept of them, leaves this a point which can probably never be determined.

Before WASHINGTON left Mount Vernon, in the spring of 1789, to repair to the Federal Capital as President elect, he visited his mother, for the last time, at Fredericksburg. We have already shown his interview with her in 1782, after years of absence in the military service of his country. Again he had come to say that his country demanded his services, but that when the public interests permitted he would return. She interrupted him by saying: "You will see my face no more. My great age, and the disease that is fast approaching my vitals, warns me that I shall not be long of this world. But go, GEORGE, fulfil the high duties which Heaven appears to assign you; go, my son, and may Heaven's and your mother's blessing always attend you."

WASHINGTON had learned during his eventful life to meet with composure the dangers of the battle-field, the frowns of adversity, and the smiles of fortune; but the tenderness of his mother's words, and the maternal look and tone with which they were spoken, overcame every restraint he had placed on his feelings; and he leaned his head upon her aged shoulder as if he were again a boy, and the furrows in his cheeks were wet with unwonted tears.

The words of his mother were indeed prophetic; for she died the following autumn, and was buried in a spot she had herself chosen. It was near a romantic ledge of rocks, where she had often resorted for prayer; and the sylvan bethel, where a mother's prayers were offered for our WASHINGTON, is now hallowed by that mother's grave. What spot on American soil should be more sacred than that?

CHAPTER VII.

WASHINGTON leaves his home to assume the presidency.—Public demonstrations during his journey.—Arrives in New York.—His inauguration.—Chancellor LIVINGSTON, Grand Master of New York, administers to him the oath of office on Bible of St. John's Lodge.—Inscription in it relating to the event.—His inaugural address.—Services at St. Paul's Church.—Other public ceremonials.—First address from the Senate.—President's title established.—Rules of presidential etiquette established.—Public jealousies thereby aroused.—WASHINGTON visits the New England States.—Incident at Boston.—Visit to Rhode Island.—King David's Lodge.—Its address to WASHINGTON.—His reply.—His visit to the Southern States.—Address to him from Grand Lodge of South Carolina.—His reply.—Importance of this correspondence.—He returns to Mount Vernon.—*South-east* corner-stone of the Federal District set with Masonic ceremonies.—Published account of it.—Jealousies as to location of Federal capital.—Its Indian name.—Its present name, "The City of Washington."—The name of WASHINGTON often used geographically, and also in naming lodges.—Masonic constitutions of Virginia dedicated to WASHINGTON.—Proceedings of Grand Lodge of Pennsylvania relative to address to WASHINGTON.—Copy of the address.—His reply.—Union of the two Grand Lodges in Massachusetts.—Their new Book of Constitutions dedicated to WASHINGTON.—Their address to him on the occasion.—His reply.—Sword presented him by FREDERICK THE GREAT.—Box presented by the Earl of Buchan.

WASHINGTON left his home on the 16th of April, 1789, to repair to New York. At Alexandria, at Georgetown, at Baltimore, at Philadelphia, at Trenton, and at Elizabethtown he was greeted by crowds of his fellow-citizens, who publicly honored him with festivities, civic decorations, and laudatory addresses.

He wished to avoid on the occasion all ostentatious display; but the great heart of America was full of love for him, and blessings were showered upon his head, and flowers strown along his pathway.

These various public demonstrations are recorded on the pages of our country's history, and need not be repeated here. It was as if he were passing through the spring fields of a country where tender plants, whose buds had been crushed by war, were now putting forth blossoms, to hide the blood stains that had been left there during the War of the Revolution.

WASHINGTON reached New York on the 23d of April, and the 30th of the same month was the day fixed for his inauguration. On that occasion, General JACOB MORTON was marshal of the day. He was the Master of St. John's, the oldest lodge in the city, and at the same time Grand Secretary of the Grand Lodge of New York. General MORTON brought from the altar of his lodge the Bible with its cushion of crimson velvet, and upon that sacred volume, ROBERT R. LIVINGSTON, Chancellor of the State of New York, and Grand Master of its Grand Lodge, administered to WASHINGTON his oath of office as President of the United States.

Having taken the oath, WASHINGTON reverently bowed and kissed the sacred volume; and the awful suspense of the moment was broken by Chancellor LIVINGSTON, who solemnly said, "*Long Live* GEORGE WASHINGTON, *President of the United States!*" A thousand tongues at once joined in repeated acclamations, "LONG LIVE GEORGE WASHINGTON!"

A memorial leaf of the sacred Book was then folded at the page on which WASHINGTON had devoutly impressed his lips; and the volume was returned to St. John's Lodge, and placed again upon its sacred altar. A few years later it was again taken from its resting place, and borne in a solemn procession by the Ma-

THE BIBLE ON WHICH WASHINGTON TOOK THE OATH OF OFFICE, AS PRESIDENT.

sonic brethren of New York city, who met to pay funeral honors to the memory of WASHINGTON. It is still in possession of St. John's Lodge No. 1, who value it highly as a sacred memento. The memory of WASHINGTON's oath of office upon it, is perpetuated by the following inscription, beautifully engrossed, and accompanied by a miniature likeness from an engraving by LENEY, which were inserted by order of the lodge. The closing poetic lines were first written by the Rev. Dr. HAVEN, of Portsmouth, New Hampshire, on WASHINGTON's visit to that town in 1789, in answer to an inquiry by what title he should be addressed. The committee appointed by the lodge to form this memorial, were sworn on the same volume to do it faithfully.

ON THIS
SACRED VOLUME,

ON THE 30TH DAY OF APRIL, A. M. 5789, IN THE CITY OF NEW YORK,

WAS ADMINISTERED TO

GEORGE WASHINGTON,

THE FIRST PRESIDENT OF THE UNITED STATES OF AMERICA,

THE OATH

TO SUPPORT THE CONSTITUTION OF THE UNITED STATES.

THIS IMPORTANT CEREMONY WAS PERFORMED BY THE MOST WORSHIPFUL

GRAND MASTER

OF FREE AND ACCEPTED MASONS OF THE STATE OF NEW YORK,

ROBERT R. LIVINGSTON,

CHANCELLOR OF THE STATE.

"Fame spread her wings, and loud her trumpet blew:
Great WASHINGTON is near! What praise HIS due?
What TITLE shall he have? She paused—and said,
Not ONE ; HIS NAME ALONE STRIKES EVERY TITLE DEAD!"

Having taken his oath of inauguration, WASHINGTON proceeded to the Senate chamber and delivered his first address as chief magistrate of the Federal Union. It was a reflex of the principles of Masonry from the mind and the heart of our greatest American brother. He seemed to imagine himself again treading the ground floor of a new apartment in the temple of human life; and he modestly reviewed his qualifications, his hopes, and fears upon entering it. He next acknowledged a Divine Ruler over all human events, and humbly invoked his guidance and blessing. Was not this a remembrance of the first lessons he had been taught in Masonry? Then, as the Mason examines the lines on his trestle-board, he proceeded to examine the requirements of the constitution, and the duties to be performed under it, and closed with a renewed acknowledgment of dependence on Divine aid. How true was all this to the character of WASHINGTON! How true to the teachings of Masonry!

As soon as these ceremonies and duties were performed, President WASHINGTON and both houses of Congress proceeded to St. Paul's Church, where divine services were held on the occasion, and the evening was spent by the citizens of New York with the most extravagant exhibitions of joy. A magnificent transparent painting, brilliantly illuminated, was suspended between the fort and Bowling Green, on the centre of which was represented WASHINGTON as the emblem of Fortitude; on his right hand, the supreme judiciary, by the emblem of Justice; and on his left, the supreme legislature, by the emblem of Wisdom.

The choice of these emblems from the chambers of Masonic science, and their appropriation at this time to these purposes, must have called the mind of

WASHINGTON and his Masonic brethren forcibly back to the silent teachings of these very emblems in the lodge-room. Our Federal Government, of which WASHINGTON was the representative head, had that day passed a threshold where fortitude, which shrinks at no pain or danger, is required; and he that day stood, as he had long before, and will ever be remembered, a personification of this cardinal Masonic virtue.

It was not until the 16th of May, that answers were returned by the Senate and House of Representatives to WASHINGTON'S inaugural address; and on such presentations, a question arose between those bodies as to the title by which he should be addressed; the lower body contending that as the constitution fixed no title beyond that of "*The President,*" etc., no other should be used; while the Senate preferred to prefix "*His Highness,*" or some other title of rank to his name and office. The republican simplicity of the lower house prevailed, and, as is well known, our presidents have ever been addressed without any addition to the title which the constitution gives them.

While this question of courtly official address was occupying the attention of Congress, a kindred one of greater importance and real necessity was forced upon the decision of WASHINGTON. It was the etiquette of presidential receptions of citizens and strangers. To establish such rules of private intercourse as these demanded, and still leave the President in command of time necessary for the fulfilment of his official duties, without encroaching upon the claims of nature for rest and refreshment, was a delicate duty for him to perform. There were those who believed that the dignity of the presidential office should be invested with many forms and courtly ceremonies; and there were others who claimed that the harmony of our new-born republican institutions required an entire abandonment of all distinction between the President and the people in social intercourse. The first were, perhaps, too fond of official show, and the latter too anxious for an unbecoming agrarianism. WASHINGTON committed the details of presidential etiquette to Colonel DAVID HUMPHREY, who had been one of his aids-de-camp during the Revolution, and was now his private secretary. Colonel HUMPHREY seems to have happily conceived appropriate rules and ceremonials for presidential intercourse; for they have remained substantially the same through each successive presidency for three-quarters of a century.

We have already noted in this sketch feelings of jealousy that arose in certain minds relative to the Society of the Cincinnati. These were again aroused by the necessary restrictions that were placed on citizens who sought interviews with the President. Many saw in them only the hated forms and ceremonies of royalty; and WASHINGTON was by some denounced as another Royal GEORGE. Trifling as such jealousies and fears may now seem to us, they even entered into the political discussions of that day; and a letter is still extant from WASHINGTON explanatory of the necessity of the restrictions of the presidential etiquette.

During the first autumn of the presidency, WASHINGTON visited the New England States which had united in the Federal Union; and on his arrival at

Boston, a misconception seems to have occurred with Governor HANCOCK, of Massachusetts, as to the relative dignity in the capital of the State, of a visiting Federal President, or the governor at his own seat of power; and he remained at the gubernatorial mansion awaiting a formal call from the President. WASHINGTON would have waived all ceremonies, in calling at the humblest abode of a soldier of the Revolution; but he would not compromise the superior dignity of the chief magistrate of the Union, by first knocking at the gubernatorial gate. It was on Saturday that WASHINGTON arrived in Boston, and on the following Monday, Governor HANCOCK yielded the point, with a plea of previous bodily indisposition.

No records are known to exist which contain any account of Masonic intercourse between WASHINGTON and his Masonic brethren in New York while he resided there as President, nor with the Fraternity in New England during his visit in 1789. In the following year the seat of the Federal Government was removed from New York to Philadelphia; and when Congress closed its last session in New York in August of that year, WASHINGTON visited Rhode Island for the benefit of his health. He was received at both Newport and Providence with much distinction. There existed at that time in Newport a lodge of Freemasons, called King David's Lodge, to which we have already alluded as having contemplated an address to WASHINGTON in 1781, on the occasion of his visit to that city as commander-in-chief. On his presidential visit in 1790, this lodge addressed him a letter, and received the reply which the enemies of Masonry, a few years ago claimed was forged long after his death. But as the records of the lodge of that date show the transaction; and as this letter from King David's Lodge, and WASHINGTON'S reply to it, were both published in Boston in 1796, while he was yet living, in an authorized collection of his various addresses, etc., to public bodies, no doubt can exist of their authenticity.

The records state, that,

"At a lodge, called by request of several brethren on Tuesday evening, August 17, 5790, an Entered Apprentice Lodge was opened, where it was proposed to address the President of the United States. The R. W. MOSES SEIXAS, HENRY SHERBURNE, and WM. LITTLEFIELD, secretary, were appointed a committee for that purpose, after which the lodge closed."

The following is a copy of their letter on that occasion, as published in the Boston Collection of Addresses, in 1796, a copy of which rare work we have before us. It contains also other Masonic letters of WASHINGTON, which some have claimed were spurious, and written long after his death. Their publication during his own lifetime, and under his sanction, falsifies such an assertion.

"To GEORGE WASHINGTON, *President of the United States of America:*

"SIR—We, the Master, Wardens, and Brethren of King David's Lodge, in Newport, Rhode Island, joyfully embrace this opportunity to greet you as a brother, and to hail you welcome to Rhode Island.

"We exult in the thought, that as Masonry has always

been patronized by the wise, the good, and the great, so hath it stood, and ever will stand, as its fixtures are on the immutable pillars of Faith, Hope, and Charity.

"With unspeakable pleasure we gratulate you as filling the presidential chair, with the applause of a numerous and enlightened people; whilst at the same time, we felicitate ourselves in the honor done the brotherhood by your many exemplary virtues, and emanations of goodness proceeding from a heart worthy of possessing the ancient mysteries of our Craft, being persuaded that the wisdom and grace with which Heaven has endowed you, will ever square all your thoughts, words, and actions, by the eternal laws of honor, equity, and truth, so as to promote the advancement of all good works, your own happiness, and that of mankind.

"Permit us then, illustrious brother, cordially to salute you with three times three, and to add our fervent supplications, that the Sovereign Architect of the Universe may always encompass you with his holy protection.

"MOSES SEIXAS, *Master*,
"HENRY SHERBURNE,
Committee.

"By order,
"WM. LITTLEFIELD, *Secretary*.

"NEWPORT, August 17, 1790."

To this truly Masonic greeting, WASHINGTON returned the same day the following reply:

"TO THE MASTER, WARDENS, AND BRETHREN OF KING DAVID'S LODGE IN NEWPORT, RHODE ISLAND:

"GENTLEMEN—I receive the welcome which you give me to Rhode Island with pleasure; and I acknowledge my obligations for the flattering expressions of regard contained in your address with grateful sincerity. Being persuaded that a just application of the principles on which the Masonic fraternity is founded, must be productive of private virtue and public prosperity, I shall always be happy to advance the interests of the society, and to be considered by them as a deserving brother. My best wishes, gentlemen, are offered for your individual happiness.

"G°. WASHINGTON."

This is the earliest presidential Masonic correspondence that exists on record; and the succeeding pages of this sketch will show, that no incumbent of the chair of the chief magistrate of the Union, ever gave so strong and multiplied proofs of his attachment to Masonry as WASHINGTON; and yet many of them had also seen before reaching that station

"That hieroglyphic bright,
Which none but craftsmen ever saw."

After the close of the session of Congress in Philadelphia in the winter of 1790–1, WASHINGTON returned to Mount Vernon, and in the spring and early summer months he made a visit as President to the Southern States. On his arrival in Charleston, in South Carolina, General MORDECAI GIST, who was Grand Master of Ancient York Masons there, addressed him the following congratulatory letter as Grand Master, in behalf of his Grand Lodge:

"SIR—Induced by a respect for your public and private character, as well as the relation in which you stand with the brethren of this society, we, the Grand Lodge of the State of South Carolina, Ancient York Masons, beg leave to offer our sincere congratulations on your arrival in this State.

"We felicitate you on the establishment and exercise of

a permanent government, whose foundation was laid under your auspices by military achievements, upon which have been progressively reared the pillars of the free Republic over which you preside, supported by wisdom, strength, and beauty unrivalled among the nations of the world.

"The fabric thus raised and committed to your superintendence, we earnestly wish may continue to produce order and harmony to succeeding ages, and be the asylum of virtue to the oppressed of all parts of the universe.

"When we contemplate the distresses of war, the instances of humanity displayed by the Craft afford some relief to the feeling mind; and it gives us the most pleasing sensation to recollect, that amidst the difficulties attendant on your late military stations, you still associated with, and patronized the Ancient Fraternity.

"Distinguished always by your virtues, more than the exalted stations in which you have moved, we exult in the opportunity you now give us of hailing you brother of our Order, and trust from your knowledge of our institution, to merit your countenance and support.

"With fervent zeal for your happiness, we pray that a life so dear to the bosom of this society, and to society in general, may be long, very long preserved; and when you leave the temporal symbolic lodges of this world, may you be received into the celestial lodge of light and perfection, where the Grand Master Architect of the Universe presides.

"Done in behalf of the Grand Lodge.

"M. Gist, *G. M.*

"Charleston, 2d May, 1791."

To this letter, Washington immediately returned the following reply:

"Gentlemen—I am much obliged by the respect which

you are so good as to declare for my public and private character. I recognize with pleasure my relation to the brethren of your Society, and I accept with gratitude your congratulations on my arrival in South Carolina.

"Your sentiments, on the establishment and exercise of our equal government, are worthy of an association, whose principles lead to purity of morals, and are beneficial of action.

"The fabric of our freedom is placed on the enduring basis of public virtue, and will, I fondly hope, long continue to protect the prosperity of the architects who raised it. I shall be happy, on every occasion, to evince my regard for the Fraternity. For your prosperity individually, I offer my best wishes.

"G°. WASHINGTON."

To understand fully at this day the value and significance of this correspondence between the Grand Master of Masons in South Carolina in behalf of his Grand Lodge and General WASHINGTON, it must be remembered that General GIST had been the friend and companion in arms of General WASHINGTON during the War of the Revolution; and that, while in command of the Maryland Brigade in 1779, he had held intimate personal and Masonic intercourse with him; had presided over a convention of Masonic brethren in the army at Morristown that desired to elevate WASHINGTON to the Grand Mastership of all American Masons; had been constituted by a warrant from the Grand Lodge of Pennsylvania, Master of a military lodge in his own brigade; and having borne the trowel and the sword together in many weary marches and many well-fought battles, had, at the close of the war, retired to a plantation near Charleston; and carrying with him, to his Southern home, a love of Masonry and a knowledge of its kindly influences during the war, had established a lodge in Charleston, been chosen Grand Master of the Ancient York Masons of South Carolina, and as such greeted WASHINGTON on his arrival there, in their behalf.

When, therefore, he said in his letter to WASHINGTON, "When we contemplate the distresses of war, the instances of humanity displayed by the Craft afford some relief to the feeling mind; and it gives us the most pleasing sensation to recollect that amidst the difficulties attendant on your late military stations, you still associated with, and patronized the Ancient Fraternity," he well knew that WASHINGTON was familiar with the instances of humanity in war to which he alluded; nor would he have adverted in this manner to his associations with the fraternity during the war, had he not known that it was a pleasing association to his distinguished brother and public guest. Nor did WASHINGTON fail on this occasion to reiterate his often declared sentiments, that Masonry was beneficial to society and the basis of public virtue.

WASHINGTON returned to Mount Vernon on the 12th of June, having performed a journey of more than seventeen hundred miles in sixty-six days with his own horses and carriage. He had in that time visited each of the States south of the Potomac, and been received by all classes of citizens with the highest honors.

During his absence his lodge at Alexandria had performed a public labor, in the ceremonials of erecting the first corner-stone of the District of Columbia near that city. As this Federal territory was required, by an act of Congress, to embrace a district of country ten miles square, lying on both sides of the Potomac, WASHINGTON had appointed commissioners to establish its boundaries, and its *south-east* corner-stone was set with Masonic ceremonies on the 15th of April, 1791. Its location was at Jones' Point near the mouth of Hunting Creek, on the bank of the Potomac, near where the Light-house at Alexandria now stands. The following account of setting this stone was written by a gentleman of Alexandria, and published in the United States Gazette at Philadelphia, April 30, 1791:

"ALEXANDRIA, April 21, 1791.

"On Friday, the 15th instant, the Hon. DANIEL CARROLL and Hon. DAVID STEUART arrived in this town to superintend the fixing of the first corner-stone of the Federal District.

"The mayor and commonalty, together with the members of the different lodges of the town, at three o'clock waited on the commissioners at Mr. WEISE's, where they dined; and after drinking a glass of wine to the following sentiment—viz., 'May the stone which we are about to place in the ground, remain an immovable monument of the wisdom and unanimity of North America'—the company proceeded to Jones' Point in the following order:

"1st. The Town Sergeant.

"2d. Hon. DANIEL CARROLL and the Mayor.

"3d. Mr. ELLICOTT and the Recorder.

"4th. Such of the Common Council and Aldermen as were not Freemasons.

"5th. Strangers.

"6th. The Master of Lodge No. 22, with Dr. DAVID STEU-

ART on his right, and the Rev. JAMES MUIR on his left, followed by the rest of the Fraternity in their usual form of procession.

"*Lastly.* The citizens, two by two.

"When Mr. ELLICOTT had ascertained the precise point from which the first line of the district was to proceed, the Master of the lodge and Dr. STEUART, assisted by others of their brethren, placed the stone. After which a deposit of corn, wine, and oil was made upon it, and the following observations were made by the Rev. JAMES MUIR:

"'Of America it may be said, as of Judea of old, that it is a good land and large,—a land of brooks of waters, of fountains, and depths that spring out of the valleys and hills,—a land of wheat, and barley, and vines, and fig-trees, and pomegranates,—a land of oil, olives, and honey,—a land wherein we eat bread without scarceness, and have lack of nothing,—a land whose stones are iron, and out of whose hills thou mayest dig brass,—a land which the LORD thy GOD careth for;—the eyes of the LORD thy GOD are always upon it, from the beginning of the year even unto the end of the year.

"'May Americans be grateful and virtuous, and they shall insure the indulgence of Providence. May they be unanimous and just, and they shall rise to greatness. May true patriotism actuate every heart. May it be the devout and universal wish: Peace be within thy walls, O America, and prosperity within thy palaces. Amiable it is for brethren to dwell together in unity; it is more fragrant than the perfumes on Aaron's garment; it is more refreshing than the dews on Hermon's Hill.

"'May this stone long commemorate the goodness of GOD in those uncommon events which have given America a name among nations. Under this stone may jealousy and selfishness be forever buried. From this stone may a superstructure arise, whose glory, whose magnificence, whose stability, unequalled hitherto, shall astonish the world, and invite even the savage of the wilderness to take shelter under its roof.'

"The company partook of some refreshments, and then returned to the place from whence they came, where a number of toasts were drank; and the following was delivered by the Master of the lodge (Dr. Dick), and was received with every token of approbation:

"'Brethren and Gentlemen—May Jealousy, that green-eyed monster, be buried deep under the work which we have this day completed, never to rise again within the Federal District.'

"It may fairly be presumed that this, or a similar sentiment pervaded the breast of every individual present on the occasion."

These Masonic incidents are of interest, not only to the personal history of Washington, but to both the general and Masonic history of those times. It is well known that Washington directed the tide of events that established the seat of the Federal Government on the Potomac; and that when the act was being passed for its location there, jealousies were aroused within the district on the subject of its boundaries, and the location of its public buildings. Georgetown and Alexandria were both rivals for the honors and advantages incident to their location; and when Washington gave his influence for placing the Capitol on the north side of the Potomac, he yielded his private interest to allay all Northern jealousies as to its location. But the sentiment in Alexandria was adverse to this; and it was befitting Masonry, in the character of WASHINGTON'S own lodge, to perform the ceremonials in the first public act of establishing the boundaries of the Federal District. Her voice was then, as it ever is, "Let public jealousies be forever buried." Would that her voice were always heeded!

The future seat of the Federal Government had at that time no name, and Mr. WOLCOTT, of Connecticut, facetiously termed it, "The Indian place, with the long name on the Potomac," in reference to its Indian name having been *Conecogeague*. It was at first called "The Federal City," and WASHINGTON thus styled it in a letter written April 13, 1791; but the commissioners appointed to superintend the laying out of the city, had employed Major L'ENFANT, a French architect, to form plans and drawings of it; and in a letter to him, bearing date September 9, 1791, they informed him that they had agreed that the Federal District should be called "The Territory of Columbia," and the Federal City, "The City of Washington," and directed him to thus designate them on his maps.

No baptismal name could have been more appropriate for the Federal city than that of Washington. It had already been geographically used in naming a county in Virginia in 1776, and one or two military points may have borne the name at an earlier period. Towns and counties without number have since borne this honored name; and the Masonic Fraternity have remembered their great American patron in adopting his name for their organizations in a multitude of instances. A curious research in Masonic nomenclature will show, that every grand jurisdiction has that name as designating some of her subordinate Masonic organizations. It was first thus used in 1778, by a lodge in the Massachusetts line of the army; and a curious instance of WASHINGTON'S memory being honored by a lodge-name, was by a lodge of Masons in North Carolina, which had borne the name of the "Royal George" while that State was a colony of England, changing it to the "American George" after the Revolution.

During the summer of 1791, the Grand Lodge of Virginia published the first edition of her Book of Constitutions, or *New Ahiman Rezon* as it was called, and dedicated it to WASHINGTON as follows:

"TO GEORGE WASHINGTON, Esq., President of the United States of America, the following work is most respectfully dedicated by his obedient and devoted servant,

"THE EDITOR."

During the same year, the Grand Lodge of Pennsylvania renewed its testimonials of respect for WASHINGTON, by directing that an address be presented to him from that body, as seen by the following extracts from its records:

"DECEMBER 27, 1791.

"The Rev. Brother Dr. SMITH and the Right Worshipful Grand Officers were appointed a committee to prepare an address to our illustrious Brother GEORGE WASHINGTON,

President of the United States. Lodge adjourned to the 2d day of January next to receive the report of the committee."

"JANUARY 2, 1792.

"The minutes of St. John's-day being read as far as relates to the appointment of a committee to prepare an address to our illustrious Brother GEORGE WASHINGTON, the Rev. Brother Dr. WILLIAM SMITH, one of the said committee, presented the draft of one, which was read; whereupon, on motion and seconded, the same was unanimously approved of, and resolved, that the Right Worshipful Grand Master and Deputy Grand Master and Grand Officers, with Brother SMITH, be a committee to present the said address in behalf of this Right Worshipful Grand Lodge, signed by the Right Worshipful Grand Master, and countersigned by the Grand Secretary."

"MARCH 5, 1792.

"The Right Worshipful Grand Master informed the brethren, that in conformity to the resolve of this Grand Lodge, he had, in company with the Grand Officers and the Rev. Brother Dr. SMITH, presented the address to our illustrious Brother GEORGE WASHINGTON, and had received an answer, which was read. Whereupon, on motion and seconded, resolved unanimously, that the said address and the answer thereunto shall be entered on the minutes."

With these prefatory extracts from the records of the Grand Lodge of Pennsylvania, we give the address and WASHINGTON's reply as therein recorded. Both were also published in the United States Gazette at Philadelphia, January 2, 1792, which, together with the record, fixes their date as that day. The address was presented to

WASHINGTON in person by a committee of the Grand Lodge, with the Grand Master at its head, which accounts for the omission of date to these documents:

"To GEORGE WASHINGTON,

President of the United States:

"SIR AND BROTHER—The Ancient York Masons of the jurisdiction of Pennsylvania, for the first time assembled in General Communication to celebrate the feast of St. John the Evangelist since your election to the chair of government of the United States, beg leave to approach you with congratulations from the East, and, in the pride of fraternal affection, to hail you as the great master-builder (under the Supreme Architect), by whose labors the temple of liberty hath been reared in the West, exhibiting to the nations of the earth a model of beauty, order, and harmony, worthy of their imitation and praise.

"Your knowledge of the origin and objects of our institution—its tendency to promote the social affections and harmonize the heart—give us a sure pledge that this tribute of our veneration, this effusion of love, will not be ungrateful to you; nor will Heaven reject our prayer, that you may be long continued to adorn the bright list of master workmen which our Fraternity produces in the terrestrial lodge; and that you may be late removed to that celestial lodge where love and harmony reign transcendent and divine; where the Great Architect more immediately presides, and where cherubim and seraphim wafting our congratulations from earth to heaven shall hail you brother!

"By order and in behalf of the Grand Lodge of Pennsylvania, in General Communication assembled in ample form.

[L. S.] "J. B. SMITH, G. M.

"Attest: P. LE BARBIER DU PLESSIS, G. Sec."

To this address, WASHINGTON returned the following written reply:

"TO THE ANCIENT YORK MASONS OF THE JURISDICTION OF PENNSYLVANIA:

"GENTLEMEN AND BROTHERS—I receive your kind congratulation with the purest sensations of fraternal affection; and from a heart deeply impressed with your generous wishes for my present and future happiness, I beg you to accept my thanks.

"At the same time I request you will be assured of my best wishes and earnest prayers for your happiness while you remain in this terrestrial mansion, and that we may hereafter meet as brethren in the celestial temple of the Supreme Architect.

"G°. WASHINGTON."

WASHINGTON'S residence was at that time in Philadelphia, and it was at the presidential mansion in that city that this address was presented. We know not that while there during his presidency, he participated in the ritualistic labors of the lodge-room; but the Masonic records of the Fraternity in that city state that they were often made the almoners of his bounty to those in distress. Charity was ever one of his distinguished Masonic characteristics.

Masonry was at that time undergoing in this country one of those silent, yet constant changes that have ever marked its progress without disturbing its grand design. Its Cyclopean, its Egyptian walls—perhaps antediluvian in their designs—had long been in ruins. The trestle-board of its masters had since borne designs of Tyrian, of Greek, and of Roman skill; and these too had taken their place among memorials of the past in the archives of Masonry. Our fathers, as Anglo-Saxon colonists, had brought with them to this country its more modern external forms; and two divided schools of design, each with cunning masters and faithful workmen, had endeavored to perpetuate forms in mystic architecture, which at most could claim no higher antiquity than a Norman or an Elizabethan age. For the purposes of our sketch, we may therefore consider the ceremonies and polity of Masonry, which were introduced into America about the third decade of the last century under HENRY PRICE, at Boston, as of the modern or Elizabethan school; while those practised a few years later under JOSEPH WARREN, by the self-styled Ancients, might be called the Norman features of Anglo-Saxon Freemasonry. Both were agreed in angular lines; they only differed in those of curvature. WASHINGTON had been familiar with both these systems. He had been made a Mason under the first, and afterwards became affiliated under the second. The veil which separated the bands of American workmen under each of these systems was rent in twain in Massachusetts in 1792, and a Book of Constitutions published for the government of the United Grand Lodge of that jurisdiction, which, by direction of that Grand Body, bore the following dedication to WASHINGTON:

"In testimony of his exalted merit, and our inalienable regard, this work is inscribed and dedicated to our illustrious BROTHER GEORGE WASHINGTON, the friend of Masonry, of his Country, and of Man."

It was a quarto volume, and besides the Masonic Constitutions of Massachusetts, it contained much of historic interest to Masonry, and was published for the Grand Lodge by ISAIAH THOMAS, afterwards Grand Master of that State, and author of the "*History of Printing.*" By resolution of the Grand Lodge, a copy of this book was presented to WASHINGTON, accompanied by the following address. The resolution bore date December 27th, and the address 29th, 1792:

"THE GRAND LODGE OF FREE AND ACCEPTED MASONS FOR THE COMMONWEALTH OF MASSACHUSETTS, TO THEIR HONORED AND ILLUSTRIOUS BROTHER GEORGE WASHINGTON, PRESIDENT OF THE UNITED STATES:

'SIR—Whilst the historian is describing the career of your glory, and the inhabitants of an extensive empire are made happy in your unexampled exertions—while some celebrate the Hero, so distinguished in liberating United America, and others the Patriot who presides over her councils—a band of brothers, having always joined the acclamations of their countrymen, now testify their respect for those milder virtues which have ever graced the man.

"Taught by the precepts of our Society that all its members stand upon a level, we venture to assume this station, and to approach you with that freedom which diminishes our diffidence without lessening our respect.

"Desirous to enlarge the boundaries of social happiness, and to vindicate the ceremonies of their institution, this Grand Lodge have published a 'Book of Constitutions,' and a copy for your acceptance accompanies this, which, by discovering the principles that actuate, will speak the eulogy of the Society; though they fervently wish the conduct of its members may prove its higher commendation.

"Convinced of his attachment to its cause, and readiness to encourage its benevolent designs, they have taken the liberty to dedicate this work to one, the qualities of whose heart, and the action of whose life, have contributed to improve personal virtue, and extend throughout the world the most endearing cordialities; and they humbly hope he will pardon this freedom, and accept the tribute of their esteem and homage.

"May the Supreme Architect of the Universe protect and bless you, give length of days and increase of felicity in this world, and then receive you to the harmonious and exalted Society in heaven.

"JOHN CUTLER, Grand Master
"JOSIAH BARTLETT, } Grand Wardens.
"MUNGO MACKAY, }

"BOSTON, December 29, A. L. 5792."

To this address, WASHINGTON returned the following reply, both of which were published during his lifetime in a volume of his speeches and addresses, issued in Boston, to which allusion has been already made:

"TO THE GRAND LODGE OR FREE AND ACCEPTED MASONS OF THE COMMONWEALTH OF MASSACHUSETTS:

"GENTLEMEN—Flattering as it may be to the human mind, and truly honorable as it is to receive from our fellow-citizens testimonials of approbation for exertions to promote the public welfare, it is not less pleasing to know that the milder virtues of the heart are highly respected by a society whose liberal principles are founded in the immutable laws of truth and justice.

"To enlarge the sphere of social happiness is worthy the benevolent design of the Masonic Institution, and it is most fervently to be wished that the conduct of every member of the Fraternity, as well as those publications that discover the principles which actuate them, may tend to convince mankind that the grand object of Masonry is to promote the happiness of the human race.

"While I beg your acceptance of my thanks for the 'Book of Constitutions' which you have sent me, and for the honor you have done me in the dedication, permit me to assure you that I feel all those emotions of gratitude which your affectionate address and cordial wishes are calculated to inspire. And I sincerely pray, that the Great Architect of the Universe may bless you here, and receive you hereafter in his immortal Temple.

"G°. WASHINGTON."

But it was not from Masons in his own country alone that WASHINGTON, at this period of his life, received testimonials of distinguished consideration. Frederic the Great, of Prussia, who was at the head of Masonry in continental Europe, sent him an elegant sword with a complimentary inscription; and the Earl of Buchan, who was Grand Master of Scotland from 1782–1785, sent him also a curious box made of wood from the oak-tree that sheltered Sir WILLIAM WALLACE after his defeat at the battle of Falkirk. These, though not strictly Masonic, but illustrate the sentiment of Masonry, that,

> "GOD hath made mankind one mighty brotherhood,
> Himself their Master, and the world their Lodge."

CHAPTER VIII.

WASHINGTON re-elected President.—Lays the corner-stone of the Capitol.—Placed at the *southeast* corner.—Accounts of the procession and ceremonies, as given by the newspapers of that day.—Address of JOSEPH CLARKE, Grand Master *pro tem.* on that occasion.—WASHINGTON'S participation as a Mason in these ceremonies justly a part of our public history.—Gave strength to the illusion that he was officially General Grand Master of the United States.—WASHINGTON'S Masonic portrait in Alexandria.—Records of Lodge No. 22 relating to it.—Inscription on the back of it.—Its sash and apron represent those presented him by LA FAYETTE.—WASHINGTON'S farewell address.—His allusion in it to secret political societies.—Attempts long after his death to make these denunciations apply to Masonry.—Extracts from records of the Grand Lodge of Pennsylvania relative to address to WASHINGTON.—Copy of the address.—His reply.—The inconsistency of the claim that he repudiated his Masonic connection.—His feelings when about to retire to private life.—His last presidential dinner.—Inauguration of Mr. ADAMS.—WASHINGTON'S valedictory.—Affecting scene on that occasion.

WASHINGTON desired to return again to private life at the close of his first presidential term, but having been unanimously re-elected, he yielded to the public wish and the strong solicitations of his friends, and again accepted the presidency. His second inauguration took place in the Senate chamber in Philadelphia, on the 4th of March, 1793. Judge CUSHING, of Massachusetts, administered to him the oath of office.

On the 18th of September of that year WASHINGTON

laid the corner-stone of the Capitol of the United States, in the city that bore his name. It was laid at the *southeast* corner of the edifice, it being the custom of our Masonic fathers to place it at that point, and not at the *northeast* as at present. The following account of the ceremonies on the occasion was published in the newspapers of that day.

"GEORGETOWN, September 21, 1793.

"On Wednesday one of the grandest Masonic processions took place, for the purpose of laying the corner-stone of the Capitol of the United States, which, perhaps, was ever exhibited on the like important occasion. About ten o'clock, Lodge No. 9 was visited by that congregation so graceful to the Craft, Lodge No. 22 of Virginia, with all their officers and regalia; and directly afterwards appeared on the southern banks of the grand river Potomac, one of the finest companies of volunteer artillery that hath been lately seen, parading to receive the President of the United States, who shortly came in sight with his suit, to whom the artillery paid their military honors; and his Excellency and suit crossed the Potomac, and was received in Maryland by the officers and brethren of No. 22 Virginia, and No. 9 Maryland, whom the President headed, preceded by a band of music; the rear brought up by the Alexandria volunteer artillery, with grand solemnity of march, proceeded to the President's square, in the city of Washington, where they were met and saluted by No. 15 of the City of Washington in all their elegant badges and clothing, headed by Brother JOSEPH CLARKE, Rt. W. G. M., P. T., and conducted to a large lodge prepared for the purpose of their reception. After a short space of time, by the vigilance of Brother CLOTWORTHY STEPHENSON, Grand Marshal P. T., the brotherhood and other bodies were disposed in a second order of procession, which took place amidst a brilliant crowd of spectators of both sexes, according to the following arrangement, viz.:

"The Surveying Department of the City of Washington;

"Mayor and Corporation of Georgetown;

"Virginia Artillery;

"Commissioners of the City of Washington and their attendants.

"Stone-cutters. Mechanics.

"The Sword-bearer.

"Masons of the first degree.
"Bible, etc., on Grand Cushions.
"Deacons, with staffs of office.
"Masons of the second degree.
"Stewards, with wands.
"Masons of the third degree.
"Wardens, with truncheons.
"Secretaries, with tools of office.
"Past Masters, with their regalia.
"Treasurers, with their jewels.
"Band of music.
"Lodge No. 22 of Virginia, disposed in their own order.
"Corn, Wine, and Oil.
"Grand Master *pro tem.*, Brother George Washington, and Worshipful Master of No. 22 of Virginia.
"Grand Sword-bearer.

"The procession marched two abreast, in the greatest solemn dignity, with music playing, drums beating, colors flying, and spectators rejoicing, from the President's square to the Capitol in the City of Washington, where the Grand Marshal ordered a halt, and directed each file in the procession to incline two steps, one to the right and one to the left, and face each other, which formed a hollow oblong square, through which the Grand Sword-bearer led the van, followed by the Grand Master P. T. on the left, the President of the United States in the centre, and the Worshipful Master of No. 22 Virginia on the right; all the other orders that composed the procession advanced in the reverse of their order of march from the President's square to the southeast corner of the Capitol, and the artillery filed off to a destined ground to display their manœuvres and discharge their cannon; the President of the United States, the Grand Master

P. T., and the Worshipful Master of No. 22 taking their stand to the east of a large stone, and all the Craft forming a circle westward, stood a short time in awful order.

"The artillery discharged a volley. The Grand Marshal delivered the commissioners a large silver plate with an inscription thereon, which the commissioners ordered to be read, and was as follows:

"'This Southeast corner-stone of the Capitol of the United States of America, in the City of Washington, was laid on the 18th day of September, 1793, in the thirteenth year of American independence, in the first year of the second term of the presidency of George Washington, whose virtues in the civil administration of his country have been as conspicuous and beneficial, as his military valor and prudence have been useful in establishing her liberties, and in the year of Masonry, 5793, by the President of the United States, in concert with the Grand Lodge of Maryland, several lodges under its jurisdiction, and Lodge No. 22 from Alexandria, Virginia.

"'Thomas Johnson, David Steuart, and Daniel Carroll, Commissioners; Joseph Clarke, R. W. G. M., P. T.; James Hoban and Stephen Hallate, Architects; Collin Williamson, M. Mason.'

"The artillery discharged a volley. The plate was then delivered to the President, who, attended by the Grand Master P. T., and three most Worshipful Masters, descended to the cavazion trench and deposed the plate, and laid it on the corner-stone of the Capitol of the United States of America, on which was deposed Corn, Wine, and Oil, when the whole congregation joined in reverential prayer, which was succeeded by Masonic chanting honors, and a volley from the artillery.

"The President of the United States and his attendant brethren ascended from the cavazion to the east of the corner-stone; and there the Grand Master P. T., elevated on a triple rostrum, delivered an oration fitting the occasion, which was received with brotherly love and commendation. At intervals, during the delivery of the oration, several volleys were discharged by the artillery. The ceremony ended in prayer, Masonic chanting honors, and a 15-volley from the artillery.

"The whole company retired to an extensive booth, where an ox of 500 lbs. weight was barbecued, of which the company generally partook, with every abundance of other recreation. The festival concluded with fifteen successive volleys from the artillery, whose military discipline and manœuvres merit every commendation. Before dark the whole company departed with joyful hopes of the production of their labor."

The following is a copy of the address of JOSEPH CLARKE on the occasion, who acted as Grand Master *pro tem.* of the Grand Lodge of Maryland, in the Masonic jurisdiction of which the Federal Capitol was built:

"MY WORTHY BRETHREN—I presume you expect I shall in some measure address you on this very important occasion, which I confess is a duty incumbent upon me, although quite inadequate to the task, and entirely unprepared; for until high meridian yesterday, I was not solicited, neither had I a conception to have performed this duty. Therefore you will accept my observations with brotherly love; they are, I assure you, sincere, and dictated by a pure Masonic heart, though very brief.

Volley from the Artillery.

"Brothers, I beg leave to disclose to you that I have, and I expect that you also have, every hope that the grand work we have done to-day will be handed down, as well by record as by oral tradition, to as late posterity as the like work of that ever memorable Temple to our order erected by our Grand Master Solomon.

Volley from the Artillery.

"The work we have done to-day, laying the corner-stone of this designed magnificent temple, the Capitol of our extensive and populous States of veteran republicans, States which were recovered, settled, and permanently established by the virtuous achievements and bravery of our most illustrious Brother George Washington—

Volley from the Artillery.

"I say, that we further hope that this work may be remembered for many ages to come, as a similar work has from the commencement of time to this remarkable moment; I mean, the work of laying the corner-stone of our ancient, honorable, and sublime order.

Volley from the Artillery.

"We also hope that the Grand Architect of all men, Freemasons and others, may continue His great gifts of ability to all those concerned, to persevere in raising, not only on this particular corner-stone, but on every other corner-stone already planted in this extensive site for a commercial Federal city—edifices so durable with strength and beauty, that with common care and nurture, they may not envy time. And we further hope that the edifices which may be erected in this territory of Columbia, may be numerously inhabited with citizens, to merit every commendation for their virtue, honor, bravery, industry, and arts.

Volley from the Artillery.

"And I hope that our super-excellent order may here be indefatigably laborious, not only to keep in good repair our hallowed dome, but be incessantly industrious to adorn it with the grand theological virtues, faith, hope, and charity, and embellish it with wisdom, strength, and beauty.

Volley from the Artillery.

"My dear brethren, it would be ungrateful, indeed I think impossible, on this occasion not to notice, under the auspices of our most glorious divine Providence, the growth of this extensive city, in so short a period, by the assiduous, indefatigable labor and industry of all those very valuable characters for virtue, honor, industry, and ability, who have had not only the supreme command, but, in every grade.

Volley from the Artillery.

"Brothers, permit me to suggest to your good understandings, if so much can be done by the local assistance of two-fifteenths of these vast States, by such an eminent Leader, excellent Director, Architects, Surveyors, and Mechanics, what ought we to conceive will be done by them, when aided by the remaining thirteen-fifteenths, who will set to work with willing and powerful hands, not in a local and sparing, but in an infinite and loving manner! And in addition thereto, an universality of individuals, like innumerable hives of bees bestowing their industrious labor on this second paradise.

Volley from the Artillery.

"Then, my dear brethren, Architecture, Masonry, Arts, and Commerce will grow with rapidity inconceivable to me; therefore incomparable. Brethren, although I have neither wishes nor pretensions to divination, yet I venture to prophesy, from such intuitive sense, that all I have suggested to you will soon come to pass; when we shall all hail, Blessed Territory of Columbia,—favored land, soon, very soon, indeed, shall the shores of thy peaceful and delightful city be visited by the commercial interests of the united world; then happy thy sons, and thrice happy those whose prudence and foresight have induced them to become thy citizens!

Volley from the Artillery.

"It must, my dear brethren, be evident to all our understandings, that not only nature, but Providence, have marked their intentions in the most indelible manner, to make the seat for the Grand Mark, the super-excellent emporium for Politics, Commerce, Arts, and Industry of the United States,—seated in the very centricity of our Republic, on the banks of one of the noblest rivers in the Universe, sufficiently capacious to erect thereon a city equal, if not superior in magnitude, to any in the world. It boasts, but then very truly, a climate the most serene and salubrious; equal of accession to all the cardinal and intermediate points, as any place that kind nature has formed, even beyond conception of art, wanting no defence, but what is in, and ever will be in, I trust, the intrepidity and bravery of its founder and citizens.

Volley from the Artillery.

"Although it is not the growth of years, yet there is already planted in this garden or nursery of the Arts, and hath blossomed numerous flowers, that bloom with high lustre in their various departments (not to mention its ever-to-be-remembered founder), but its financiers, conductors, projectors, delineators, and executive gennises without number, and many of them not only brethren of our order, but brothers of superior, excellent, and sublime estimation.

Volley from the Artillery.

"Certainly, my dear brethren, it must be as grateful to you, as it is to me, to possess the great pleasure of laying the corner-stone, which we hope, expect, and sincerely pray to produce innumerable corner-stones; and that on every one of them may spring edifices, we fervently pray to the Great Grand Master of heaven, earth, and all things, of His immense wisdom, strength, goodness, and mercy, to grant. So mote it be."

WASHINGTON, although holding at this time no official rank in Masonry, except that of Past Master of Lodge No. 22, at Alexandria, clothed himself for the occasion with an apron and other insignia of a Mason, and, as the foregoing account shows, was honored with the chief place in the procession and ceremonies. The gavel which he used on the occasion was ivory, and is now in possession of Lodge No. 9, at Georgetown, which was represented by its officers and members in the procession. No act of WASHINGTON was more historic than this, and yet it has found no place on the pages of our country's history. It was he who was first in the hearts of all men, honoring Masonry by his presence as a brother, and sanctioning by his participation as the chief actor in its highest public ceremonies, its claims as an institution worthy of national confidence and regard. And yet the compilers of our country's annals have ignored the fact, or left it unrecorded on their pages, until their silence has been made to testify that WASHINGTON disdained to publicly avow himself a Mason. But he stood on that occasion before his brethren and the world as the representative of SOLOMON of old, who, the Jewish historian says, "laid the foundation of the Temple very deep in the ground; and the materials were strong stones, and such as would resist the force of time." Those who would blot the record of the mystic labors of WASHINGTON, would blush at the memory of one wiser than he.

There is no doubt but that this was one of the Masonic incidents in WASHINGTON's history which aided in establishing and perpetuating the illusion that he was the official General Grand Master of the United States; and yet, as we have already stated, such an office in American Masonry is only a historic fiction. Many American brethren have at various times advocated such a centralization of Masonic power and dignity; but to WASHINGTON only has been accorded the worthiness to hold it. He lived and died the patron *par excellence* of American Masonry; and her voice as spoken by her orators on public occasions, her muse as breathed in her songs and festive toasts, have sometimes appropriated to him a proposed, but never invested title. When another WASHINGTON shall enroll his name upon our American records, and engrave his virtues upon our hearts, perhaps then, but not till then, will all accord united Masonic homage to a General American Grand Master.

There is a striking representation of the features and person of WASHINGTON at this period of his life, and perhaps the Masonic dress that he wore at the laying of the corner-stone of the Capitol, still in possession of his old lodge, No. 22, at Alexandria. We have given an accurate copy of this almost unknown original portrait of WASHINGTON at the commencement of this volume, and we trust the following extracts from the old records of Alexandria Lodge will justify us in so doing:

"*August* 29, 1793.—ELISHA C. DICK, Master. The Worshipful Master informed the lodge that he convened them in consequence of an offer of Mr. WILLIAMS to compliment them with the portrait of the President of the United States, provided they make application to him (the President) for that purpose; and upon taking into consideration the proposal of Mr. WILLIAMS, they determined that the following address, signed by the officers of the lodge, be immediately forwarded to our illustrious Brother, the President of the United States."

We regret much that we are unable to give the letter or address, as the above record calls it, of the lodge to WASHINGTON, and his reply; but they are not recorded, nor do we know that they are preserved, or any copies of them in existence. That the application met with a favorable response is seen from the following further extracts from the records:

"*October* 25, 1794.—Mr. WILLIAMS having offered to the

lodge a drawing of our worthy Brother George Washington, President of the United States, the same is received; and in consequence of the trouble and expense Mr. Williams was at in going to and coming from Philadelphia, it is proposed that the members of the lodge pay him fifty dollars, to be raised by voluntary subscription. Brother Gillis having offered to receive the subscriptions, a list of the members, both town and country, is presented him for that purpose."

"*November* 22, 1794.—Received and read a letter from Mr. Williams, portrait painter, praying for further compensation for painting the President's picture. Ordered to lie over till next lodge-night, or until the Worshipful Master returns."

"*December* 20, 1794.—A letter from Mr. Williams was read, praying (as stated last lodge-night) a further compensation for drawing the President's picture. The lodge are of opinion that in the sum of fifty dollars paid him, he has received full compensation for the same. The lodge, moreover, consider the fifty dollars already paid him a mere gratuity, inasmuch as application was made to the President to sit for his portrait at the request of Mr. Williams, who proposed, should the application be successful, to compliment them with his portrait, promising himself great pecuniary advantages by the sale of copies. The lodge having taken into consideration the propriety of paying the fifty dollars for the President's picture by voluntary subscription, have resolved the same shall be paid out of the funds of the lodge."

On the back of the canvas is the following inscription, apparently in the handwriting of Mr. Williams:

"His Excellency GEORGE WASHINGTON, Esquire, President of the United States. Aged 64. WILLIAMS, *Pinxit ad vivum* in Philadelphia, September 18, 1794."

This portrait was placed in an elegant gilt frame, and hung upon the walls of the lodge-room. Its collar and jewel are those of a Past Master, a rank which WASHINGTON held in his lodge; and its sash and apron represent those presented to him by Messrs. WATSON & CASSOUL.

WASHINGTON's second term of the presidency was now drawing to a close, and he deemed it his duty publicly to announce to his fellow-citizens his determination to retire from public life. He accordingly, in the summer of 1796, prepared, while at Mount Vernon, his Farewell Address, which he caused to be published in the Philadelphia Advertiser in September of that year. No document ever came from the pen of an American statesman with words of more profound wisdom; and it has ever been regarded as the richest legacy which WASHINGTON bestowed on the citizens of America. It was widely circulated by public printers; legislative bodies ordered it enrolled on their journals, and it has come down to us as sacred as any writings from an uninspired pen.

In contemplating the then existing state of American society, and the dangers in introducing and cultivating principles of foreign growth, WASHINGTON had, in allusion to certain political societies in Europe which were seeking to propagate their pernicious doctrines by secret organizations for political purposes, cautioned his fellow-citizens to beware of them. As in later years a set of political zealots attempted to torture his expression of "beware of secret societies," into a denunciation against the Masonic institution, it will be only necessary for the candid reader to see that such an idea, with such facts as we have already given in WASHINGTON'S Masonic history, and such as will follow unto the close of this sketch, could not have been conceived by him, or so understood by his fellow-citizens at that day.

The address was published in Philadelphia in September, and on the 5th of the following December, at an extra Grand Communication of the Grand Lodge of Pennsylvania, in the same city, its records state—

"A committee was appointed to form an address to be presented on the ensuing feast of St. John, December 27, to the Great Master Workman, our illustrious Brother WASHINGTON, on the occasion of his intended retirement from public labors, to also be laid before the said Grand Lodge on St. John's day; and the Right Worshipful Grand Master, Deputy Grand Master, and Brothers SADLER, MILNOR, and WILLIAMS were accordingly appointed."

December 27, 1796.—St. John's day, the records state—

"The committee to prepare an address to our Brother GEORGE WASHINGTON, President of the United States, presented an address by them drawn up, which was ordered to be read.

"It was then moved and seconded, that the same be adopted; and upon the question being taken, it appeared that it was approved of.

"On motion and seconded, it was agreed that a committee be appointed to wait on Brother WASHINGTON to acquaint him that it is the intention of this Grand Lodge to present an address to him, and to know at what time he shall be pleased to receive it.

"The committee appointed to perform this duty were Brothers WILLIAM SMITH, PETER LA BARBIER DUPLESSIS, and THOMAS PROCTOR, who after having waited on him, reported that he had appointed to-morrow at twelve o'clock to receive it.

"The committee—to wit, Brothers WILLIAM SMITH, DUPLESSIS, and PROCTOR—together with the Right Worshipful Grand Master, Deputy Grand Master, Senior and Junior Grand Wardens, Grand Secretary, and the Masters of the different lodges in the city, were then appointed a deputation to present the said address."

At the time appointed this grand committee met WASHINGTON at his residence, where the following address was presented in writing, and his written reply was soon afterwards returned:

"To GEORGE WASHINGTON, *President of the United States:*

"MOST RESPECTED SIR AND BROTHER—Having announced your intention to retire from public labor to that refreshment to which your pre-eminent services for near half a century have so justly entitled you, permit the Grand Lodge of Pennsylvania at this last feast of our Evangelic Master, St. John, on which we can hope for immediate communication with you, to join the grateful voice of our country in acknowledging that you have carried forth the principles of the lodge in every walk of your life, by your constant labor for the prosperity of that country; by your unremitting endeavors to promote order, union, and brotherly affection amongst us; and, lastly, *by the views of your farewell address*, which we trust our children's children will ever look upon as a most valuable legacy from a *friend*, a *benefactor*, and a *father*.

"To these our grateful acknowledgments (leaving to the pen of history to record the important events in which you have borne so illustrious a part), permit us to add our most fervent prayers, that after enjoying to the utmost span of human life, every felicity which the terrestrial lodge can afford, you may be received by the Great Master Builder of this world, and of worlds unnumbered, into the ample felicity of that celestial lodge, in which alone distinguished virtues and distinguished labors can be eternally rewarded.

"By the unanimous order of the Grand Lodge of Pennsylvania.

"WILLIAM MOORE SMITH, G. M.

"December 27, Anno Lucis 5796."

The original of the following reply in WASHINGTON'S handwriting is still in the archives of the Grand Lodge of Pennsylvania:

"FELLOW-CITIZENS AND BROTHERS OF THE GRAND LODGE OF PENNSYLVANIA—I have received your address with all the feelings of brotherly affection, mingled with those sentiments for the society, which it was calculated to excite.

"To have been in any degree an instrument in the hands of Providence to promote order and union, and erect upon a solid foundation the true principles of government, is only to have shared, with many others, in a labor, the result of which, let us hope, will prove through all ages a sanctuary for brothers, and a lodge for the virtues.

"Permit me to reciprocate your prayers for my temporal happiness, and to supplicate that we may all meet thera-after, in that eternal temple, whose builder is the Great Architect of the Universe.

"G°. WASHINGTON."

Let those commentators on WASHINGTON'S Farewell Address, who would torture his caution to "beware of secret societies" into an allusion to Freemasonry, place this record, which was made but a few months after it, by its side, and they will see how erroneous and unjust their conclusions have been. With such a foreign idea banished from the mind, the reader, to understand fully the import of this correspondence between WASHINGTON and the Grand Lodge of Pennsylvania, and the Farewell Address, must remember that the closing scenes of his administration were so embittered with party strife, that when the subject of a reply to his last address to the House of Representatives was before that body, some of its members opposed the common courtesies that were due to the retiring President. The members of the Grand Lodge of Pennsylvania were mostly residents of the city where such base ingratitude was manifested for the past services of WASHINGTON, and probably belonged to both of the political parties of that day. But as Masons they rose above the warfare of politicians, and tendered to him their grateful acknowledgments for his past services, leaving (to use their own significant language) "to the pen of history to record the important events in which he had borne so illustrious a part." WASHINGTON'S reply shows that he fully appreciated their kind sentiments. How ardently he sought rest at this period from his public labors may be seen from a letter written to his friend, and Masonic Brother, General

KNOX, two days before his retirement from the presidency. To him he could confide the most sacred feelings of a Mason's heart; and it is singular to remark in all his epistolary correspondence that the tenderest effusions of his pen were for those friends who were bound to him by the ties of Masonic brotherhood. On this occasion he says:

"To the wearied traveller who sees a resting-place, and is bending his body to lean thereon, I now compare myself; but to be suffered to do this in peace, is too much to be endured by some. To misrepresent my motives, to reprobate my politics, and to weaken the confidence which has been reposed in my administration, are objects which cannot be relinquished by those who will be satisfied with nothing short of a change in our political system. The consolation, however, which results from conscious rectitude, and the approving voice of my country, unequivocally expressed by its representatives, deprives their sting of its poison, and place in the same point of view, the weakness and malignity of their efforts."

The closing scene of WASHINGTON'S administration was on the 4th of March, 1797. Upon the day previous he had given his last presidential dinner, at which many official dignitaries and personal friends were present. On this occasion when the cloth was removed, he took a glass of wine, and raising it to his lips, said: "Ladies and gentlemen, this is the last time I shall drink your health as a public man. I do it with sincerity, wishing you all possible happiness." There was profound silence when this toast was drank, and tears stained the cheeks of many guests at the farewell dinner of WASHINGTON.

WASHINGTON's administration closed on the following day, and Mr. ADAMS was inaugurated his successor. On this occasion he publicly appeared for the last time as President, and having introduced Mr. ADAMS to the assemblage before him, he read to them a brief valedictory which he had prepared. His parting words met with responsive sobs from the audience, and his own great heart swelled with emotions till the tears fell from his cheeks. As he retired from the scene before him, he was followed by a multitude of citizens, all eager to catch the last look of one they loved so well. At his own door he turned to express his acknowledgment to the people; but his voice failed him, and it was only by a wave of his hand that he could convey a farewell blessing.

CHAPTER IX.

WASHINGTON leaves Philadelphia and returns to Mount Vernon.—Engages in domestic pursuits.—Letter to General KNOX.—Receives address from Grand Lodge of Massachusetts.—His reply.—Receives letter from Master of his own lodge inviting him to an entertainment.—Accepts it.—Account of this entertainment as published at the time.—His employments.—Unpleasant position of France towards our Government.—WASHINGTON appointed commander of the provisional army.—Letter to him from the Grand Lodge of Maryland, with copy of Constitutions.—His reply.—Public mind excited by the writings of BARRUEL and ROBISON on the subject of Illuminism.—Attempts made to implicate Masonry with it.—Rev. Mr. SNYDER sends WASHINGTON "proofs of a conspiracy."—Copy of accompanying letter from Mr. SNYDER.—WASHINGTON'S reply.—Mr. SNYDER writes him a second letter.—His reply.—Contents of these letters considered.—Other clergymen seek to alarm the public in regard to Masonry.—Grand Lodge of Massachusetts address a letter to President ADAMS.—His reply.—Grand Lodges of Vermont and Maryland also write letters to Mr. ADAMS, to which he replies.—Extract from letter of Grand Lodge of Maryland to Mr. ADAMS.—Extract from his reply.—Rev. Mr. MORSE qualifies his sermon when published.—France assumes a more pacific attitude.—WASHINGTON'S last celebration of his birthday at Mount Vernon.—Marriage of his adopted daughter.—His birthday anniversaries became National holidays.—Also Masonic holidays.—Dr. SEABURY dedicates sermon to him.—Curious pamphlet by Rev. Mr. WEEMS dedicated to him.—Copy of Mr. WEEMS' letter to him, and his reply.

WASHINGTON left Philadelphia in a few days and returned to Mount Vernon, where he at once engaged in superintending the improvement of his estate, and arranging his domestic affairs, which had been neglected during the eight years of his presidency. He had said in a letter to General KNOX:

8*

"The remainder of my life, which in the course of nature cannot be long, will be occupied in rural amusements; and though I shall seclude myself as much as possible from the noisy and bustling crowd, none would more than myself be regaled by the company of those I esteem at Mount Vernon—more than twenty miles from which, after I arrive there, it is not likely I shall ever be."

He had scarcely settled himself in his domestic enjoyments, when the voice of Masonry—ever grateful to his ear—reached him in an address from the Grand Lodge of Massachusetts, which bore date March 21, 1797, of which the following is a copy:

"The *East*, the *West*, and the *South*, of the Grand Lodge of Ancient Free and Accepted Masons, for the Commonwealth of Massachusetts, to their most worthy Brother GEORGE WASHINGTON.

"Wishing ever to be foremost in testimonials of respect and admiration of those virtues and services with which you have so long adorned and benefited our common country, and not the last nor least to regret the cessation of them in the public councils of the Union, your brethren of this Grand Lodge embrace the earliest opportunity of greeting you in the calm retirement you have contemplated to yourself.

"Though as citizens they lose you in the active labors of political life, they hope as Masons to find you in the pleasing sphere of fraternal engagement. From the cares of State, and the fatigues of public business, our institution opens a recess, affording all the relief of tranquillity, the harmony of peace, and the refreshment of pleasure. Of these may you partake in all their purity and satisfaction;

and we will assure ourselves that your attachment to this social plan will encrease; and that, under the auspices of your encouragement, assistance, and patronage, the Craft will attain its highest ornament, perfection, and praise. And it is our earnest prayer, that when your light shall be no more visible in this earthly Temple, you may be raised to the *All Perfect Lodge* above, be seated on the right of the Supreme Architect of the Universe, and receive the refreshment your labors have merited.

"In behalf of the Grand Lodge, we subscribe ourselves, with the highest esteem, your affectionate brethren,

"PAUL REVERE, Grand Master.
"ISAIAH THOMAS, Senior Grand Warden.
"JOSEPH LAUGHTON, Junior Grand Warden.
"DANIEL OLIVER, Grand Secretary.

"BOSTON, March 21, 5797."

To this address WASHINGTON returned the following reply, which was communicated to the Grand Lodge on the 12th of the following June:

"TO THE GRAND LODGE OF ANCIENT FREE AND ACCEPTED MASONS IN THE COMMONWEALTH OF MASSACHUSETTS:

"BROTHERS—It was not until within these few days that I have been favored by the receipt of your affectionate address, dated in Boston, the 21st March.

"For the favorable sentiments you have been pleased to express on the occasion of my past services, and for the regrets with which they are accompanied for the cessation of my public functions, I pray you to accept my best acknowledgments and gratitude.

"No pleasure, except that which results from a consciousness of having, to the utmost of my abilities, discharged the trusts which have been reposed in me by my country, can equal the satisfaction I feel for the unequivocal proofs I continually receive of its approbation of my public conduct; and I beg you to be assured that the evidence thereof, which is exhibited by the Grand Lodge of Massachusetts, is not among the least pleasing or grateful to my feelings.

"In that retirement which declining years induces me to seek, and which repose, to a mind long employed in public concerns, rendered necessary, my wishes that bounteous Providence will continue to bless and preserve our country in peace, and in the prosperity it has enjoyed, will be warm and sincere; and my attachment to the Society of which we are members will dispose me always to contribute my best endeavors to promote the honor and interest of the Craft.

"For the prayer you offer in my behalf, I entreat you to accept the thanks of a grateful heart, with assurances of fraternal regard, and my best wishes for the honor, happiness, and prosperity of all the members of the Grand Lodge of Massachusetts.

"G°. WASHINGTON."

Although this Masonic greeting from the Grand Lodge of Massachusetts antedates any other Masonic intercourse on record after his retirement from the presidency; yet before its reception by him, his own lodge at Alexandria also took measures to welcome his return. For this purpose they addressed him the following letter:

"ALEXANDRIA, March 28, 1797.

"MOST RESPECTED BROTHER—Brothers RAMSEY and MARSTELLER wait upon you with a copy of an address which has been prepared by the unanimous desire of the Ancient York Masons of Lodge No. 22. It is their earnest request that you will partake of a dinner with them, and that you will please appoint the time most convenient for you to attend.

"I am, most beloved Brother,
"Your most obd't and humble serv't,
"JAMES GILLIS, M.

"GENERAL GEORGE WASHINGTON."

WASHINGTON accepted the invitation, and designated the following Saturday as the time when he would meet the brethren of his lodge. The following account of the addresses and ceremonies on the occasion is given in the "Freemasons' Magazine," published in London in June, 1797:

"UNITED STATES OF AMERICA,
ALEXANDRIA, April 4, 1797.

"In consequence of an invitation from the Ancient York Masons of the Alexandria Lodge No. 22 to General GEORGE WASHINGTON, he joined the brethren on Saturday last, when the following address was delivered:

"'MOST RESPECTED BROTHER—The Ancient York Masons of Lodge No. 22 offer you their warmest congratulations, on your retirement from your useful labors. Under the Supreme Architect of the Universe, you have been the Master Workman in erecting the Temple of Liberty in the West, on the broad basis of equal rights. In your wise administration of the Government of the United States for the space of eight years, you have kept within the compass of our happy constitution, and acted upon the square with foreign nations, and thereby preserved your country in peace, and promoted the prosperity and happiness of your fellow-citizens. And now that you have returned from the labors of public life, to the refreshment of domestic tranquillity, they ardently pray that you may long enjoy all the happiness which the Terrestrial Lodge can afford, and finally be received to a Celestial Lodge, where love, peace, and harmony forever reign, and cherubim and seraphim shall hail you Brother!

"'By the unanimous desire of Lodge No. 22.

"'James Gillis, Master.

"'General George Washington.'

"To which the following reply was made:

"'Brothers of the Ancient York Masons No. 22—While my heart acknowledges with brotherly love your affectionate congratulations on my retirement from the arduous toils of past years, my gratitude is no less excited by your kind wishes for my future happiness. If it has pleased the Supreme Architect of the Universe to make me an humble instrument to promote the welfare and happiness of my fellow-men, my exertions have been abundantly recompensed by the kind partiality with which they have been received. And the assurances you give me of your belief that I have acted upon the square in my public capacity, will be among my principal enjoyments in this Terrestrial Lodge.

"'G°. Washington.'

"After this the lodge went in procession from their room to Mr. Albert's tavern, where they partook of an elegant dinner prepared for the occasion, at which the utmost harmony prevailed. The following were the principal toasts:

"1st. Prosperity to the Most Ancient and Honorable Craft.

"2d. All those who live within the Compass and the Square.

"3d. The Temple of Liberty—may its pillars be the poles, its canopy the heavens, and its votaries all mankind.

"4th. The virtuous nine.

"5th. The United States of America.

"6th. The Grand Master of Virginia.

"7th. All oppressed and distressed, wherever dispersed.

"8th. Masons' wives, and Masons' bairns, and all who wish to lie in Masons' arms.

"9th. May brotherly love unite all nations.

(By Brother WASHINGTON.)

"10th. The Lodge at Alexandria, and all Masons throughout the world.

"After which he retired.

"11th. Our most respected Brother GEORGE WASHINGTON. Which was drunk with all Masonic honors."

These Masonic incidents in WASHINGTON's life occurred while he was busily preparing to rearrange the domestic concerns of his estate, which had been somewhat neglected during the presidency. In a letter to a friend he says:

"I find myself in the situation of a new beginner; for although I have not houses to build (except one which I must erect for the accommodation and security of my military, civil, and private papers, which are voluminous, and may be interesting), yet I have scarcely any thing else about me that does not require considerable repairs. In a word, I am already surrounded with joiners, masons, and painters; and such is my anxiety to get out of their hands, that I have scarcely a room to put a friend into or to sit in myself, without the music of hammers or the odoriferous smell of paint."

But WASHINGTON was not permitted to enjoy the quietness of Mount Vernon undisturbed by public cares. Before his administration had closed, the government of France assumed an unpleasant position towards our own, and the clouds of war were again gathering thick above our horizon, and threatening to burst upon our country with all their complicated gloom. So imminent had the danger become, that in 1798 a provisional army was ordered to be raised, and all eyes in America were turned on WASHINGTON as its commander. He received and reluctantly accepted the appointment, and in the fall of that year again left his own quiet home and repaired to Philadelphia to arrange the details of a perfect military organization of the country for the anticipated contest. While he was engaged in these duties, he received from the Grand Lodge of the State of Maryland a copy of its Book of Constitutions, which had been published the previous year, accompanied by a letter from that Grand Lodge, to which he returned the following reply, dated November 8, 1798:

"TO THE RIGHT WORSHIPFUL GRAND LODGE OF FREEMASONS OF THE STATE OF MARYLAND:

"BRETHREN AND BROTHERS—Your obliging and affectionate letter, together with a copy of the 'Constitutions of Masonry,' has been put in my hands by your Grand Master, for which,

I pray you, to accept my best thanks. So far as I am acquainted with the principles and doctrines of Freemasonry, I conceive them to be founded on benevolence, and to be exercised only for the good of mankind. I cannot, therefore, upon this ground, withdraw my approbation from it. While I offer my grateful acknowledgments for your congratulations on my late appointment, and for the favorable sentiments you are pleased to express of my conduct, permit me to observe, that, at this important and critical moment, when high and repeated indignities have been offered to the Government of our country, and when the property of our citizens is plundered without a prospect of redress, I conceive it to be the *indispensable* duty of every American, let his station and circumstances in life be what they may, to come forward in support of the Government of his choice, and to give all the aid in his power towards maintaining that independence which we have so dearly purchased; and, under this impression, I did not hesitate to lay aside all personal considerations and accept my appointment.

"I pray you to be assured that I receive with gratitude your kind wishes for my health and happiness, and reciprocate them with sincerity.

"I am, gentlemen and brothers, very respectfully,

"Your most obed't serv't,

"G°. WASHINGTON."

"November 8, 1798."

The student of Masonic history will remember that this reply from WASHINGTON to the Grand Lodge of Maryland was written when our country was agitated with a threatened war with France; and that the intestine commotions that had distracted that republic, were ascribed to the influence of German and French "illuminism," which a BARRUEL and a ROBISON asserted had been planted and fostered there through the influence of Masonic lodges.

BARRUEL—who was a French Jesuit, used all his professional cunning to implicate Masonry in the excesses of the Jacobins of France—and ROBISON, who was a Scotchman of some literary notoriety, had each issued a work in which they they sought to demonstrate that Masonic lodges were all schools of *illuminism*, in which *infidelity* and *red-republicanism* were taught. These works had just made their appearance in this country, and the excesses of the French at home, and their hostile and insolent attitude to our Government, caused them to receive an attention and make an impression on the public mind which would have been impossible under other circumstances. It is worthy of note that the author of one of these productions was a Papist, and that of the other a Scotch Presbyterian.

Masonic lodges in this country had multiplied since the Revolution to an extent unknown before; their membership embraced men in all the honorable walks of life, and higher organizations and Masonic grades of office were being formed in many of the States. ROBISON had openly asserted that illuminism was a grade in Masonry, which had already been introduced in the United States; and public agitators in this country sought to identify the infidelity of Germany, and the excesses of France, with Masonry in America.

While the public mind was poisoned with these insinuations, and the country was threatened with an invasion by France, WASHINGTON received from a clergyman, by the name of SNYDER, who resided at Fredericktown, in Maryland, a copy of Mr. ROBISON'S work, which had just been republished in America, entitled "Proofs of a Conspiracy against all the Religions and Governments of Europe, carried on in the secret meetings of Freemasons, Illuminati, and Reading Societies.") The book was also accompanied by the following letter to him from Mr. SNYDER:

"SIR—You will, I hope, not think it presumption in a stranger, whose name, perhaps, never reached your ears, to address himself to you, the commanding general of a great nation. I am a German born, and liberally educated in the city of Heidelberg, in the Palatinate of the Rhine. I came to this country in 1776, and felt soon after my arrival a close attachment to the liberty for which these Confederated States then struggled. The same attachment still remains, not glowing, but burning in my breast. At the same time that I am exulting in the measures adopted by our Government, I feel myself elevated in the idea of my adopted country. I am attached, both from the best of education and mature inquiry and research, to the simple doctrines of Christianity, which I have the honor to teach in public; and I do heartily despise all the cavils of infidelity. Our present time is pregnant with the most shocking evils and calamities, which threaten ruin to our liberty and Government. Secretly the most secret plans are in agitation; plans calculated to ensnare the unwary, to attract the gay and irreligious, and to entice even the well-disposed to combine in the general machine for overturning all government and religion.

"It was some time since that a book fell into my hands, entitled 'Proofs of a Conspiracy, etc., by JOHN ROBISON,' which gives a full account of a Society of Freemasons, that distinguishes itself by the name of 'Illuminati,' whose plan is to overturn all government and all religion, even natural, and who endeavor to eradicate every idea of a Supreme Being, and distinguish man from beast by his shape only.

"A thought suggested itself to me that some of the lodges in the United States might have caught the infection, and might co-operate with the Illuminati, or the Jacobine clubs in France.

"FAUCHET is mentioned by ROBISON as a zealous member; and who can doubt GENET and ADET? Have not these their confidants in this country? They use the same expressions, and are generally men of no religion. Upon serious reflection I was led to think that it might be within your power to prevent the horrid plan from corrupting the brethren of the English lodges over which you preside. I send you the 'Proofs of a Conspiracy,' etc., which, I doubt not, will give you satisfaction, and afford you matter for a train of ideas that may operate to our national felicity. If, however, you have already perused the book, it will not, I trust, be disagreeable to you that I address you with this letter, and the book accompanying it. It proceeded from the sincerity of my heart, and my ardent wishes for the common good.

"May the Supreme Ruler of all things continue you long with us in these perilous times; may He endue you with strength and wisdom to save our country in the threatening storms and gathering clouds of factions and commotions; and after you have completed His work on this terrene spot, may He bring you to the full possession of the glorious liberty of the children of GOD, is the hearty and most sincere wish of

"Your Excellency's

"Very humble and devoted servant,

"G. W. SNYDER.

"His Excellency General GEORGE WASHINGTON.

"FREDERICKTOWN, Maryland, August 22, 1798."

To this letter WASHINGTON replied as follows:

"MOUNT VERNON, 25th September, 1798.

"THE REV. MR. SNYDER: SIR—Many apologies are due to you for my not acknowledging the receipt of your obliging favor of the 22d ult., and not thanking you, at an earlier period, for the book you had the goodness to send me.

"I have heard much of the nefarious and dangerous plan and doctrines of the Illuminati, but never saw the book until you were pleased to send it to me. The same causes which have prevented my acknowledging the receipt of your letter have prevented my reading the book hitherto—namely, the multiplicity of matters which pressed upon me before, and the debilitated state in which I was left after a severe fever had been removed, and which allows me to add but little more than thanks for your kind wishes and favorable sentiments, except to correct an error you have run into, of my presiding over the English lodges in this country. The fact is, I preside over none, nor have I been in one more than once or twice within the last thirty years. I believe, notwithstanding, that none of the lodges in this country are contaminated with the principles ascribed to the society of the Illuminati.

"With respect, I am, sir,

"Your obedient, humble servant,

"G°. WASHINGTON."

Mr. SNYDER wrote a second letter to WASHINGTON, in the following month, on the same subject; and for this we have also made strict search in the archives of the Federal State Department, where the Washington papers are deposited; but it is nowhere to be found. A copy of WASHINGTON's reply to this second letter, however, we are able to lay before our readers.

"MOUNT VERNON, 24th October, 1798.

"REVEREND SIR—I have your favor of the 17th instant before me, and my only motive for troubling you with the receipt of the letter is to explain and correct a mistake which, I believe, the hurry in which I am obliged often to write letters has led you into.

"It was not my intention to doubt that the doctrines of the *Illuminati*, and the principles of *Jacobinism* had not spread in the United States. On the contrary, no one is more fully satisfied of this fact than I am.

"The idea I meant to convey was, that I did not believe that the lodges of Freemasons in this country had, as societies, endeavored to propagate the diabolical tenets of the former, or the pernicious principles of the latter, if they are susceptible of separation. That individuals of them may have done it, or that the founder, or instruments employed to found, the democratic societies in the United States may have had these objects, and actually had a separation of the people from their Government in view, is too evident to be questioned.

"My occupations are such that little leisure is allowed me to read newspapers or books of any kind. The reading of letters and preparing answers absorbs much of my time.

"With respect, I remain, sir, etc.,

"G°. WASHINGTON."

The first letter of General WASHINGTON to Mr. SNYDER has been often quoted, in some of its parts, to attempt to show that WASHINGTON disclaimed all connection with Masonry during his mature and latter years. His statement, that he presided over none of the English lodges of this country, nor had been in one more than once or twice in the last thirty years, is given as if the qualifying designation of *English* lodges was not there written and fully meant by him. It is well known, as any fact in history, that previous to the Revolution all regular lodges of Masons in this country derived their authority, either directly or indirectly, from one of the Grand Lodges of Great Britain, and Masonry in this country was known as English Masonry, in contradistinction to some of the existing systems of Continental Europe. When the independence of the United States was fully confirmed, Masonry, as an institution, conformed its organizations and government to the new existing political state of the country; and its lodges, with but few exceptions, relinquished all dependence on their English progenitor and head. American lodges, therefore, in 1798, were as distinct from English lodges, as the independent States were from their former colonial dependence, except in a few instances, where individual lodges, like St. Andrew's in Boston, still continued their fealty to the foreign Grand Lodge, to which they owed their birth, and declined to acknowledge the supremacy or legitimacy of any independent American Grand Lodge. Some of these lodges thus continued until after the commencement of the present century.

There were also many lodges in America, while the

Provincial Grand Lodge system was in vogue here, which had their warrants from the Grand Lodges of England direct, and were never subject to the government of the American Provincial Grand Bodies; and there were other English Military Lodges in this country, both during the Revolution and previous to it, which had no connection with the Provincial Grand Lodges in America, except in owing a common allegiance to the English Grand Easts, from which they sprung. In which of these WASHINGTON may "once or twice" have been, we have no record to determine, while we have abundant records to show that he often met with his *American* brethren in their lodges, and was to the close of his life an affiliated member, and as such received Masonic burial at their hands.

Mr. SNYDER was not the only clergyman in America whose fears were aroused by the artful statements of Mr. ROBISON'S book, for it pervaded to a great extent among the Scotch Presbyterians; and in New England many of all classes suffered themselves to be very much alarmed by its statements. Mr. ADAMS, as President of the United States, had recommended a national fast-day to be observed on the 9th of May, 1798; and on that occasion many clergymen introduced the subject of Illuminism into their discourses, and attempted to show from the writings of BARRUEL and ROBISON, that Masonry was an institution dangerous to civil and religious liberty. Much feeling was aroused in New England by these discourses, and the fears of many were excited that Masonry in this country was about to work the same evils here that had been falsely attributed to it in Europe.

To counteract this false impression on the public mind, the Grand Lodge of Massachusetts, at their session on the 11th of June of that year, addressed the following communication to JOHN ADAMS, as President of the United States:

"BOSTON, June 11, 1798.

"TO THE PRESIDENT OF THE UNITED STATES:

"SIR—Flattery and a discussion of political opinions are inconsistent with the principles of our Fraternity; but while we are bound to cultivate benevolence, and extend the arm of charity to our brethren of every clime, we feel the strongest obligations to support the civil authority which protects us. And when the illiberal attacks of a foreign enthusiast, aided by the unfounded prejudices of his followers, are tending to embarrass the public mind with respect to the real views of our society, we think it our duty to join in full concert with our fellow-citizens in expressing our gratitude to the Supreme Architect of the Universe, for endowing you with that wisdom, patriotism, firmness, and integrity which has characterized your public conduct.

"While the independence of our country, and the operation of just and equal laws, have contributed to enlarge the sphere of social happiness, we rejoice that our Masonic brethren throughout the United States have discovered by their conduct a zeal to promote the public welfare, and that many of them have been conspicuous for their talents and unwearied exertions. Among those, your *venerable predecessor* is the most illustrious example; and the memory of our beloved WARREN, who from the chair of this Grand Lodge has often urged the members to the exercise of patriotism and philanthropy, and who sealed his principles with his blood, shall ever animate us to a laudable imitation of his virtues.

"Sincerely we deprecate the calamities of war, and have fervently wished success to every endeavor for the preservation of peace. But, sir, if we disregard the blessings of liberty, we are unworthy to enjoy them. In vain have our statesmen labored in their public assemblies and by their midnight tapers; in vain have our mountains and valleys been stained with the blood of our heroes, if we want firmness to repel the assaults of every presumptive invader. And while, as citizens of a Free Republic, we engage our utmost exertions in the cause of our country, and offer our services to protect the fair inheritance of our ancestors, as Masons we will cultivate the precepts of our institution, and alleviate the miseries of all who by the fortunes of war, or the ordinary concerns of life, are the objects of our attention.

"Long may you continue a patron of the useful arts, and an ornament to the present generation; may you finish your public labors with an approving conscience, and be gathered to the sepulchres of your co-patriots with the benedictions of your countrymen; and finally, may you be admitted to that celestial temple, where all national distinctions are lost in undissembled friendship and universal peace.

"JOSIAH BARTLETT, Grand Master.
"SAMUEL DUNN, D. G. Master.
"JOSEPH LAUGHTON, } G. Wardens.
"WM. LITTLE, }

"Attest: DANIEL OLIVER, G. Secretary."

To this address, Mr. ADAMS sent the following courteous and respectful reply.

"GENTLEMEN—As I never had the honor to be one of your ancient fraternity, I feel myself under the greater obligations to you for your respectful and affectionate address. Many of my best friends have been Masons, and two of these, my professional patron, the learned GRIDLEY, and my intimate friend, your immortal WARREN, whose life and death are lessons of patriotism and philanthropy, were Grand Masters. Yet so it has happened, that I never had the felicity to be initiated. Such examples as these, and a greater still in my *venerable predecessor*, would have been sufficient to induce me to hold the Institution and Fraternity in esteem and honor, as favorable to the support of civil authority, if I had not known their love of the fine arts, their delight in hospitality, and devotion to humanity.

"Your indulgent opinion of my conduct, and your benevolent wish for the fortunate termination of my public labors, have my sincere thanks.

"The public engagement of your utmost exertions in the cause of your country, and the offer of your services to protect the fair inheritance of your ancestors, are proofs that you are not chargeable with those designs, the imputation of which, in other parts of the world, has embarrassed the public mind with respect to the real views of your society.

"JOHN ADAMS.

"PHILADELPHIA, June 22, 1798."

Mr. ADAMS had, a few months previous, received a similar letter from the Grand Master of Maryland, in behalf of the Fraternity of that State, to which he also replied. From this letter and reply, we give the following extracts. Mr. BELTON, the Grand Master, in his letter, bearing date Baltimore, July 12, 1798, said:

* * * * * * * * * "Permit us to offer our most sincere congratulations on an occurrence the most interesting to Americans. We again behold *our* WASHINGTON !—the glory of his country—the boast, the honor of our Society and of mankind, relinquishing in old age the tranquil scene. Summoned by the voice of his country, we again behold the Hero and the Patriot, willing and forward to sacrifice his private ease for her safety! What heart can be so cold, what heart can so languidly move, as not to beat high and strong at the thought of being once more commanded by that highest ornament of the human character—our true, ever-beloved Brother GEORGE WASHINGTON ! The name alone will form a sure defence."

To this sentiment Mr. ADAMS replied under date of July 18, 1798:

* * * * * * "With heartfelt satisfaction, I reciprocate your most sincere congratulations on an occasion the most interesting to Americans. No light or trivial cause would have given you the opportunity of beholding your WASHINGTON again relinquishing the tranquil scenes in delicious shades. To complete the character of French philosophy and French policy, at the end of the eighteenth century, it seemed to be necessary to combat this *Patriot* and *Hero*."

These addresses and replies show that WASHINGTON'S connection with Masonry was as fully recognized at this period by all classes of American citizens as it was proudly claimed by his brethren, and that the misinterpretation of his views by its enemies had not then been attempted. Even the Rev. JEDEDIAH MORSE, who in his fast-day sermon at Boston, on the 9th of

May, had entered largely into the spirit of BARRUEL and ROBISON, when he permitted the sermon to appear in print a few months later, softened his accusations in a marginal note by saying:

"Judging from the characters in general who compose the Masonic Fraternity in America, at the head of which stands the immortal WASHINGTON, and particularly the characters of the Masons in New England, who, as a body, have ever shown themselves firm and decided supporters of civil and religious order, we may presume that this *leaven* has not found its way into our American lodges, especially in the Eastern States. If it has been introduced among us, it has probably been insinuated through different channels."

Thus was WASHINGTON'S fame as a Mason publicly acknowledged and unimpeached, even by those of his contemporaries who assailed the integrity and objects of the institution.

The last year of WASHINGTON'S life was spent in quietness at his home on the Potomac. His duties as lieutenant-general of the Provisional army did not call him into the field, for France assumed a more pacific attitude towards our Government, and he was spared the necessity of directing a bloody conflict with our former ally. The 22d of February, 1799, was a gala-day at Mount Vernon. It was WASHINGTON'S last celebration of his birthday; and on this occasion his adopted daughter, NELLY CUSTIS, was given by him as the bride of his nephew, LAWRENCE LEWIS. She was the daughter of his stepson, JOHN PARKE CUSTIS, who died near Yorktown in 1781. His two youngest children, a son and a daughter, as before stated, had on that occasion been adopted by WASHINGTON; and of these NELLY was his favorite, and the bridal flower that graced Mount Vernon on his last birthday.

While the States were English colonies, the king's birthday anniversaries were public holidays; and as such, the 4th of June was King GEORGE's day with the people: but after the close of the Revolution, the celebration of WASHINGTON'S birthday took the place of that; and the 22d of February became a festival day in our country. It was thus observed in Alexandria as early as 1784; and the birth-night balls of February 22d have been successively continued there. We have also seen notices of it in Richmond as early as 1786, and in Philadelphia, 1790. It also became, during WASHINGTON'S presidency, a Masonic festival. St. John's Lodge at Newark, New Jersey, kept it as such as early as 1792; and that venerable lodge has, from that time to the present, yearly convened on that day to commemorate the Masonic virtues of WASHINGTON. Little did those brethren, who first met to celebrate it as Masons, reflect how many millions in after-years would regard it as

"The gayest festival in all the year."

Even at the yearly festivals of more ancient origin to commemorate the two St. Johns, it had become the custom to remember WASHINGTON in one of the standing Masonic toasts at that day. He was also still remembered in published Masonic addresses dedicated to him. One of these, delivered before a special session of the Grand Lodge of Connecticut, at Norwich, on the 24th of June, 1795, by Dr. SAMUEL SEABURY, the first consecrated Bishop in America, bore the following dedication by him to WASHINGTON:

"To the Most Worshipful GEORGE WASHINGTON, President of the United States of America, the following discourse is respectfully inscribed, by his affectionate brother, and most devoted servant,

"SAMUEL SEABURY."

It is a curious fact in the Masonic history of our country during WASHINGTON'S lifetime, that most dedications of Masonic literature were made to him, while other publications also were in some instances thus dedicated. A curious semi-dedication of a quaint pamphlet, by the Rev. MASON L. WEEMS, an early biographer of WASHINGTON, published in 1799, was thus given, which we here reproduce as the last written correspondence with WASHINGTON in which Masonic allusions are made. The pamphlet was entitled,

"The PHILANTHROPIST, or *Political Peace-Maker* between all honest men of both parties. With the recommendation prefixed by GEORGE WASHINGTON in his own handwriting, by M. L. WEEMS, Lodge No. 50, Dumfries."

It was prefaced with the following letter to WASHINGTON, and a *fac-simile* copy of his reply, which were as follows:

"TO HIS EXCELLENCY GEORGE WASHINGTON, ESQUIRE, *Lieutenant-General of the Armies of the United States:*

"MOST HONORED GENERAL—Scarcely was I delivered of this young republican philanthropist before I began, according to good Christian usage, to look about for a suitable god-father for it. My thoughts, presumptuously enough, I confess, instantly fixed upon you, for two reasons: *First*, I was desirous of paying to you (the first benefactor of my country) this little mite of grateful and affectionate respect; and *secondly*, because I well know there exists not, on this side of heaven, the man who will more cordially than General WASHINGTON approve of whatever tends to advance the harmony and happiness of Columbia.

"GOD, *I pray him, grant!* that you may long live to see us *all* catching from your fair example that reverence for the Eternal Being, that veneration for the laws, that infinite concern for the *national Union*, that unextinguishable love for our country, and that insuperable contempt of pleasures, of dangers, and of death itself, in its service and defence, which have raised you to immortality, and which alone can exalt us to be a GREAT and HAPPY REPUBLIC.

"On the square of Justice, and on the scale of Love, I remain, honored general, your very sincere friend, and Masonic brother,

"M. L. WEEMS."

WASHINGTON replied:

"MOUNT VERNON, 29th August, 1799.

"REV'D SIR—I have been duly favored with your letter of the 20th instant, accompanying 'The Philanthropist.'

"For your politeness in sending the letter, I pray you to receive my best thanks. Much indeed it is to be wished that the sentiments contained in the Pamphlet, and the doctrines it endeavors to inculcate, were more prevalent. Happy would it be for *this country at least*, if they were so. But while the passions of mankind are under so little restraint as they are among us, and while there are so many motives and views to bring them into action, we may wish for, but never see the accomplishment of it.

"With respect,

"I am your most obed't humble servant,

"G°. Washington.

"The Rev'd M. L. Weems."

CHAPTER X.

WASHINGTON'S last autumn.—His sickness.—Death.—Who present at the time.—Preparations for the funeral.—Ceremonies arranged by a committee of Lodge No. 22.—Emergent meeting of this lodge.—Meeting of Lodge No. 47.—Other lodges in the district requested to attend the funeral.—Military of Alexandria invited to join as an escort.—Citizens assembled at the funeral.—Inscription on the coffin.—Masonic ceremonies at the house.—Vessel on the river furls its sails.—Formation of the procession.—Clergy present on the occasion.—Who of them were Masons.—Moving of the procession.—Arrival at the tomb.—Religious services.—Masonic ceremonies.—A salute fired.—Entombment concluded.—Lodge No. 22 meets on the following day.—Colonel DENEALE elected its Master.—Its former Masters.—Dr. DICK'S address.—Lodges go to the Presbyterian church to hear sermon by Rev. Mr. MAFFIT.—Lodges attend on two succeeding Sabbaths to hear sermons from various clergymen.—Celebration at Alexandria on the following 22d of February.—Masonic lodges attend in mourning.—Other attendance.—Ceremonies.—Extracts from Dr. DICK'S address on the occasion.—Prayers delivered on the occasion by Rev. Brothers Dr. MUIR, THOMAS DAVIS, and WILLIAM MAFFIT.

WASHINGTON'S last summer and autumn were spent in arranging the minutest details of his domestic affairs and private business. Whether he had a premonition that it was his last year, no one can determine; but like a wise man, he set his house in order. December came, and with its chilling breath and wintry mantle came also the messenger of death for WASHINGTON!

His sickness was sudden, short, and painful. It

commenced on the evening of Thursday, the 12th of December, as a common cold, with soreness of the throat. Upon the succeeding day the inflammation there had increased, and in the night became alarming. He was urged to send to Alexandria for Dr. Craik, his family physician, but the night was stormy, and his humanity for his servant induced him to defer it until Saturday morning, using, in the mean time, all the usual domestic remedies in such cases. But these were of no avail, and his physicians came too late. It was eleven o'clock on the forenoon of Saturday before Dr. Craik arrived, and the disease had made so alarming a progress, that two eminent consulting physicians, Dr. Dick, of Alexandria, and Dr. Brown, of Port Tobacco, were also sent for. But none of them could afford relief. The chilling hand of death was already upon him. Fully aware that his last mortal hour had come, he met it with a composure of mind that astonished those about him, saying to his physician, who assured him that he had not long to live: "It is well, doctor: I am not afraid to die." Then calmly crossing his arms upon his breast, he closed his eyes, and, with a few shortening breaths, expired without a struggle, between ten and eleven in the evening.

Mrs. Washington was sitting at the time at the foot of the bed, and as his spirit ebbed away, she buried her face in the enfolded curtains and silently prayed that it might peacefully pass. The stillness of the death-chamber was first broken by her words, as she raised her head and asked in a firm and collected, but mournful voice: "Is he gone?" Mr. Lear, who was standing by the bedside, by a motion of his hand, silently signified that he was no more. "'Tis well," said she in the same voice; "all is now over; I shall soon follow him; I have no more trials to pass through."

Few were present as witnesses of the scene. It was only the domestic circle of his own household, with, perhaps, a few family friends, and his attending physicians who were there. Of these, Dr. CRAIK, his life-long friend and family physician, and Dr. DICK, were Masons; the latter being at the time the Master of WASHINGTON's own lodge at Alexandria. What Masonic requests may have been made to them during his last hours we know not. But it is well known to every Mason, that the mystic rites of a Masonic burial are not performed, except at a brother's request while living, or by desire of his family after his death. It was believed at the time, by intelligent brethren, that WASHINGTON had signified that to be his wish; and the holy rites of the Christian Church of which he was a member, and the mystic rites of Masonry, were each performed in their beautiful simplicity at the tomb of this distinguished brother.

At midnight—*the low twelve of Masonry*—the body was taken from the chamber of death to a large drawing-room below, clothed in burial robes. The death dew had been wiped from its brow, and the pale taper at its head threw a flickering light on the marble features where death had set his signet. From midnight until morning there was stillness there. Words were spoken only in whispers, as if accents from human lips would fall discordant on the sleeper's ear. America, too, in that dread interval from midnight to

Sabbath morn, lay in slumber, unconscious of her loss. Morning came, and the hurrying footsteps of family friends, who hastened to Mount Vernon, were heard mingling with those that left to carry the tidings of a Nation's loss! My pen cannot describe what followed. A pencil painted it:

Washington in Glory;—America in Tears!

During the day a plain mahogany coffin was ordered from Alexandria, and mourning for the family, overseers, and domestics at Mount Vernon. The funeral was appointed for Wednesday, the 18th, at meridian; and the Rev. Mr. DAVIS, the Episcopal clergyman at Alexandria, was invited to perform the burial rites of that Church on the occasion. The selection was an appropriate one; for Mr. DAVIS was not only the rector of WASHINGTON'S church, but he was also a member of the same Masonic lodge.

The funeral procession and burial ceremonies were arranged by a committee of Lodge No. 22, at Alexandria, consisting of Dr. ELISHA CULLEN DICK, its Master; Colonel GEORGE DENEALE, its Senior Warden; and Colonels CHARLES LITTLE and CHARLES SIMMS, who were members. On Monday, the 16th, an emergent meeting of this lodge was called, at which Dr. DICK, its Master, presided. Forty-one of its members were present, and two visiting brethren, one from Fredericksburg, where WASHINGTON was made a Mason, and the other from Philadelphia.

Dr. DICK addressed the brethren in a feeling manner, on the event which had called them together. It was their first recorded meeting on an occasion like this. They sat in sorrow there. The death-angel's alarm at their tiled door had found none to withstand his approach, or ask from whence he came, or what he came thither to do. With step unseen, and salutation strange to all, he had approached their midst, removed from before their altar a mystic taper, and taken it to the Grand Lodge above. To arrange for commemorating, in the burial of their departed WASHINGTON, the extinguishing of that light in their lodge, and their confident hope of finding it shining with brighter rays before the Grand Orient of the Holy One on High, they were now met.

There was also another Masonic lodge at that time in Alexandria, called Brooke Lodge No. 47, which was convened at the same hour. A committee from No. 22, consisting of Brothers JOSEPH NEALE and THOMAS PETREKIN was appointed to confer with No. 47; and the joint committee of both lodges agreed upon the ceremonies as arranged by the former committee of Lodge No. 22. There were also two other lodges at that time in the Federal District, held under warrants from the grand Lodge of Maryland. These were Potomac Lodge No. 9, at Georgetown, and Federal Lodge No. 15, at Washington. A messenger was appointed by No. 22 to wait on these lodges on Tuesday, "and invite them to join the funeral procession at Mount Vernon on Wednesday at twelve o'clock, if fair, or on Thursday at the same hour." The deacons of the lodge were directed to have the *Orders* cleaned and prepared, and to furnish spermaceti candles for them. The secretary was also directed to have the case in which the charter was kept repaired and gilded for the occasion. It was also arranged that the military companies of Alexandria should join in the procession as an escort and guard of honor. They were at that time under command of Colonel DENEALE, the Senior Warden of WASHINGTON'S lodge. These arrangements having been signified to the family, Mr. LEAR, WASHINGTON'S late private secretary, ordered, as was the custom at that day, provisions and other refreshments to be provided at Mount Vernon for the funeral assembly.

Upon the next day, Wednesday, December 18th, the citizens about Mount Vernon commenced assembling there at eleven o'clock, and the encoffined body of the illustrious dead was placed in the piazza of the grand old mansion, where, while living, he had been accustomed to walk and muse, or converse with visitors. On an ornament at the head of the coffin was inscribed, SURGE AD JUDICITUM, and beneath it GLORIA DEO; and upon a silver plate on the middle of the lid was inscribed,

GENERAL

GEORGE WASHINGTON

DEPARTED THIS LIFE ON THE 14TH DECEMBER,

1799, ÆT. 68.

The sun had passed its meridian height before the Fraternity and military escort arrived from Alexandria. The Masonic apron and two crossed swords were then placed upon the coffin, a few mystic words were spoken, and the brethren one by one filed by the noble form, majestic even in death, and took a last sad look on one they had loved so well. Alas, the light of his eye and the breathing of his lips in language of fraternal greeting were lost to them forever on this side of the grave!

Adown the shaded avenues that led from the mansion to the Potomac might then be seen a vessel at anchor, with its white sails furled, awaiting the procession's forming. The cavalry took its position in the van, and next came the infantry and guard, all with arms reversed. Behind them followed a small band of music with muffled drums; and next the clergy, two and two. They were four in number—viz., the Rev. Dr. MUIR and the Rev. Messrs. DAVIS, MAFFIT, and ADDISON—the first three of whom were Masons and members of Lodge No. 22, at Alexandria. Then followed WASHINGTON'S war-horse, led by two grooms dressed in black. It was riderless that day, but carried saddle, holsters, and pistols. Next was placed the body on its bier, covered with a dark pall. Six Masonic brethren attended it as pall-bearers. They were Colonels GILPIN, MARSTELLER, and LITTLE on the right, and Colonels SIMMS, RAMSEY, and PAYNE on the left, all members of WASHINGTON'S own lodge. Each of them wore on his left arm an ample badge of black crape, which may still be seen, together with the bier on which the body was borne, in the Museum at Alexandria. The relatives of the deceased and a few intimate family friends then followed as principal mourners. Then came the officers and members of his lodge and other Masonic brethren, all too as mourners.

The officers of the corporation of Alexandria then

took their places behind the Masonic Fraternity; citizens followed, preceded by the overseers of the Mount Vernon estate, and its domestics closed the procession.

It was between three and four o'clock before the procession moved. The booming cannon from the vessel on the river was the signal, and then with slow and measured steps that melted their souls in all the tenderness of woe, their way was taken to the family vault at the bottom of the lawn near the bank of the Potomac. The military escort there halted and formed their lines. The body, the clergy, the mourning relatives, and the Masonic brethren then passed between them, and approached the door of the tomb. There the encoffined WASHINGTON rested on his bier before them. Dr. DICK, the Master of the lodge, and the Rev. THOMAS DAVIS, rector of Christ Church, stood at its head, the mourning relatives at its foot, and the Fraternity in a circle around the tomb.

The Rev. Mr. DAVIS broke the silence by repeating from sacred writings, "I am the resurrection and the life; he that believeth in Me, though he were dead, yet shall he live." Then with bowed and reverent heads all listened to the voice of prayer; and as the holy words went on, as used in the beautiful and expressive burial-service of the Episcopal Church, their soothing spirit was echoed in the responses of the multitude around. Mr. DAVIS closed his burial-service with a short address. There was a pause;—and then the Master of the lodge performed the mystic funeral rites of Masonry, as the last service at the burial of WASHINGTON. The apron and the swords were removed from the coffin, for their place was no longer there. It was ready for entombment. The brethren one by one cast upon it an evergreen sprig; and their hearts spoke the Mason's farewell as they bestowed their last mystic gift. There was a breathless silence there

MASONIC FUNERAL CEREMONIES.

during this scene. So still was all around in the gathered multitude of citizens, that they might almost have heard the echoes of the acacia as it fell with trembling lightness upon the coffin-lid. The pall-bearers placed their precious burden in the tomb's cold embrace, earth was cast on the threshold, and the words were spoken: "*Earth to earth—ashes to ashes—dust to dust!*" and the entombment of WASHINGTON was finished. The mystic public burial honors of Masonry were given by each brother with lifted hands, saying in his heart, "Alas! my Brother! *we have knelt with thee in prayer, we have pressed thee to our bosoms, we will meet thee in heaven!*" The mystic chain was reunited in the circle there, the cannon on the vessel and on the banks above them fired their burial salute, and Mount Vernon's tomb was left in possession of its noblest sleeper. The sun was then setting, and the pall of night mantled the pathway of the Masonic brethren as they sadly returned to their homes.

Lodge No. 22, at Alexandria, had then left on its roll of membership sixty-nine Masons, sixty of whom were Master Masons, and nine Entered Apprentices. It met on the following day in regular communication, and elected Colonel GEORGE DENEALE its Master. It had been presided over while under its Pennsylvania Warrant by three Masters—viz.: ROBERT ADAM, ROBERT McCREA, and Dr. DICK. Under its Virginia Warrant it had also had the same number—GEORGE WASHINGTON, JAMES GILLIS, and Dr. DICK.

> "Three there were, but one was not,—
> He lay where Cassia mark'd the spot."

It had been the custom of this lodge from its first organization to meet on the festivals of St. John the Evangelist in December and listen to charity sermons, collect contributions for the indigent, and partake of social refreshments. St. John's day in December, 1799, was duly observed, but all hilarity was dispensed with. It was made a mourning day for the loss of WASHINGTON. Dr. DICK installed Colonel DENEALE as his successor in the chair; but before doing that duty, he addressed the lodge as its retiring Master. Having made the customary demands for charity, he closed by saying in a feeling manner:

"Whilst every recurrence of this festival demands that we distribute a portion of the comforts we possess among those of our more immediate neighbors who are unhappily destitute, it has also, hitherto, invited us to social and convivial enjoyment. After having fulfilled the primary duties of the day, it has been heretofore our custom to indulge in festive gayety; and, indeed, nothing can either so fully sanction such an indulgence, or capacitate the mind for a real and rational enjoyment of it, as the due observance of this preliminary injunction.

"But on the present occasion, my brethren, a cloud of sorrow surrounds our prospects. A recent and heavy calamity has obstructed every avenue to mirth. Our great and good Grand Master is no more! He who hath so often united in our annual celebrations is gone, to return not again. He whose presence was wont to inspire surrounding multitudes with reverence and admiration—he who was but lately the boast of his own country and the wonder of the world, now lies cold and prostrate in his tomb! Thus, my brethren, is lost from the treasury of the Universal Lodge its brightest jewel!

"Feeble is the language of eulogium when applied to a character of such uncommon worth. Statues of marble will prove the love and gratitude of his survivors; but his own virtues and his services have already implanted a monument far more durable than these in the bosoms of his countrymen. May it be particularly nurtured by the Fraternity of Free and Accepted Masons to the end of time. So mote it be."

When this address and the ceremonies of instalment were concluded, the lodge, accompanied by Lodge No. 47, walked in procession to the Presbyterian Church, where a sermon was preached on the occasion by the Rev. Bro. WM. MAFFIT, after which they returned to the lodge-room. On the two succeeding Sabbaths the Masonic brethren of Alexandria met in their lodges, clothed themselves in mourning, and repaired in procession to the Presbyterian Church, where sermons on the occasion of WASHINGTON's death were preached, on the first by the Rev. Bros. THOMAS DAVIS and Dr. MUIR, and on the second by the Rev. Mr. TOLLISON.

The funeral of WASHINGTON at Mount Vernon, and memorial ceremonies at Alexandria, had thus far been conducted by the Masonic Fraternity; but on the 22d of the following February, the citizens there assembled in all their various capacities; Masonic, military, civic, and religious bodies uniting in accordance with a recommendation of Congress, to honor the memory of him whom all had loved, and whose loss all mourned. Lodge No. 22 had, at its meeting on the 20th of this month,

"*Resolved*, That the members belonging to this lodge wear on the 22d instant, and for thirty days thereafter, a white ribbon through two button-holes on the left side of their coats, and that the columns, orders, and deacon's staffs be shrouded with black; * * * * * * * and that the members of this lodge do assemble at our lodge-room precisely at ten o'clock on Saturday, the 22d instant, in order to evince the respect they owe to their late departed brother, General GEORGE WASHINGTON."

Colonel DENEALE, the Master of Lodge No. 22, was selected by the citizens as the officer of the day for the anniversary, and his lodge joined with Brooke Lodge, and united with the military and various other bodies of citizens, and walked through several of the principal streets of Alexandria to the Presbyterian meeting-house, where Dr. DICK, late Master of Lodge No. 22, who had been appointed the orator for the occasion, delivered a feeling and eloquent address. We have already given his eulogium before his brethren in the lodge-room, at their first meeting after the funeral of WASHINGTON, and we here give an extract from his portraiture of him as a man on this public occasion—a day set apart for a united homage of all American citizens to his memory.

"Four millions of the human race—free in their thoughts and affections, unrestrained in their actions, widely dispersed over an extensive portion of the habitable globe—are seen devoted to a single purpose;—a people detached by local causes; actuated in common life by opposite views, or rivals in the pursuit of similar objects; jealous in all other matters of general concern, are offering the tribute of affection to the memory of their common friend. In vain shall we examine the records of antiquity for its parallel. Worth so transcendent as to merit universal homage, with a correspondent desire to bestow it, mark an event in the history of our country that may be considered as a phenomenon in the annals of man.

"Modest and unassuming, yet dignified in his manners; accessible and communicative, yet superior to familiarity; he inspired and preserved the love and respect of all who knew him. For the promotion of all public and useful undertakings, he was singularly munificent. The indigent and distressed were at all times subjects of his sympathy and concern. His charity flowed in quiet, but constant streams from a fountain that was at no time suffered to sustain the smallest diminution. No pursuit or avocation, however momentous, was permitted to interrupt his systematic attention to the children of want. His anxious solicitude on this score is pathetically exemplified in a letter, written in 1775, at a time when the unorganized state of the army might have demanded his exclusive concern. Addressing himself to the late LUND WASHINGTON, he writes: 'Let the hospitality of the house be kept with respect to the poor. Let no one go away hungry. If any of this kind of people should be in want of corn, supply their necessities, provided it does not encourage them in idleness. I have no objection to your giving my money in charity, when you think it will be well bestowed. I mean, that it is my desire that it should be done. You are to consider that neither myself nor my wife are now in the way to do these good offices.'

"Such, my fellow-citizens, was the man whose memory we have assembled to honor. It has been your peculiar felicity often to have seen him on the footing of social intimacy. That the inhabitants of Alexandria held a distinguished place in his affection, you have had repeated testimony. You have seen his sensibility awakened on occasions calculated to call forth a display of his partiality. The last time we met to offer our salutations and express our inviolable attachment to the venerable sage, on his retiring from the chief magistracy of the Union, you may remember that in telling you how peculiarly grateful were your expressions, the visible emotions of his great soul had almost deprived him of the power of utterance.

"But Heaven has reclaimed its treasure, and America has lost its first of patriots and best of men, its shield in war, in peace its brightest ornament; the avenger of its wrongs; the oracle of its wisdom, and the mirror of its perfection. His fair fame, secure in its immortality, shall shine through countless ages with undiminished lustre. It shall be the statesman's polar-star, the hero's destiny, the boast of age, the companion of maturity, and the goal of youth. It shall be the last national office of hoary dotage to teach the infant, that hangs on his trembling knee, to lisp the name of WASHINGTON!"

Masonic records state that prayers were also delivered on this occasion by the Rev. Bros. Dr. Muir, Thomas Davis, and Wm. Maffit, after which the brethren returned to their rooms, and the lodge was closed in harmony at three o'clock.

CHAPTER XI.

Rumor of WASHINGTON's death reaches Congress at Philadelphia.—Becomes certain.—Becomes known in all parts of the country.—General sorrow.—Societies of the Cincinnati and Masonic lodges deeply mourn his death.—Congress decrees a national mourning and funeral ceremonies at Philadelphia.—Masonic Fraternity invited to attend.—Grand Lodge of Pennsylvania convened on the occasion.—Grand Master's address.—Resolutions of the Grand Lodge.—It unites with its subordinates in the procession.—General LEE delivers the oration.—Grand Lodge of Pennsylvania meet on the following day.—Resolutions to wear mourning.—Sorrow lodge held by French Lodge in Philadelphia.—Oration before it by SIMON CHAUDRON.—Oration published and sent to public officers and MRS. WASHINGTON.—Her acknowledgment of it by Mr. LEAR.—First news of WASHINGTON's death in New York.—Action of the Common Council.—The Grand Lodge of New York convened.—Its action and resolutions on the occasion.—Masonic Fraternity of New York join in the public funeral ceremonies.—Bible on which WASHINGTON's first oath as President was taken carried in the procession.—News of WASHINGTON's death reaches Boston.—Celebration of the "Landing of the Pilgrims" then being held.—Sensations produced.—Action of the Grand Lodge of Massachusetts.—Lodges unite with citizens in funeral ceremonies.—Grand Lodge of Massachusetts address a letter of condolence to MRS. WASHINGTON, soliciting a lock of her husband's hair.—Her reply, granting the request.—Masonic celebration at Boston, February 11.—Ceremonies on that occasion.—Ceremonies by St. John's Lodge at Boston.—Masonic funeral ceremonies in New Hampshire.—In Vermont.—In Rhode Island.—In Connecticut.—Masonic Fraternity on all such occasions given a post of honor.—Funeral ceremonies in Fredericksburg, Va., by the lodge in which WASHINGTON had been made a Mason.—Address by Major BENJAMIN DAY, Grand Master of Virginia, on that occasion.—Public ceremonials at Fredericksburg.—Inventory of WASHINGTON's personal estate shows various Masonic articles.—List and price of them as given.—Conclusion.

RUMOR of WASHINGTON's death reached Philadelphia, where Congress was sitting, on Wednesday, December 18th, the day of his funeral. The next day the sad news became painfully certain, and was formally announced by the President to Congress. It soon became known in all parts of the country, and produced more profound emotions of sorrow than had been felt by the American people for the loss of any citizen. The great heart of the nation swelled for a moment with grief, and then beat with rapid throbs of unwonted agony. The National Congress, State legislatures, municipal bodies, religious societies, civic and scientific associations, military organizations, and all classes of citizens felt and manifested a common bereavement.

But while these all combined to express their deep sense of the national affliction, two other associations, with which WASHINGTON had been intimately connected, joined in the common bewailment with deep expressions of fraternal grief. These were the societies of the Cincinnati and the Masonic Lodges of America. With the Cincinnati, WASHINGTON had held from its first organization the highest official membership, and they mourned their chief with processions, eulogies, and sable habiliments suited to the genius of that institution. The Masonic Fraternity, too, had long regarded him as the chief ornament of their society, and wherever funeral ceremonies were held, they joined their fellow-citizens, with their emblems draped in symbolic sorrow, and expressed a mournful remembrance of their loved and departed brother by many ancient and hallowed forms peculiar to their fraternity.

The genius of America lent its aid to express a nation's woe. The artisan gave his cunning skill, the artist all the rich hues of his pencil, the poet all the inspiration of his pen, the orator all his melting pathos, and fancy wove its fairest garlands to express in every varied form one common sorrow; and eulogies and dirges, catafalcos and urns, gave expression to the grief of America at her first great national bereavement.

Congress designated the 26th of December as the day on which a national tribute should be paid by that body to the memory of WASHINGTON, and all other public bodies in and about Philadelphia were invited to join on the occasion. The Masonic Fraternity were assigned a distinguished place in the procession on that day, it being among the chief mourners. Major-General HENRY LEE, who was the orator of the day, was himself a Mason and member of Hiram Lodge No. 59, at Westmoreland Court House, Virginia.

The invitation by Congress to the Masonic Fraternity to join in the funeral solemnities having been received by the Grand Master of Pennsylvania, he issued his orders on the 24th, convening his Grand Lodge at ten o'clock on the day appointed. That body accordingly met in extra Grand Communication on that day, and were thus addressed by their Grand Master JONATHAN BAYARD SMITH:

"Right Worshipful Deputy Grand Master, Senior and Junior Grand Wardens, and Brethren. You have been called to hold this special convention in consequence of an invitation to join the representatives of a great and grateful people in a solemn act of duty. With respect to the unexpectedly early moment of executing this duty, we have been anticipated; but by the death of General GEORGE WASHINGTON, we have felt ourselves impelled, irresistibly impelled, to yield to the strongest emotion of the heart, and cordially to join our fellow-citizens in public evidences of estimation and regret.

"The interesting event having been officially communicated to the public, I immediately directed that the sable emblements of our order should be borne in Grand Lodge by the members at our next communication, then to take place in a few days, wishing to give to ulterior orders on the occasion the force and the dignity of the spontaneous voice of the collected craft of Pennsylvania.

"While we respectfully leave to abler hands, to the appointed organ of the councils of the United States, to the common voice of his country and of mankind, and to succeeding ages, which will venerate his name as long as they shall experience the happy effects of his civic virtues and public services, duly to appreciate his worth, the Masons of Pennsylvania, impressed with their more immediate Masonic connections and character, may be allowed to deplore that their friend, their brother, their father is gone. Yes, my brethren, as such the Masons of Pennsylvania did long ago recognize him. It is now twenty-one years since they, by an unanimous suffrage, proposed him as Grand Master of Masons for the United States. They have on sundry occasions, and very lately, given attestations of unabated attachment to his person, and a high sense of his unremitting endeavors in promoting order, union, and brotherly affection among us, and in carrying forth the principles of the lodge into every walk of life. In our archives are found flattering evidences of his reciprocated esteem and approbation of our order, as relative more especially to those two chiefest concerns of man, religion and government. The public have seen him gracing and dignifying our processions by his attendance. We have been made the almoners and dispensers of his charitable beneficence. But, my brethren, this pleasing intercourse is suspended. Since our last communication, this our brother has been removed from a terrene to expand his ample mind in the boundless duties and enjoyments of a celestial lodge of that eternal temple (to use his own expression to our Grand Lodge), whose builder is the Great Architect of the Universe. The Old as well as the New World reveres his name. He was indeed an illustrious brother, citizen, and chief,—in peace and in war, in council and in action, pre-eminent. The Masons of Pennsylvania have exulted that the name of WASHINGTON stood enrolled on their list of brethren; and they will cherish the remembrance of his virtues and his services as a rich legacy for their emulous example. If devotion of time and talents to ameliorate the state of man be a virtue; if obeying the calls of his country in times of the greatest difficulty and danger, at every risk, be a Masonic duty; of that virtue may Masonry boast that this our WASHINGTON has exhibited an instance beyond former example brilliant, and for the exercise of this duty will our WASHINGTON ever stand conspicuous in the foremost rank. Is a love of order and sacred regard to the laws of the social compact characteristic of Masons? For his exemplary adherence to these Masonic virtues, through all the vicissitudes and variegated difficulties of a Revolutionary War, has our WASHINGTON received the plaudits of thirteen sovereign States.

"It now remains, my brethren, that in our several spheres we do likewise as our brother has done; that by showing respect to merit, it appear that we value it; that by cordial regret on the translation of virtue from among us, we evidence that we revere it; and while we drop our portion amid the universal effusion of sorrow on this mournful occasion, we anticipate for our lamented brother the applause of nations and the veneration of ages.

"I detain you no longer. The government of our country has this day honorably distinguished us as among the chief mourners of WASHINGTON,—its friend, its protector, and its ornament. The destined hour has come, and we move to the summons."

It was then

"*Resolved,* That this Grand Lodge are deeply and sincerely afflicted with the melancholy event which has occasioned this communication, and will immediately proceed to join in the honors about to be shown to the memory of our illustrious deceased brother."

The Grand Master then appointed Colonel THOMAS PROCTOR master of ceremonies for the day. The brethren then formed in due order in the Grand Lodge-room, and moving from thence joined the general procession, which proceeded to Zion Church, where religious services were performed by the Rev. Dr. WHITE, and the oration was delivered by General LEE; after which they returned to the Grand Lodge-room, and their labors for the day were closed.

Upon the following day the Grand Lodge again met, the Grand Master recalled their attention to the mournful occasion of the preceding day, and it was unanimously

"*Resolved,* That the room committee be directed to put the Grand Lodge-room in mourning, in such a manner as they shall conceive to be most suitable and proper to testify our fraternal attachment to our late Brother WASHINGTON, and the high veneration we entertain for his memory and virtues.

"*Resolved,* That as a further mark of our warm regard

for the memory of our deceased brother, and deep affliction for the loss we have sustained by his death, the members of the Grand Lodge wear black crape on their left arm, as recommended by the President and Congress to the citizens of the United States; and that the emblems on their aprons be covered with black for the term of six months, being until St. John's day next; and that the same be recommended to all the lodges under the jurisdiction of this Grand Lodge."

There existed in Philadelphia at that time, under a warrant from the Grand Lodge of Pennsylvania, a French Lodge of Ancient York Masons, known as "*L'Aménité*, No. 71." On the following week (January 1, 1800), a *sorrow lodge* was held by these brethren, which was attended by the officers of the Grand Lodge and a great number of the Fraternity in that city. After the conclusion of ceremonies peculiar to such a lodge, an oration was delivered by its orator, SIMON CHAUDRON, in the French language, which was followed by an address in English by the Master, JOSEPH DE LA GRANGE. This oration was published in both the French and English languages, and copies were sent to the President and Vice-president of the United States, to the governor of Pennsylvania, and to Mrs. WASHINGTON at Mount Vernon. They all acknowledged their receipt by letter; and Mrs. WASHINGTON'S, by the hand of the private secretary of her late husband, was as follows:

"MOUNT VERNON, May 15, 1800.

"SIR—In compliance with Mrs. WASHINGTON'S request, I have the honor to acknowledge the receipt of your letter to her of the 15th of March, with three copies of the funeral oration which the French Lodge, L'Aménité, in Philadelphia, have consecrated to the memory of her husband.

"Impressed with a lively sense of this testimonial of respect and veneration paid to the memory of the partner of her heart, Mrs. WASHINGTON begs the lodge will be assured of her grateful acknowledgments; and you will be pleased to accept her best thanks for the obliging manner in which you have communicated their sympathy in her affliction and irreparable loss.

"I am, sir,
"Very respectfully,
"Your obedient servant,
"TOBIAS LEAR,
"Secretary to the late General WASHINGTON."

The news of WASHINGTON's death reached New York on Friday, December 20th. The Common Council on that day publicly announced it to the citizens, and signified to the different religious societies of the city their wish that their churches be draped in mourning, and their bells muffled and tolled every day from twelve till one o'clock until the 24th inclusive.

Upon Monday, the 23d, the Grand Lodge of New York was convened in an extra Grand Communication. General JACOB MORTON, the Deputy Grand Master, presided on the occasion, and

"Announced that the reason for convening this extra meeting of the Grand Lodge was, the mournful intelligence of the death of their illustrious and much beloved Brother GEORGE WASHINGTON, late President of the United States, and commander-in-chief of the army; and urged with energy and respectful expressions the duties which belong to every Mason on such a painful event, and the necessity of this Grand Lodge to take such steps as are proper and Masonic, to pay the tribute of respect due to a brother, who, being called to the Celestial Lodge above, lives in the heart of the virtuous and the wise.

"Whereupon the following was decreed: 'The Grand Lodge, with the deepest and sincerest sorrow, announces to the Lodges under its jurisdiction the death of their illustrious and much beloved Brother GEORGE WASHINGTON, late President of the United States, and commander-in-chief of its army. He closed his useful and honorable life at his seat at Mount Vernon on the night of the 14th instant, in the 68th year of his age.

"'When, in the dispensations of Providence, the great and the good, when those whom we love and revere sink into the silent tomb, the afflicted heart seeks its solace in rendering to their memories every honorable tribute which affectionate gratitude can devise. This is a feeling engrafted in our natures, as an incentive to honorable ambition; and the expression of those feelings is a duty which the customs of civil society have enjoined; but in decreeing a tribute of respect to our deceased brother on this occasion, there is naught we can devise which will fully evince our veneration of his virtues or our sorrow for his loss.

"'To decree honor to that illustrious name upon which glory hath already exhausted all her store; to render a tribute of affection to his memory who lived in the hearts of a grateful people, are duties which we feel we can never satisfactorily perform. That humble tribute which we are enabled to pay, we decree.

"'*Resolved*, Therefore, that all the lodges under our jurisdiction be clothed in mourning for the space of six months, and that the brethren also wear mourning for the same space of time.

"'*Resolved*, That a committee be appointed to erect at the expense of this Grand Lodge a monumental memorial to the virtues of our illustrious brother, to be placed in the room occupied by the Grand Lodge for its sittings; and that the Right Worshipful JACOB MORTON, Deputy Grand Master; the Right Worshipful MARTIN HOFFMAN, Senior Grand Warden; the Right Worshipful ABRAHAM SKINNER, Junior Grand Warden; the Right Worshipful REVIER JOHN VANDEN BROECK, Grand Secretary; and the Worshipful Brethren CADWALADER D. COLDEN and PETER IRVIN be a committee for that purpose.

"'*Resolved*, That the said committee have authority to meet and concur with such other committees of our fellow-citizens, as shall be appointed to devise some public testimonials of respect and veneration to the memory of our departed brother.

"'*Resolved*, That the Grand Secretary be directed to write circular letters to the different Grand Lodges in the United States, condoling with them on the loss which we have sustained in the death of our beloved brother, who was the chief ornament of his country, and the pride of our institution.

"'*Resolved*, That the Grand Secretary be directed to forward immediately a copy of these resolutions to the several lodges in this city.'"

In accordance with these resolutions, the Masonic Fraternity joined in the public proceedings held in the city of New York on the 31st of December, to express sorrow at the death of WASHINGTON. The place assigned them was among the chief mourners. The

Bible on which WASHINGTON had taken his first oath of office as President of the United States was borne before the Grand Master, and all the decorations they carried in the procession were mournfully impressive. They marched to St. Paul's Church, where an oration was delivered by GOUVERNEUR MORRIS, accompanied by appropriate music.

The tidings of WASHINGTON'S death reached Boston on the 23d of December, during a celebration held that day to commemorate the landing of the Pilgrims in 1620. In the morning a rumor came that WASHINGTON was dead! Before noon its truth was confirmed. Common festivals upon such intelligence would have been omitted. But the impressions arising from the celebration were thought not inconsistent with a due sensibility to the sad event which was announced. The usual expressions of gayety had no place, and the guests assembled together rather for condolence than festivity.

On the 28th of this month the following circular was issued by the Grand Master of Massachusetts to the Fraternity in that State:

"GRAND LODGE OF MASSACHUSETTS,
BOSTON, December 28, A. D. 1799.

[L. S.] "To testify their veneration of the exalted character and pre-eminent virtues, and their respect for the memory of their highly distinguished Brother GEORGE WASHINGTON, it is recommended to the brethren of the Fraternity of Free and Accepted Masons in the Commonwealth of Massachusetts to wear, for the term of six weeks, commencing on the 1st day of January, 1800, a black crape on the left arm below the elbow, interwoven with a narrow ribbon running direct.

"By order of the Most Worshipful,

"SAMUEL DUNN, Esq.,

"DANIEL OLIVER, *Grand Secretary.*"

Some of the lodges in and about Boston solemnized the event of WASHINGTON'S death, either in their private meetings or by uniting with citizens in public ceremonies soon after this order was given; but the Grand Lodge of that jurisdiction took no steps towards a public testimonial of their respect for his memory until the 15th of the following month (January, 1800), when they resolved to pay funeral honors to his memory on the 22d of February. But finding that the authorities of the General and State governments had also designated that day for public ceremonies in honor of WASHINGTON, it was subsequently thought by the Grand Lodge, that distinct Masonic ceremonies were more appropriate for the Fraternity, and they changed the time of their own funeral ceremonies from the 22d to the 11th of February.

The Grand Lodge of Massachusetts had, however, previous to this, written a letter of condolence to Mrs. WASHINGTON, and solicited a lock of her deceased husband's hair. This she complied with, as the following correspondence shows:

"BOSTON, January 11, 1800.

"MADAM—The Grand Lodge of the Commonwealth of Massachusetts have deeply participated in the general grief of their fellow-citizens, on the melancholy occasion of the death of their beloved WASHINGTON.

"As Americans, they have lamented the loss of the chief who led their armies to victory, and their country to glory; but as *Masons* they have wept the dissolution of that endearing relation by which they were enabled to call him their friend and their brother. They presume not to offer you those consolations which might alleviate the weight of common sorrows, for they are themselves inconsolable. The object of this address is not to interrupt the sacred offices of grief like yours; but whilst they are mingling tears with each other on the common calamity, to condole with you on the irreparable misfortune which you have individually experienced.

"To their expressions of sympathy on this solemn dispensation, the Grand Lodge have subjoined an order, that a *Golden Urn* be prepared as a deposit for a lock of hair, an *invaluable relique* of the Hero and the Patriot whom their wishes would immortalize; and that it be preserved with the jewels and regalia of the society.

"Should this favor be granted, madam, it will be cherished as the most precious jewel in the cabinet of the lodge, as the memory of his virtues will forever be in the hearts of its members. We have the honor to be, with the highest respect, your most obedient servants,

"JOHN WARREN,
"PAUL REVERE,
"JOSIAH BARTLETT.

"MRS. MARTHA WASHINGTON."

To this request Mrs. WASHINGTON replied through Mr. LEAR, inclosing a lock of WASHINGTON'S hair, which was duly received.

"MOUNT VERNON, January 27, 1800.

"GENTLEMEN—Mrs. WASHINGTON has received, with sensibility, your letter of the 11th instant, inclosing a vote of the Grand Lodge of Massachusetts, requesting a lock of her deceased husband's *hair*, to be preserved in a *Golden Urn*, with the jewels and regalia of the Grand Lodge.

"In complying with this request by sending the lock of hair which you will find inclosed, Mrs. WASHINGTON begs me to assure you that she views with gratitude the tributes of respect and affection paid to the memory of her dear deceased husband; and receives with a feeling heart the expressions of sympathy contained in your letter.

"With great respect and esteem, I have the honor to be, gentlemen, your most obedient servant,

"TOBIAS LEAR.

"JOHN WARREN,
"PAUL REVERE,
"JOSIAH BARTLETT, } Past Grand Masters."

Agreeably to previous notice, upon the 11th of February, the Grand Lodge performed Masonic funeral ceremonies in honor of their illustrious brother. At eight o'clock in the morning the bells commenced tolling, and at eleven a grand procession, composed of upwards of sixteen hundred brethren, was formed at the Old State House, and moved in Masonic order. Each brother bore a sprig of acacia, and the Golden Urn that contained the lock of WASHINGTON's hair was borne by six distinguished brethren. Many appropriate devices and emblems decorated the procession, and it was probably the most imposing one the Fraternity had ever formed in America. It passed through several of the principal streets of Boston to the Old South Meeting House, where public solemnities were performed, with prayers, odes, dirges, and a eulogy by Dr. TIMOTHY BIGELOW. From the Old South Church the procession then moved to the Stone Chapel, where a funeral service was performed by the Rev. Brother BENTLEY, Grand Chaplain, assisted by the Rev. Brother Dr. WALTER. Flowers were then strewn, the acacia deposited, and the brethren returned to the Old State House, where the procession had formed, and there separated. The Golden Urn, with its precious treasure was deposited in the archives of the Grand Lodge, where it has since remained.

St. John's Lodge, at Boston, the oldest Masonic daughter of England on this continent, held in its hall, one week previous to the above Grand Lodge proceedings, private funeral solemnities, at which a eulogy was delivered by Bro. GEORGE BLAKE. At a meeting of that lodge, held on the 26th of March, it was voted that a copy of that eulogy, handsomely bound, together with a *Golden Medal*, be transmitted to the Grand Lodge of England, accompanied with an address; and a committee was appointed to form the address and transmit these memorials to their mother Grand Lodge; but we have failed to find the evidence that it was carried into effect.

In New Hampshire, Masonic funeral honors to WASHINGTON were shown by most of the lodges in that State, by joining with the citizens at large, in testifying grief for his loss and respect for his memory. The New Hampshire Gazette of January 8, 1800, contains the following paragraph:

"The Grand Lodge of New Hampshire are unanimous in opinion, that to mourn with our fellow-citizens at large, would be more respectable to our late illustrious brother, and more honorable, than particular society lodges of mourning. The loss is deep and universal; so ought to be our testimonials of respect decent and uniform throughout the United States. But in our lodges will be the seat of sorrow."

NATHANIEL ADAMS was at that time the Grand Master of Masons in New Hampshire, and in his "Annals of Portsmouth" he says:

"1799.—Tuesday, the 31st day of December, was set apart to commemorate the death of the illustrious WASHINGTON, who departed this life on the 14th of this month. At an early hour all public offices, stores, and shops were closed. Business and pleasure were suspended. At eleven o'clock a procession moved from the Assembly-room to St. John's Church, in the following order:

"The companies of Artillery, Light Infantry, and Governor Gilman's Blues, with muffled drums, music in crape, arms reversed, side-arms with black bows; martial music playing the Dead March in Saul; the Grand Lodge of New Hampshire, accompanied by St. John's Lodge, and many visiting brethren in the habiliments of their order; the orator and rector of St. John's Church; United States military officers; commissioned officers of the militia; selectmen; clergy; citizens and strangers two and two.

"When the procession reached the church, a solemn piece of music was performed on the organ. Rev. Mr. WILLARD read the service of the church, and JONATHAN MEWELL, Esq., pronounced an eulogy on the sorrowful occasion. A vast concourse of people attended, and almost every individual of respectability wore a crape as a badge of mourning, and all the shipping in the harbor hoisted their flags half-mast high."

Although the ceremonies on this occasion were not designed as Masonic, yet the ode which was sung was strictly so. It was composed by the Rev. Brother GEORGE RICHARDS; and so highly did the brethren of St. John's Lodge appreciate it, that, at their next meeting, they voted that it be sung each lodge-night for the three following months, and that all other songs be excluded during that time.

The news of the death of WASHINGTON reached Bennington, Vermont, on the 25th of December. The court of the county was there in session, and upon the sad event being therein announced, it was adjourned for the day, and in the evening a large meeting was held, at which ISAAC TICHNEOR, the governor of the State, presided; and it was determined that a public demonstration of sorrow should be made by a procession and suitable discourses on Friday the 27th.

At two o'clock on that day, a large number of citizens convened at the courthouse, and a procession was formed, in which the Masonic Fraternity occupied a conspicuous place. With muffled drums and music playing a solemn dirge, the procession moved to the church, where the Rev. Mr. SWIFT delivered a discourse to the general audience, after which, ANTHONY HASWELL delivered an oration in behalf of the Masonic brethren. The ceremonies at the church were closed by an ode prepared by Brother HASWELL for the occasion. The procession then returned to the courthouse, where the Fraternity partook of a repast prepared for them. By recommendation of the Grand Master of Vermont, the brethren there wore a badge of mourning for WASHINGTON six months.

In Rhode Island, also, the principal demonstrations of sorrow for the death of WASHINGTON, were in conjunction with the public ceremonies of all classes of citizens in that State. As soon as his death became known, the Grand Master of Masons in that jurisdiction issued the following order:

"By order of the Most Worshipful PELEG CLARK, Grand Master of the State of Rhode Island.

"All brethren under the jurisdiction of this Grand Lodge, are required to wear a black scarf on the left arm for nine days, as a token of regard for the loss of our late illustrious Brother GEORGE WASHINGTON.

"By order,

"JOHN HANDY, G. Secretary.

"NEWPORT, December 28, 1799."

The records of the subordinate lodges, both in Rhode Island and Connecticut, show that a general mourning was adopted on the sad event;.and that in all the numerous public processions and ceremonies, the Fraternity were assigned a post of dignity, in consideration of the well-known connection WASHINGTON had with their Society. It is impossible in this sketch to give even a synopsis of the rich treasures such records in the various States contain, relating to funeral ceremonies on that occasion. They are worthy of a volume. From our portfolio of these rich memorials of merited regard, we will select but one other. It is the mourning of the brethren at Fredericksburg, where WASHINGTON had been made a Mason nearly fifty years before. Youthful craftsmen had in those long years taken the places of most of the ancient brethren of that lodge; but there were some who still remembered, how, when youth and manhood were mingling their lines upon his brow, he sought their altar and bound himself to them in vows of brotherhood. These unbroken vows had been kept in their memory. There was now sadness in their hearts when they were summoned by their Master to meet and commemorate his loss. It was the second Sabbath after his death, and amidst the tolling of bells, which had commenced at sunrise, they met in their lodge-room at ten o'clock. The Grand Master of Virginia, Major BENJAMIN DAY, was with them, and having taken the chair in the East, he thus addressed the lodge:

"We are now, brethren, to pay the last tribute of affection and respect to the eminent virtues and exemplary conduct that adorned the character of our worthy deceased Brother, GEORGE WASHINGTON. He was early initiated in this venerable lodge, as I am respectably informed, in the mysteries of our ancient and honorable profession; and having held it in the highest and most just veneration, the fraternal attention we now show to his memory is the more incumbent on us. He is gone forever from our view; but gone to the realms of celestial bliss, where the shafts of malice and detraction cannot penetrate, where all sublunary distinctions cease, and merit is rewarded by the scale of unerring justice. While the tear of sympathy is excited for a loss so generally and deservedly lamented, let us recollect that posterity will not less justly appreciate the talents and virtues he possessed. As a man, he was frail; and it would be a compliment to which human nature cannot aspire to suppose him free from peculiarities, or exempt from error. But let those that best know him determine the measure to which they extend. In the offices of private life, he was most endeared to those who were most in his familiarity and intimacy. In the various important appointments of public confidence, let not the sin of ingratitude sully the historic page, by denying him the incense of public applause. Abler panegyrists will attend at the sacred altar, and do that justice to his memory to which his merits entitle him; while attendant angels await his immortal spirit in the mansions of eternal peace.

"Suffer me, brethren, on this solemn occasion, to remind you of the instability of all human concerns, and the uncertainty of our continuance in this transitory state of our existence. Let the example of our worthy deceased brother, and the amiable precepts of our institution, guide us in our conduct to each other; and the *sacred volume*, always open for our instruction in our duty to the inconceivably great, omnipotent, and merciful Architect of the Universe! That when it shall please Him to relieve us from the cares and solicitude of this probationary state, we may not be dismayed, but with a well-grounded hope, familiarized to the expectation of a change, the awful, yet the inevitable lot of mortality, and the entrance into a lodge of perfect harmony and eternal happines."

The lodge then formed a procession, and moved from their hall, preceded by music playing a solemn dirge, to the public parade-ground, where they were received by the military with reversed arms, who escorted them to the church, where a discourse was delivered by the Rev. Mr. STEPHENSON, from the words: "*And the Lord spake unto Joshua, the son of Nun, Moses' minister, saying, Moses my servant is dead.*" The solemnities of the day were concluded by the military firing sixteen minute-guns as the brethren returned to their lodge-room.

The official inventory of WASHINGTON'S estate after his death was duly entered in the records of Fairfax County, and from it we are able to show that he treasured in his cabinet and in his library, to the close of his life, the Masonic souvenirs he had at various times received from his brethren, thus verifying also our records and traditions of his reception of them. The statements which we have given in the foregoing sketch, embrace his reception of Masonic regalia from Messrs. WATSON & CASSOUL; a box containing a Masonic apron and sash from LA FAYETTE; the Pennsylvania *Ahiman Rezon* from the Grand Lodge of Pennsylvania; the Book of Constitutions of the Grand Lodge of Massachusetts, from that Grand Lodge; "Proofs of a Conspiracy," from the Rev. Mr. SNYDER; and an *Ahiman Rezon*, or Book of Constitutions, from the Grand Lodge of Maryland. All of the above books we find inventoried by the appraisers of his personal estate, as follows: The Pennsylvania Ahiman Rezon, one dollar; the Massachusetts Grand Lodge Constitution, one dollar; "Proofs of a Conspiracy," one dollar and fifty cents; Maryland Ahiman Rezon, one dollar and fifty cents. We also find in the same inventory, a volume of Masonic Sermons, fifty cents. The same list also contains a "Japan box containing a Mason's apron," inventoried at fifty dollars; and a "Piece of oil-cloth containing Orders of Masonry," fifty dollars. The first of these was probably the box and apron sent by LA FAYETTE,—the term *Japan* referring to the fine exterior polish of the box. The last was doubtless what is called the *Mason's carpet* or *floor-cloth*. We have never met with any other mention of this last Masonic relic of WASHINGTON'S, except in this official inventory, and are at loss to know when it came into his possession, and what finally became of it. So interesting and valuable a relic of WASHINGTON should not be lost; and we here request that if its history or existence be known, it be communicated to the Fraternity of which our illustrious brother was the pride and ornament.

Reader, we have sketched for you WASHINGTON as a MASON. Learn from it, that—

"Ere mature manhood marked his youthful brow,
He sought our altar and he made his vow—
Upon our tesselated floor he trod,
Bended his knees, and placed his trust in GOD!
Through all his great and glorious life he stood
A true, warm brother, foremost e'er in good;
And when he died, amid a nation's gloom,
His mourning brethren bore him to the tomb!'

PART II.

WASHINGTON'S MASONIC COMPEERS.

MAJOR HENRY PRICE.

FIRST GRAND MASTER IN NEW ENGLAND.

THE introduction of Freemasonry into America has neither written nor traditionary date. From a period extending so far back into the gray ages of antiquity that it antedates the twilight of written history, its mystic rites are said to have been practised in the eastern world; and when the first explorers of the western continent formed their infant settlements here, they may have brought with them some knowledge of its mysteries.

For more than a century after the English commenced their settlements in America, Masonic lodges were held in all countries without any written warrants, but by the inherent right of Masons, sanctioned by immemorial usage. Such lodges kept no written records of their proceedings, and American history is silent on the subject of Freemasonry until about the commencement of the third decade of the last century. At that time the Masonic chronicles of England state, that a deputation was granted to DANIEL COXE, constituting him Provincial Grand Master of New Jersey. A copy of this deputation, recently obtained by the Grand Lodge of New Jersey from the Grand Lodge at London, shows, that it constituted DANIEL COXE, Provincial Grand Master of the provinces of New York, New Jersey, and Pennsylvania. This deputation was granted by the Duke of Norfolk, Grand Master of Masons in England, and bore date the 5th day of June, 1730. From the same source we also learn, that DANIEL COXE was present at the meeting of the Grand Lodge in London on the 29th of the following January, where his health was proposed and drank as "Provincial Grand Master of *North America.*" Of his personal history, we only know that he was the son of Dr. DANIEL COXE, of England, who was physician to the queen of Charles the Second, and to Queen ANNE, and who held extensive proprietary claims to lands in New

Jersey and other American colonies; and that he was his father's agent and representative in this country. His residence is believed to have been in Burlington, New Jersey. He was for many years a member of the council of that province under Lord CORNBURY, and the speaker of the House of Assembly during a part of the administration of Governor HUNTER. He was also, it is historically stated, for a time, deputy governor of Western New Jersey. He represented his father's claims to an extensive tract of country lying on the Gulf of Mexico, which he made some attempts to colonize. In furtherance of this object, he wrote a dissertation on this territory, entitled, "A Description of the English Province of *Carolana*, by the Spaniards called *Florida*, and by the French, *La Louisaine*." This, we believe, was first published in England in 1741, although some authorities state it was published in 1722. Two existing proprietary claims to this territory were possessed by his father, the first of Spanish, and the second of English origin. It was Mr. COXE's desire to hold and settle it as an English province; and he accordingly, in the preface to his pamphlet, proposed a colonial alliance of all the English settlements as a defence against the Indians, and also the French and Spanish colonies in the vicinity. The terms of this proposition for an English colonial union in America, we believe, antedate any such ideas by others; and we cannot forbear to insert them here as curious in the civil history of our country, being published prior to the Union recommended by Dr. FRANKLIN at the Colonial Congress in Albany in 1754. Mr. COXE's proposition was—

"That all the colonies appertaining to the crown of Great Britain, on the northern continent of America, be united under a legal, regular, and firm establishment; over which a lieutenant or supreme governor may be constituted and appointed to preside on the spot, to whom the governors of each colony shall be subordinate." "It is further humbly proposed," he continued, "that two deputies shall be annually elected by the Council and Assembly of each province, who are to be in the nature of a great council, or general convention of the estates of the colonies; and by the order, consent, or approbation of the lieutenant or governor-general, shall meet together, consult and advise for the good of the whole, settle and appoint particular quotas or proportions of money, men, provisions, etc., that each respective government is to raise for their mutual defence and safety, as well as, if necessary, for offence and invasion of their enemies; in all which cases the governor-general or lieutenant is to have a negative, but not to enact any thing without their concurrence, or that of a majority of them."

May not this proposition of our Masonic brother and first American Grand Master, have been the germ of thought from which sprung our present form of civil government? Mr. COXE, we believe, died at Burlington, New Jersey, and was there buried; for there is said to exist in the east transept of the old Episcopal Church there, a marble slab bearing this inscription:

"DANIEL COXE,

DIED, APRIL 25, 1739.

ÆTAT 65."

To this digression from the Masonic design of our

sketch, we will only add, that so little has been left on record of the Masonic history of DANIEL COXE, that even his Grand Mastership has been deemed a myth. His name stands in the annals of American Masonry, like the morning-star at dawn rising above the mountain's misty top, and then fading from our vision in the sunlight of the bright skies that followed.

In 1733, three years later, the written records of Freemasonry in America commence. Upon the 30th of April of that year, a deputation was granted by Lord MONTACUTE, Grand Master of the Grand Lodge of England, to HENRY PRICE, the subject of this sketch, "in behalf of himself and *several other brethren*" then residing in New England, appointing him "Provincial Grand Master of New England aforesaid, and dominions and territories thereunto belonging." From the powers contained in this *deputation* sprang the first existing lodges in this country, and HENRY PRICE is regarded as the father of American lodges of Freemasons.

The deputations or commissions to DANIEL COXE in 1730, and HENRY PRICE in 1733, were in form and verbiage nearly the same; but they differed somewhat in powers conferred. That to Mr. COXE confined his powers to the provinces of New York, New Jersey, and Pennsylvania; while that to Mr. PRICE, gave him Masonic authority in New England, and "dominions and territories thereunto belonging." That to Mr. COXE also continued his powers for two years from the following feast of St. John the Baptist; "after which time," it continues, "it is our will and pleasure, and we do hereby ordain, that the brethren who do now reside, or who may hereafter reside, in all or any of the said provinces, shall, and they are hereby empowered every other year, on the feast of St. John the Baptist, to elect a Provincial Grand Master, who shall have the power of nominating and appointing his Deputy Grand Master and Grand Wardens." That of Mr. PRICE was unlimited in time, and revokable at the pleasure of the authority that issued it. We have no Masonic lodge records in this country previous to 1733; but it is a curious fact, that newspapers printed in Philadelphia as early as 1732, state the existence of a Masonic lodge in that city at that date, and that WILLIAM ALLEN, then recorder of the city (and afterwards chief-justice of the province), was, on St. John the Baptist's day of 1732, elected *Grand Master in Philadelphia.* Were the brethren in that city at that time holding lodges under authority from DANIEL COXE, or by the old immemorial right and usage of Masons? It is an interesting point in our Masonic history, but one which we are not called upon to consider further in this sketch. Our task is to give a brief memoir of the Masonic history of HENRY PRICE, and even this would embrace more of the history of the early progress of Masonry in this country than our limits admit.

History has recorded but little of his life, except what is found on its Masonic pages. He was a native of England, and was born in London about the year 1697. He came to America about 1723, and settled in Boston, where he commenced business as a merchant tailor. He was then about twenty-six years of age, and had doubtless been made a Mason in London, in one of the four old lodges of that city. It was about ten years, therefore, from the time he came to America, before he received the deputation granted him by Lord MONTACUTE to assemble the brethren of the Masonic Fraternity and constitute lodges in New England.

At that time, nearly three months were required to transmit documents from London to Boston, and the promptness with which he entered on his new duties is seen from the record, that on the 30th of July, 1733, just three months from the date of his commission, he assembled the brethren then residing in Boston, at the "Bunch of Grapes Tavern," and causing his deputation to be read, he appointed ANDREW BELCHER his Deputy Grand Master, and THOMAS KENNELLY and JOHN QUANN his Grand Wardens. We have few written records from which to give the social position of the members of this Grand Lodge. Mr. PRICE, its Grand Master, was the same year appointed "cornet in the governor's troop of guards, with the rank of major." He was also at one time paymaster in Queen ANNE's regiment. JONATHAN BELCHER was the governor of Massachusetts, and ANDREW BELCHER, the Deputy Grand Master, was his son.

The same day that Mr. PRICE organized his Grand Lodge, he received a petition from eighteen Masons in Boston, in behalf of themselves and "*other brethren,*" asking to be established as a regular lodge. They had probably often convened and worked as Masons in that city before, without any authority except the ancient immemorial right which the Craft had formerly exercised, of meeting when and where circumstances permitted or required, and choosing the most experienced one present as Master, form for the occasion a lodge. In such assemblages of the Craft, temporarily convened, with little ritualistic labor, but with simple forms, it is probable most of the old Masons in America had been admitted to the knowledge of our mystic rites. But having now an opportunity to conform to the newly established custom in England of working under the sanction of a Grand Lodge, composed of a Grand Master and other officers, and representatives of all the brethren in the jurisdiction, they seem at once to have availed themselves of the privilege. Their petition was accordingly granted, and they were formed and constituted by Mr. PRICE a regular lodge the same evening, their officers being installed by him in person. This lodge was denominated "*First Lodge*" in Boston until 1783, when it took the name of St. John's Lodge, by which it has since been known. As it was constituted by Grand Master PRICE in person, it was not at that day thought necessary that it should have a *written warrant*, his own act of personally constituting it, being at that time a sufficient authority for perpetuating itself as a legal lodge.

Early in the following year, Major PRICE granted warrants to brethren in Philadelphia and in Portsmouth, New Hampshire, to hold lodges in those places, and for this purpose *written* instruments of authority were first used by him in America. He also received an extension of his authority in 1734 from the Grand Master of England, giving him jurisdiction over all North America. Under it he granted a warrant, on the 27th of December, 1735, for a lodge at Charleston,

South Carolina. It is probable that some, if not all these warrants, were to confirm and bring under regular Masonic government, bodies of Masons that had previously met and worked as lodges in their several localities.

Major PRICE was superseded as Provincial Grand Master, in 1737, by a like commission granted by the Grand Master of England to ROBERT TOMLINSON. Mr. TOMLINSON held the office for seven years, and was succeeded by THOMAS OXNARD, who held it about ten years, and died with his commission unrevoked. Upon the death of Mr. OXNARD, Major PRICE, as the oldest Provincial Past Grand Master in America, was called to the vacant Grand East until a new appointment could be made by the Grand Master of England. He therefore held the office at this time, by virtue of his priority in that position, from the 26th of June, 1754, until October 1, 1755, when JEREMY GRIDLEY was duly commissioned and installed. Mr. GRIDLEY continued as Provincial Grand Master until his death in September, 1767, when Major PRICE again resumed the office until the 25th of November, 1768, when JOHN ROWE was regularly appointed to it by the Grand Master of England.

Such is a brief sketch of the connection Major PRICE had with American Masonry as Provincial Grand Master. But his Masonic labors were not confined to his duties in his Grand Lodge. By an early regulation of the mother Grand Lodge in England, Apprentices could be made Fellow-crafts and Master Masons only in the Grand Lodge, unless by special dispensation from the Grand Master. This rule was soon afterwards relaxed, and "Master's Lodges" were instituted to confer the second and third degrees on candidates who had received the first in regular lodges of the Craft.

About the year 1738 a "Master's Lodge" was instituted in Boston, which met monthly. Major PRICE was its first Master, and he occupied this position and performed its labors until 1744, when he resigned the office. During this period the record shows that he was absent but one evening; and after he resigned the chair, he was generally present at the meetings of the lodge, and frequently officiated as master *pro tem.*, until 1749, when he again held it one term by election. He frequently performed the duties of the minor offices of the lodge, and was ever an active member. He was also a member of the "First Lodge," and gave it his active support.

Major PRICE had been successful in his mercantile business in Boston, and was able to support a country-seat a few miles from the city. The records of the Grand Lodge of Massachusetts show, that in April, 1751, that Grand Body resolved to celebrate the coming St. John's Day at "Brother PRICE's house" in Menotomy (West Cambridge); but when the day arrived, the record further shows, that his house "being encumbered by sickness," the celebration was held at the house of another brother in Cambridge. Soon after this he lost his wife, and also a daughter of about the age of nineteen years; and on the 20th of April, 1766, he lost his only surviving child, a son, who was apprenticed to an apothecary. This son died suddenly in a fit. The stricken father was now childless and lonely, and he wrote to his friends in London, in 1771, that as soon as his affairs in Boston could be intrusted to a suitable person, he contemplated returning to England. He was then nearly seventy-five years old; yet he again married, and in 1774 he relinquished his business in Boston, and retired to a farm in Townsend, a few miles from the city, which town he afterwards represented in the General Court. The second wife of Major PRICE was a widow, LYDIA ABBOT, of Townsend, who had at the time of this marriage two daughters by her former husband, and she afterwards had two daughters more by Major PRICE. He continued his residence in Townsend until his death at about the age of eighty-three years, which occurred on the 20th of May, 1780. He was buried in the public burial-ground of that town, where his tombstone still stands, bearing this inscription:

"IN MEMORY OF HENRY PRICE, ESQ.,

"Was born in London about the year of our LORD 1697. He removed to Boston about the year 1723; received a deputation appointing him Grand Master of Masons in New England; and in the year 1733 was appointed a Cornet in the Governor's Troop of Guards, with the rank of Major. By his diligence and industry in business, he acquired the means of a comfortable living, with which he removed to Townsend in the latter part of his life. He quitted mortality the 20th of May, A. D. 1780, leaving a widow and two young daughters, with a numerous company of friends and acquaintances to mourn his departure, who have that ground of hope concerning his present lot, which results from his undissembled regard to his Maker, and extensive benevolence to his fellow-creatures, manifested in life by a behavior consistent with his character as a MASON, and his nature as a Man."

Major PRICE provided by his will equally for his two step-daughters as for his own, giving to the four all his property after having made suitable provision for his widow. His descendants still live in Massachusetts; and one of them, a few years ago, presented to the Grand Lodge of that State an original portrait of their first Grand Master, taken in middle life. It is a valuable memento of one who is justly regarded as the *Father of Freemasonry in America.*

SIR WILLIAM JOHNSON,

THE ENGLISH SUPERINTENDENT OF INDIANS IN NEW YORK; AND FIRST MASTER OF ST. PATRICK'S LODGE ON THE MOHAWK.

FREEMASONRY has its traditions and historic allusions to lodges in New York, which are older than any of its authentic records in that colony. Like footprints on the shores of time, they seem to point to unrecorded dynasties of craftsmen, whose labors, like those of the pioneer in some primeval forest, who erects the first rude habitation in the place where busy cities afterwards arise, are all obliterated and forgotten. These traditions seem to point to the Palatines on the Hudson as the first mystic temple builders of New York. The Masonic annals of England then give us the names of DANIEL COXE, in 1730; RICHARD RIGGS, in 1737; FRANCIS GOELET, in 1751, as each having authority to congregate the brethren and establish Masonic lodges in the province of New York. There is no recorded certainty that either of these, except Mr. GOELET, acted on their commissions, and the only record of his proceedings in his Provincial Grand-mastership that we have met with, is a newspaper account of that day, which states that on St. John the Evangelist's day, in 1753, when his successor, GEORGE HARRISON, was installed in the city of New York, a Grand Lodge, which had previously existed in the province, was convened on the occasion. GEORGE HARRISON presided as Provincial Grand Master for eighteen years, and during that time he established lodges in the city of New York, and others in towns upon the Hudson, where the population was numerous, and one in an infant settlement on the Mohawk. He also granted warrants in Connecticut, New Jersey, and at Detroit.

The lodge which he chartered upon the Mohawk, was located at Caughnawaga, the residence of Sir WILLIAM JOHNSON, who was its first Master. It was called St. Patrick's Lodge, and its charter bore date May 23d, 1766. Caughnawaga was an English and German settlement on the extreme western verge of civilization, and in the vicinity of the Six Nations of

Indians, of whom Sir WILLIAM was the English superintendent. Sir WILLIAM JOHNSON was a native of Ireland, and born in 1714. He inherited no title of nobility by birth, but was a nephew upon his mother's side of Sir PETER WARREN, the naval commander who distinguished himself at the siege of Louisburg in 1745. Sir PETER had previously married a sister of Chief-Justice DE LANCY of New York, and had further identified himself with American interests by the purchase of a large tract of wilderness country upon the Mohawk River; and he sent for his nephew, who is the subject of this sketch, to come to America and take charge of his landed estate. Young JOHNSON had just been disappointed in a love affair in Ireland, and listened willingly to his proposal.

He was then about twenty years of age, and he came to America and settled on his uncle's lands at Caughnawaga on the Mohawk about the year 1735, two years after the first lodge was established in Boston. The Mohawk country was at that time but sparsely settled by white men, and for many years his principal neighbors and associates were the native Indians of the Six Nations, known in history as the confederacy of the Iroquois. He learned their language, and often joined with them in hunting, fishing, and other recreations; and by his adroitness obtained an almost unbounded influence over them. He was adopted by them according to their customs, and given by them an Indian name—*Warraghiiyagey.* For their amusement, it is said, he introduced among them many novel diversions, among which were foot-races, in which the competitors had meal-bags drawn over their legs and tied under their arms; turning a hog loose with his tail greased, and giving it as a prize to the one who would catch and hold it by that extremity; a half-pound of tea to the one who would make the ugliest face; and a bladder of snuff to the old woman who could scold the hardest. These were hilarities for the multitude. For the chiefs in council he had a demeanor silent, thoughtful, and grave as a sachem; and when he joined them in their mystic religious rites, no Indian devotee was more expert and devoted. He was skilled in their diplomacy, in their traditionary legends, and in their religious ceremonies. The English government had appointed him its superintendent of Indian affairs in the colony of New York, an office which he held until his death. His official position, his locality, and his intimacy with the various tribes around him, gave great advantages for trafficking in the productions of the forest, and he made large gains by exchanging European goods for the rich furs of the Indian hunters.

Many amusing anecdotes have come down to us of the artful manner in which Sir WILLIAM managed to increase his own wealth at the expense of his Indian neighbors, and at the same time preserve their kind feelings. On one occasion HENDRICK, the chief of the Mohawks, was charmed with the sight of a fine gold-laced coat which JOHNSON had just procured for himself from England. The cupidity of the chief was excited, and he went to its owner the next day saying, *he had dreamed.*

"Well, what did you dream?" said JOHNSON.

"I dreamed," said the chief, "that you gave me the fine coat."

The hint was too strong to be mistaken or unheeded, and the proud chief went away wearing the coat, and well pleased with his pretended dream. Soon afterwards meeting the chief, JOHNSON said to him, *he also had dreamed.*

"Well, what what did *you* dream?" said HENDRICK.

"I dreamed that you gave me a tract of land," said JOHNSON, describing it.

The chief paused a moment at the enormity of the amount; but soon said, "You may have the land, but me no dream again; you dream too hard for me."

The tract of land thus obtained is said to have been about twelve miles square, and the title was subsequently confirmed to him by the king of England, and was called the Royal Grant.

But the young Irish cavalier did not seem at all times content with the rich furs and lands of his Indian neighbors, for traditions also affirm, that he often gained the favor of the dark-eyed daughters of the forest, and that his intercourse with them was such as would be construed by the code of civilization, at least, a lapse of morality. Sir WILLIAM was yet far from being indifferent to the social and religious improvement of the tribes under his care. He encouraged the labors of teachers and missionaries among them; and while, in his own views, he was a high churchman, his patronage was often extended to an opposing New England association that was laboring to evangelize, or *gospelize*, as they termed it, the American Indians. His position and sentiments were often made matters of comment in the correspondence of the New England Society, an extract from which, in a letter from Colonel BABCOCK to the Rev. Dr. COOPER, we cannot refrain from giving in this sketch:

"Why," says he, "may not Sir WILLIAM be the means of introducing learning and religion amongst the Indians and civilize them, as well as PETER the Great did the Muscovites? And though Sir WILLIAM, like SOLOMON, has been eminent for his pleasures with the brown ladies, yet he may lay the foundation for a building in the Mohawk country that may be of more real use than the very splended temple that SOLOMON built; and I dare say that the queens of the Senecas, Oneidas, Onondagas, Cayugas, Tuscaroras, and Mohawks may join in their observations with the queen of Sheba, and say with the same truth, that not one-half was told them."

Sir WILLIAM was twice married. His first wife was a young German girl who had been sold on her arrival in America for her passage-money as a *redemptioner*, to a Mr PHILLIPS in the Mohawk Valley. She was so beautiful as to attract the attention of Sir WILLIAM, and on a friend's advising him to get the pretty German girl for a housekeeper, he determined to do so. His friend soon after missed the girl at the house of PHILLIPS, and asked him what had become of her. He replied, "JOHNSON, that tamned Irishman, came t'other day and offered me five pounds for her, threatening to horsewhip me and steal her if I would not sell her. I thought five pounds petter than a flogging, so I took it, and he's got the gal." She was the mother of his son, Sir JOHN JOHNSON, and two daughters who afterwards became the wives of GUY JOHNSON and Colonel CLAUS; and Sir WILLIAM subsequently married her to legitimatize her children.

There is also a spice of romance connected with his second wife, who was a sister of BRANT, an Indian *protegée* of Sir WILLIAM. She was a Mohawk girl of rare beauty and sprightliness, and being present one day at a military review, she playfully asked an officer who was riding on parade to allow her to ride upon his horse with him. He gave his assent, without thinking she would have the courage to attempt it; but she sprang with the swiftness of a gazelle upon the horse behind him, and, with her dark hair streaming in the wind, and her arm around his waist, rode about the parade-ground to the amusement and admiration of all present, except the young officer who became so unexpectedly the gallant of the forest fairy. Sir WILLIAM, who witnessed the spectacle, became enamored with the wild beauty before him, and soon after took her to his house as his wife in a manner consistent with Indian customs. He treated her with kindness and affection, and she is said to have made him a devoted and faithful wife, and to have borne him several children, which he legitimatized by marrying her with the ceremonies of the Episcopal Church a short time before his death. Many of the descendants of Sir WILLIAM and MOLLY BRANT, it is said, are still living in respectability in Canada.

During the times embraced in these digressive narrations of his domestic life, he was constantly employed in active public service, either in superintending Indian affairs, or in military command. In 1755, during the war between France and England, he was invested with the command of provincial troops, and for a fortunate victory over the French forces, was rewarded by the English government with a commission as major-general, and by the king with a baronetcy. His military talent, however, is not believed to have been of a high order.

We know nothing of the Masonic history of Sir William Johnson until 1766, when he obtained the warrant from George Harrison to establish St. Patrick's Lodge. He organized it on the 23d of August of that year at Johnson's Hall (now Johnstown), his residence on the Mohawk, and Guy Johnson and Daniel Claus became its Wardens. The whole number of the original members of the lodge was fifteen, many of whom, and perhaps all, were made Masons in Albany, where a lodge had been organized the year before. Sir William presented his lodge with a set of Masonic silver jewels, which he obtained for that purpose from England.

St. Patrick's Lodge was the first to erect a Masonic altar in the wilderness of New York west of the Hudson, although it had been preceded by military travelling lodges during the French and Indian war. It soon enrolled in its membership many names in the Mohawk Valley which are to be found in the history of our country, and it still maintains an honored and useful existence. Sir William continued to preside over it as Master until the 6th day of December, 1770, when the records show, that having previously informed his lodge that his duty as Master of the "*Ineffable Lodge*" at Albany did not render it convenient for him to continue longer as Master of St. Patrick's

Lodge, his son-in-law, GUY JOHNSON, was elected in his stead. Sir WILLIAM had been appointed Master of this so-called "*Ineffable*" Lodge as early as 1769, and he held that station until 1773, if not till his death. He died at Johnson's Hall, July 11, 1774, aged sixty years.

Whatever may have been the errors of his early years, his memory has been cherished for his many virtues; and he was spared from seeing the desolation that overspread the Mohawk Valley during the war of the Revolution, when his family and former friends became scattered, and the towns and villages he had seen grow up around him were laid in ruins by infuriated bands of wild savages and misguided loyalists. His death was regarded by our Government as a public loss; for it was believed that had he lived, he would have lent his aid and powerful influence with the Indians to prevent their taking up the tomahawk in behalf of the English in the then impending conflict. His influence had been powerful with them while living, and at his death he left a large sum of money to be expended in providing mourning dresses for them; and the chiefs at the Mohawk castles, and their women and children, all were provided with some badge to wear by which to express their sorrow for his loss. His authority on the Mohawk had been almost kingly, and no white man ever attained a greater influence with the American Indians than Sir WILLIAM JOHNSON.

SIR JOHN JOHNSON,

THE LAST PROVINCIAL GRAND MASTER OF THE FIRST GRAND LODGE OF NEW YORK.

THE pre-revolutionary Provincial Grand Lodge of the old colony of New York, was held by authority granted by the Grand Lodge of England, sometimes called *Moderns*, to distinguish it from the Dermott Grand Body, who denominated themselves *Ancients*. Under this authority New York had four Provincial Grand Masters, of whom Sir JOHN JOHNSON was the last.

He was the son of Sir WILLIAM JOHNSON by his first wife, was born at Johnstown in 1742, and upon the death of his father, in 1774, succeeded him in his titles and estate. Few records have come to us of his early history, but he probably was sent to England to complete his education, and there our earliest history of him as a Mason commences. He was made a Mason in London at about the age of twenty-five years, and soon after received a commission as Provincial Grand Master of New York from Lord BLANEY, Grand Master of England, and immediately returned to America.

The earliest American Masonic records of Sir JOHN are those of St. Patrick's Lodge at Johnstown, New

York, of which his father, Sir WILLIAM, was at the time Master. These records of December 5, 1767, state:

"Sir JOHN JOHNSON, knight (son of Sir WILLIAM), being lately arrived from London, where he had been entered, passed, and raised to the degree of a Master Mason in the Royal Lodge at St. James, and received his Constitution as Provincial Grand Master of New York, applied to visit the lodge, and being examined, was admitted agreeable to his degree."

From this time onward the records of St. Patrick's Lodge show that Sir JOHN was a constant visitor at its stated communications until May the 3d, 1773. They also state, December 1, 1768:

"Lord BLANEY'S warrant appointing Sir JOHN JOHNSON, knight, Grand Master for the province of New York, read; upon which he was congratulated by the members present."

November 7, 1771:

"The Worshipful Master acquainted the brethren that the Right Worshipful Sir JOHN JOHNSON, knight, Provincial Grand Master of New York, by virtue of a commission from Lord BLANEY, Grand Master of England, had lately been installed into that office by the Grand Officers in New York, and intended them the honor of a visit as such. He was accordingly introduced and received by the body, and placed in the chair with the usual ceremonies."

From the foregoing records of St. Patrick's Lodge, it appears that although commissioned as Provincial Grand Master of New York by Lord BLANEY in 1767, he was not installed as such until 1771; a conclusion which is further supported by the fact that GEORGE HARRISON, who preceded him as such, granted a charter to King Solomon's Lodge, at Poughkeepsie, on the 18th of April, 1771.

No records of the Provincial Grand Lodge of New York during the Grand Mastership of Sir JOHN JOHNSON have been preserved, nor do we know how many subordinate lodges existed in his jurisdiction. St. George's Lodge, at Schenectady, was chartered by him December 13, 1774. New York embraced at that time a far greater extent of territory than is contained in its present limits, its acknowledged boundaries containing all of Canada which lies south of the thirty-fifth parallel of north latitude, extending west as far as Detroit; and it also claimed the present State of Vermont as within its civil jurisdiction.

Of the entire number of lodges then in this district, no satisfactory account can be given. It is not probable that many had been formed, except in the eastern part of the colony, for all else was a nearly unbroken wilderness, dotted here and there with a military station. At the station at Detroit, a lodge had been chartered in 1764. Four lodges also existed in Connecticut, and one in New Jersey, which held warrants under the Grand Lodge of New York, having been chartered by HARRISON, the predecessor of Sir JOHN JOHNSON.

No records are known to exist of the doings of the Grand Lodge of New York under the Grand Mastership of JOHNSON. Doctor PETER MIDDLETON was his Deputy Grand Master, and his authority as such continued to be respected during the War of the Revolution; while Sir JOHN, by his adherence to the royal cause, was compelled to leave his home and seek the protection of the British army.

He had inherited little of his father's amiable qualities with his title and estate, and when the political storm gathered in the horizon, he gave all his energies and influence to the support of royalty, and sought to embitter his neighbors on the Mohawk, where he lived, against all who opposed its authority; nor did his efforts stop here, for he infused the same malignant spirit into the minds of many of the Indian tribes in that vicinity, and finally became the leader of predatory bands of Tories and Indians during the war.

We cannot follow him in this sketch through his military history during this seven years' struggle; suffice it to say, that he became the acknowledged leader of the Tories of central New York, was commissioned as a colonel by the British, and directed the movements of as bloody a band of savages and outlaws as existed during the Revolution. The following oath which he administered to the Indians, shows his almost unbounded influence with them, as well as his own vanity. We do not commend its purity of diction, but give it as a literary curiosity:

"By the grace of GOD unconquerable; Six Nations and loyal refugees, swear by the highest almighties, and almighty GOD's holiness, by his kingdom, by the substance of the heavens, by the sun, moon, and stars, by the earth and all under the earth, by the brains and all the hairy scalps of our mothers, by our heads, and all the strength of our souls and bodies, by the death of the great Sir WILLIAM

JOHNSON, that we, our brother and son, Sir JOHN JOHNSON, succeeding superintendent of Indian affairs, in no manner of ways in thy great and weighty affairs will leave thee ; and though it be to the o'erthrow of our nations, to be brought to nothing until there shall be left but ourselves, four or five Indians at the most, yet will we defend thee, and all those that do any ways appertain to thee ; and if thou shalt have need of us, we shall always go with thee : and in case this our promise in any way be frustrated, then let GOD's justice fall upon our heads and destroy us and our posterity, and wipe away whatsoever belongeth unto us, and gather it together into a rock of stone or substance of earth ; and that the earth may cleave asunder and swallow our bodies and souls."

This was signed by the chiefs in behalf of the Six Nations. Sir JOHN was possessed of a princely estate when the Revolution commenced; but it was confiscated, and he and his family became exiles. At the public sale of his property, JOHN TAYLOR, the lieutenant-governor of New York, purchased several of the articles, and among them the family Bible. Perceiving it contained the family record, he wrote a civil note to Sir JOHN and kindly offered its restoration. Some time afterwards a messenger from Sir JOHN rudely called for the Bible, saying, "I have come for Sir WILLIAM's Bible, and there are four guineas which it cost." The Bible was delivered, and the messenger was asked what message Sir JOHN had sent. The reply was, "Pay four guineas, and take the book!"

After the close of the war, Sir JOHN went to England, but returned and settled in Canada in 1784. Here he held several important civil offices, one of which was governor-general of Canada; and to compensate him for the loss of his property, the English government made him several grants of land. He died in Montreal in 1830, at the age of eighty-eight years, and was succeeded in his title by his son, Sir ADAM GORDEN JOHNSON.

Peyton Randolph

PEYTON RANDOLPH,

FIRST PRESIDENT OF THE CONTINENTAL CONGRESS, AND LAST PROVINCIAL GRAND MASTER OF VIRGINIA.

AMONG the honored names that adorn both the public and Masonic annals of Virginia, that of RANDOLPH has a proud distinction. Two eminent citizens of the Old Dominion who bore it were the compeers of WASHINGTON in public life and Masonic labors. These were PEYTON and EDMUND RANDOLPH. The RANDOLPHS were an old and influential family of Virginia, and we often meet the name in her Masonic as well as general records.

The first of that name who settled in Virginia was WILLIAM, of Warwickshire, or, as some authorities say, of Yorkshire, in England. He came to America about 1670, and settled at Turkey Island, on the James River, below Richmond. There he accumulated a large landed estate, and became a member of the House of Burgesses, and of the Council. His wife, whom he married after he came to Virginia, was MARY ISHAM, of Bermuda Hundred, who was descended from an ancient English family in Northamptonshire. Several sons by this marriage became men of distinction, one of whom, the sixth, was Sir JOHN RANDOLPH, who was the father of PEYTON, the subject of this sketch. His mother was SUSAN BEVERLEY.

PEYTON RANDOLPH, who was the second son of Sir JOHN, was born in Virginia in the year 1723, and was therefore nearly ten years the senior of GEORGE WASHINGTON. His father, Sir JOHN, died in 1737, when PEYTON was but fourteen years of age. He was, at the time of his death, speaker of the House of Burgesses, treasurer of the colony, and the representative of William and Mary College, where he had been educated. He was buried in its chapel, and an elegant marble tablet was placed there to perpetuate his memory.

It was the custom of the wealthy families of Virginia, at that period, to send their sons to England to be educated, and PEYTON RANDOLPH was sent there for that purpose during his minority. He graduated at Oxford with college honors, and received at that distinguished seat of learning the degree of Master of Arts. He studied law, returned to America, and was made king's attorney for Virginia in 1748, at the age of twenty-five years. He had risen rapidly in his profession, and was often the competitor at the bar with the first legal gentlemen of the colony at that early age. In his person he was tall and stately; in his manners, grave and dignified. His features were pleasing, and every look bespoke a patrician. In his profession he was noted for his accuracy, in his official capacity for his incorruptible integrity, and in his social intercourse for his generous and hospitable disposition.

Connected thus by paternal and maternal descent with the first families of the colony, and enjoying official and professional advantages for influence which few gentlemen at that time possessed, he did not fail to secure for himself high consideration in the sober councils of the colonial government; and the social circles that the *élite* of Virginia society formed, were often graced and enlivened by his presence.

The French and Indian war, which commenced soon after the middle of the last century, called many citizens of Virginia into the field to defend the western frontier. The defeat of BRADDOCK in 1755 cast a gloom on that colony, which required the wisest and boldest to step forth in its military defence; and the names enrolled as its defenders in that war, are those of the heroes who a few years later won for our country its independence. WASHINGTON was then the commander and the idol of the Virginia soldiery. PEYTON RANDOLPH, though attorney-general of the commonwealth, did not hesitate to bare his breast too in its defence. Aroused at the accounts of devastations and massacres on the western borders of the colony, Mr. RANDOLPH, in

1756, collected a band of one hundred men, and marched at their head to the scene of action in aid of WASHINGTON.

After retiring from the military service, he was elected a member of the House of Burgesses, and became its speaker in 1766, as the successor of Mr. ROBINSON. He continued to preside over that body until it was superseded by the conventions. He was thus the last presiding officer of the colonial government of Virginia. His influence there was great, and always on the side of public rights. The crumbs which royalty scattered in the pathway of its favorites in the colonies had no charms for him, and he boldly advocated popular liberty in the face of ministerial frowns.

In 1773 committees of correspondence began to be formed in the different colonies, to ascertain the true position and sentiments of each. Of that of Virginia Mr. RANDOLPH was chairman, and through him the cavaliers of Virginia became first united in political sentiment with the puritans of New England. We cannot attempt in this personal sketch of Mr. RANDOLPH to give a portraiture of the events of those times, or of the influences that produced them. Suffice it to say, that there is an unwritten history of the silent influences of Masonry in producing the political associations of that period. The mighty brotherhood of Masonry, ever the friend of freedom, was omnipotent for good.

In 1774 the first colonial convention of Virginia assembled at Williamsburg, and Mr. RANDOLPH was chosen its chairman. Delegates were elected by it to the Continental Congress soon to be held in Philadelphia; and at the head of these stands the name of PEYTON RANDOLPH for Virginia. When that body met in September of that year, fifty-five delegates were present, representing twelve different colonies, and Mr. RANDOLPH was unanimously elected its president. He was then fifty-one years of age, in the prime of dignified manhood, with experience as a presiding officer, and warmly enlisted in the cause of freedom. No step towards perfecting an American Union was so important as the one taken that day. We have already shown, in a previous sketch, that both DANIEL COXE and Dr. FRANKLIN had on previous and different occasions recommended a union of the English colonies in America. Both these had failed to gain a general approval of their plans, for want of a deep-felt common interest. In the present instance, there was an interest and purpose combined, that formed an era in the history of the western world.

PEYTON RANDOLPH was at that time a distinguished Mason, and Provincial Grand Master of Virginia. When and where the veil that had hid from his manhood's eye Masonic light was drawn, we have now no records to show. Williamsburg, where he resided, had long been the seat, perhaps the centre of Masonry in Virginia. In 1773, PEYTON RANDOLPH received from Lord PETRE, Grand Master of England, a warrant constituting him Master of the lodge in Williamsburg. It bore date in London on the 6th of November, and ist registry number was 457. For the benefit of the curious Masonic reader, we give a copy of the singular old English warrant of this lodge a place in our sketch:

"PETRE, GRAND MASTER.

[L. S.] "To all and every our Right Worshipful, Worshipful, and loving Brethren, We, ROBERT EDWARD PETRE, Lord PETRE, Baron of Writtle, in the County of Essex, Grand Master of the Most Ancient and Honorable Society of Free and Accepted Masons, send Greeting.

"*Know Ye*, That we, at the humble petition of our right trusty and well beloved Brethren, the Honorable PEYTON RANDOLPH, Esquire, JOHN MINSON GALT, EDWARD CHARLTON, WILLIAM WADDILL, JOHN TURNER, HARRISON RANDOLPH, JOHN ROWSEY, THOMAS HARWOOD, and several other Brethren residing in and near Williamsburg, in the colony of Virginia, North America, do constitute the said Brethren into a regular Lodge of Free and Accepted Masons, to be held in Williamsburg aforesaid; and do further, at their said petition, and of the great trust and confidence reposed in every of the said above-named Brethren, hereby appoint the said PEYTON RANDOLPH to be Master, JOHN MINSON GALT Senior Warden, and EDWARD CHARLTON Junior Warden for opening the said Lodge, and for such further time only as shall be thought proper by the Brethren thereof. It being our will that this appointment of the above officers shall in no wise affect any future election of officers of the Lodge, but that such election shall be regulated agreeably to such By-Laws of the said Lodge as shall be consistent with the General Laws of the Society contained in the Book of Constitution. And we hereby will and require you, the said PEYTON RANDOLPH, to take special care that all and every of the said Brethren are or have been regularly made Masons, and that they do observe, perform, and keep all the Rules and Orders contained in the Book of Constitution; and further, that you do, from time to time, cause to be entered in a book kept for that purpose, an account of your proceedings in the Lodge, together with all such Orders, Rules, and Regulations as shall be made for the good government of the same; that in no wise you omit once in every year to send to us, or to our successors, Grand Masters, or to the Honorable CHARLES DILLEN our Deputy Grand Master, or to the Deputy Grand Master for the time being, an account in writing of your proceedings, and copies of all such Rules, Orders, and Regulations as shall be made as aforesaid, together with a list of the Members of the Lodge, and such a sum of money as may suit the circumstances of the Lodge, and reasonably be expected towards the Grand Charity. Moreover, we hereby will and require you, the said PEYTON RANDOLPH, as soon as conveniently may be, to send an account in writing of what may be done by virtue of these presents.

"GIVEN at London under our hands and the seals of MASONRY this sixth day of November, A. L. 5773, A. D. 1773.

"By the Grand Master's command,

"CHARLES DILLEN, Deputy Grand Master.

"Witness,

"JAMES HUSSELTINE, Grand Secretary."

The first recorded meeting under this warrant was held on St. John's Day, June 24, 1774. Mr. RANDOLPH was not present, and JOHN MINSON GALT presided as "*Deputy Master.*" It appears from the record of this date, that previous meetings had been held, at the last of which, officers had been elected for the following year, who were as follows: JOHN BLAIR, Master; WILLIAM WADDILL, Deputy Master; WILLIAM FINNIE, Senior Warden; HARRISON RANDOLPH, Junior Warden; JOHN ROWSEY, Treasurer; WILLIAM RUSSELL, Secretary; and HUMPHREY HAYWOOD and JAMES GALT, Stewards, who "being duly qualified, took their seats in due form."

On the 5th of July, 1774, the name of PEYTON RANDOLPH first appears on the records as present at the lodge, where, the records state, he presided as *Provincial Grand Master*, with JOHN BLAIR as Master, WILLIAM WADDILL as Deputy Master, etc. From this it appears that Mr. RANDOLPH had at this time been appointed Provincial Grand Master of Virginia, a rank, which records show, he held till the time of his death. The first Continental Congress therefore was presided over by the highest Masonic officer present, and he a Provincial Grand Master. What number of Masons were members of the body we know not, for the Masonic records of that day were mostly lost during the revolutionary struggle which followed. Even the record-book of the Williamsburg Lodge, from which the foregoing extracts and facts are drawn, is lost to our Virginia Brethren, and is now in possession of an antiquarian in another jurisdiction who is not a Mason! We well know that WASHINGTON and many of his Masonic compeers were members. From the bright list of the members of that body we can say, from existing Masonic records of some, *they were our brothers;* and of others, where no records verify the fact,

"I know thee, from thy apron white,
An architect to be.
I know thee, from thy trowel bright,
Well skilled in Masonry."

After a secret session of less than two months, this Congress adjourned to meet again when occasion should require. On the 4th of October of this year the records of Williamsburg Lodge give the following interesting account of laying the corner-stone of Williamsburg Bridge:

"The design of this meeting being to lay the foundation-stone of the stone bridge to be built at the Capitol Landing, the lodge accordingly repaired thereto, and after the usual libations, and having placed the medal under the corner-stone, and laid the same in due form, closed the lodge; the inscription of which medal is as follows:

"'GEORGIO TERTIO REGE;
COMITE DUNMORE PROFECTO;
PEYTON RANDOLPH LATAMORUM PROSIDE SUPREMO;
JOHANNE BLAIR PROSIDE.
A. L. 5774.'"

At the meeting of the Williamsburg Lodge on the 15th of December following, the officers present stand recorded:

"PEYTON RANDOLPH, Grand Master.
"JOHN BLAIR, Master.
"WILLIAM WADDILL, Deputy Master.
"WILLIAM FINNIE, Senior Warden.
"EDMUND RANDOLPH, Junior Warden Pt.
"JOHN ROWSEY, Treasurer.
"WILLIAM RUSSELL, Secretary.
"HENRY J. HARWOOD, } Stewards.
"JAMES GALT, }
"JOHN MINSON GALT, Past Master."

On the 16th of June, 1775, the records state:

"On the petition of Brother PEALE, desiring the loan of the picture belonging to this lodge, which was taken for our Worshipful Provincial Grand Master, the same was granted him upon his giving security for the safe return of the same at the appointed time."

Such are the existing records of PEYTON RANDOLPH as a Mason at this interesting period of his life. Congress had in May, 1775, reassembled in Philadelphia, and Mr. RANDOLPH was again elected its President; but his health failing him, he resigned the position, and JOHN HANCOCK was elected his successor. He visited Virginia, but soon returned and took his seat as a member of the National Council. While in the performance of his duties there, he died suddenly of apoplexy, on the 22d of October, 1775, in the fifty-third year of his age. His body was placed in a vault in Philadelphia, to await the orders of his family.

Upon receiving notice of his death, the lodge in Williamsburg took the following action, as seen by its record of November 6, 1775:

"*Ordered*, That the lodge go into mourning for our late worthy Grand Master, and continue till his corpse shall arrive; and that this lodge attend in procession, and that the order be published in the Virginia Gazette."

On the 21st of December the lodge ordered,

"That Brother WILLSON PEALE be wrote to, to return the *speaker's picture*."

Mrs. RANDOLPH presented to the lodge, after her husband's death, his jewel, sash, and apron, and when the lodge met on the 27th of December of that year, it was—

"*Ordered*, that the lodge return their thanks for the present made this lodge by Mrs. RANDOLPH, of the Provincial Grand Master's jewel, sash, and apron."

On this occasion an address was delivered before the lodge by the Reverend Brother WILLIAM BLAND, its chaplain, from which we give the following extract relating to the death of Mr. RANDOLPH:

"Our forefathers cultivated Masonry with devotion, and made the dreary wilderness of America smile with the brotherly love that she inculcated; but to the disgrace of moderns, she is now almost exiled.

"Few are the places in this western world in which she can claim rest for her blest feet; fewer still are there where her votaries are sincere. The genius of Masonry, my brethren, does not consist in frequenting established meetings, or decorating ourselves with the insignia belonging to our profession. If there be a brother that dare pass by his neighbor in distress, or because he himself possesses the light, would turn the blind man out of his way, acknowledge him not. The name of a brother is an empty sound, indeed, if we refuse our hand to one fallen into a pit, disdain to relieve the sorrows of the widow and the orphan, or discard from our lives the exercise of patriotism—the highest refinement of brotherly love.

"But wherefore was I about to draw the character of a true Mason! For not long time since you had a bright example to imitate and admire,—surely, I am not called upon for his name, for it can never be forgotten. All North America was under his wing, but we his peculiar care. Write a virtue which he had not faithfully transcribed into his practice, or enumerate an excellence to which his heart was a stranger. If malice could be found within these walls, she would be silenced by the contemplation of his memory, and envy herself bear no fangs against him. That great man—great let me call him—revived the drooping spirit of Masonry. The few remaining of the Elect he concentrated in this place, and to him must we ascribe the present numerous appearance of Brethren.

"I could dwell forever on the remembrance of him, but I fear that my short acquaintance with the sublime parts of Masonry, prevent me from doing justice to him. We all know how gracefully he filled that chair, and I congratulate my brethren that we once had such a head, such a father."

The remains of Mr. RANDOLPH lay in the tomb at Philadelphia until November, 1776, when they were taken by his nephew, EDMUND RANDOLPH, to Williamsburg, where they were interred by the side of those of his father in the college chapel with Masonic ceremonies. On their arrival the lodge met, and from its records of November 26th we make the following extract:

"Met and agreed on the form of the procession of our late worthy Brother PEYTON RANDOLPH, Grand Master of Virginia, deceased, and then repairing to the Lodge Chapel; after the corpse was interred, returned to the lodge, and adjourned till a lodge in course."

The following further account of the ceremonies on that occasion we copy from the public prints of that day:

"WILLIAMSBURG, November 29, 1776.

"On Tuesday last the remains of our late amiable and beloved fellow-citizen, the Honorable PEYTON RANDOLPH, Esquire, were conveyed in a hearse to the college chapel, attended by the Worshipful Brotherhood of Freemasons, both Houses of Assembly, a number of other gentlemen, and the inhabitants of the city. The body was received from the bearers by gentlemen of the House of Delegates, who conveyed it to the family vault in the chapel, after which an excellent oration was pronounced from the pulpit by the Reverend THOMAS DAVIS* in honor of the deceased, recommending to the respectable audience to imitate his virtues. The oration being ended, the body was deposited in the vault, when every spectator paid their last tribute of tears to the memory of their departed and much honored friend,—may we add, to whom he was a father and able counsellor, and one of our firmest patriots. The remains of this worthy man were brought hither from Philadelphia by EDMUND RANDOLPH, Esq., at the earnest request of his uncle's afflicted and inconsolable widow."

PEYTON RANDOLPH was the second Provincial Grand Master whose death had been enrolled in the list of the active defenders of American liberty at this period. WARREN had fallen on the early battle-fields of our country, RANDOLPH in its council chambers. The death of each was a prelude to the great change which soon after took place in the polity of Masonry in our country. Hitherto all American Grand Masters held their authority by appointment from the Mother Grand Lodge in Great Britain. Now, for the first time, the Craft in America began to inquire into their own inherent powers to assume an elective supremacy. It

* The Reverend THOMAS DAVIS, years afterwards, officiated as rector of Christ's Church and chaplain of Alexandria Lodge, at the burial of WASHINGTON.

has been assumed by Masonic writers in our country, that the Craft in Massachusetts were the first to contemplate the election of American Grand Masters. This we believe to be a historical error, for Masonic records of Virginia show, that the earliest proposition for such action came from that State. Massachusetts records show the Craft for the first time contemplating this question there, when assembled in Boston on the 27th of December, 1776, by the Deputy Grand Master of the late Dr. JOSEPH WARREN, to celebrate the festival of St. John the Evangelist. The records of the old lodge in Williamsburg show, on the 3d of the same month, a prior record of interest to this question. It was their first meeting after the burial of Mr. RANDOLPH. We give an extract from the Williamsburg records to verify this statement:

"*December* 3, 1776.—WM. WADDILL, Master.

"On motion made, *Resolved*, That the Master of this lodge be directed to write to all the regular lodges in this State, requesting their attendance by their deputies, at this lodge, in order to form a convention to *choose a* GRAND MASTER *for the State of Virginia*, on the first day of the next Assembly."

The limits of our sketch do not admit of further connecting lines between the death of PEYTON RANDOLPH and the elective supremacy of Masonry in our country. We have already stated, in our sketch of WASHINGTON, that when the convention of Masonic delegates in Virginia met a few months later, they proposed his name first, as the most worthy to wear the earliest jewel of an elective American Grand Master.

The closing record of the old colonial lodge of Williamsburg relating to PEYTON RANDOLPH, is as follows, under date June 3, 1777:

"*Resolved*, That there shall be an elegant frame made to the picture of our late worthy and Honorable Provincial Grand Master; and that the Treasurer be appointed to employ some person to make it."

This portrait of Mr. RANDOLPH, or the copy by Mr. PEALE, afterwards became one of the treasures of the Congressional Library, but was destroyed by fire a few years ago. It was adorned, as we show in our engraving, with a Masonic sash, and Master's jewel hanging pendent from its angle.

EDMUND RANDOLPH,

GOVERNOR OF VIRGINIA, AND GRAND MASTER OF MASONS IN THAT COMMONWEALTH.

EDMUND RANDOLPH was a nephew of PEYTON RANDOLPH. His father was JOHN, the brother of PEYTON, son of Sir JOHN, and grandson of WILLIAM, the first of the Virginia RANDOLPHS. He was the fourth in descent of the American family. Both his father and his grandfather, and also PEYTON his uncle, had held the office of king's attorney in the commonwealth, and were all noted lawyers; consequently he was bred to the same profession. PEYTON RANDOLPH had succeeded Sir JOHN in that office, and while holding it, he went to England as the agent of Virginia, just before the Revolution. While in London, his independent spirit led him to speak his mind too freely on the subject of colonial rights to please the English ministry, and he was displaced as attorney-general, and his brother JOHN, the father of EDMUND, who is the subject of this sketch, was appointed in his stead. JOHN had been doing the duties of the office for his brother PEYTON during his absence to England, and superseded him, by being the pliant advocate of the English ministry in their obnoxious taxation measures. When the Revolution commenced, he was a decided royalist, and supported Lord DUNMORE, the royal governor of the commonwealth, in all his efforts to maintain the king's power in Virginia. In this they failed, and JOHN RANDOLPH disinherited his son EDMOND for his joining the patriot cause, and soon left, with Lord DUNMORE and other royalists, for England. He, however, bitterly repented his choice, died of a broken heart in 1784, and his remains were, by his request, brought to Virginia and buried at Williamsburg.

Deserted and disowned by his father, EDMUND RANDOLPH was adopted by PEYTON, his uncle. We know not his age at this time, for we have no record of his birth before us. He had grown to manhood, for he succeeded his father as attorney-general of the commonwealth. He was also a Mason at that time, and was a member of the lodge at Williamsburg, of which his uncle was first Master. His name appears on its records at its organization, June 24, 1774; and on the 4th of the following October he was appointed by the lodge to revise its by-laws. Upon the sudden death of his uncle, PEYTON RANDOLPH, at Philadelphia, his relatives not being present, his remains were deposited in a tomb in that city. In the following year, EDMOND RANDOLPH, who was then with the army at Cambridge as one of WASHINGTON'S aids, repaired to Philadelphia, and removed the body to Williamsburg, where it was interred in St. Mary's Chapel with Masonic honors.

In 1776 he married, and this event was thus announced in the Virginia Gazette, accompanied by the following poetic lines.

"EDMUND RANDOLPH, Esq., Attorney-General of Virginia, to Miss BETSEY NICHOLAS, a young lady, whose amiable sweetness of disposition, joined with the finest intellectual accomplishments, cannot fail of rendering the worthy man of her choice completely happy.

"Fain would the aspiring muse attempt to sing
The virtues of this amiable pair;
But how shall I attune the trembling string,
Or sound a note that can such worth declare?
Exalted theme! too high for human lays!
Could my weak verse with beauty be inspired,
In numbers smooth I'd chant my Betsey's praise,
And tell how much her Randolph is admired.
To light the hymenial torch since they've resolved,
Kind Heaven, I trust, will make them truly blest;
And when the *Gordian* knot shall be dissolved,
Translate them to eternal peace and rest."

In 1779 Mr. RANDOLPH was elected by his State a delegate to the Continental Congress, and he served in that station until March, 1782. While a member of that body, he offered the resolution, after the defeat of CORNWALLIS at Yorktown in 1781, to publicly return thanks to Almighty God for crowning our army with success.

An independent Grand Lodge of Masons had been formed in Virginia in 1778, and of that Grand Body EDMUND RANDOLPH was elected Deputy Grand Master, in 1784. He held the office for two years, and upon the 27th of October, 1786, he was elected Grand Master of Masons in Virginia. He held this office by re-election until October 28th, 1788. During the last year of his Grand Mastership, he had the honor of granting a warrant to the lodge at Alexandria, constituting WASHINGTON its Master.

In 1786, while he was Deputy Grand Master of Virginia, he was elected to succeed PATRICK HENRY as governor of the commonwealth. While holding that office, and also that of Grand Master of Masons, he represented his State, in conjunction with WASHINGTON and other distinguished delegates, in the convention at Philadelphia, that formed the Federal Constitution in 1787.

As a member of the convention, his views on political science coincided with those of PATRICK HENRY, and other members, who believed the rights of individual States had been too far yielded in that instrument. But when its ratification came before the people of Virginia, his desire for a harmonious union overcame his apprehension of its imperfections, and his vote was given for its adoption. When the new government was organized under this constitution, in 1789, WASHINGTON made Governor RANDOLPH his attorney-general; and in 1794, under the second administration of WASHINGTON, he succeeded Mr. JEFFERSON as secretary of state. In 1795 he resigned this office on account of some misunderstanding with the Administration, and withdrew from public life. He never again entered the political field, but died in Frederick County, in his native State, on the 12th of September, 1813.

Governor RANDOLPH was a devoted member of the Episcopal Church, being many years one of his vestrymen. All of his Virginia ancestors had been members of the same Church, and for four generations they had been vestrymen also in it. The following extract from a paper written by him soon after the death of his wife, and addressed to his children, is an interesting commentary on his religious history and character.

"Up to the commencement of the Revolution, the Church of England was the established religion, in which your mother had been educated with strictness, if not with bigotry. From the strength of parental example, her attendance on public worship was unremitted, except where insuperable obstacles occurred; the administration of the sacrament was never without a cause passed by; in her closet, prayer was uniformly addressed to the throne of mercy; and the questioning of the sacred truths she never permitted herself, or heard from others without abhorrence. When we were united, I was a deist, made so by my confidence in some whom I revered, and by the labors of two of my preceptors, who, though in the ministry, poisoned me with books of infidelity. I cannot answer to myself that I should ever have been brought to examine the genuineness of Holy Writ, if I had not observed the consoling influence which it wrought upon the life of my dearest Betsey. I recollect well that it was not long before I adopted a principle which I have never relinquished:—that woman, in the present state of society, is, without religion, a monster. While my opinions were unsettled, Mr. —— and Mrs. —— came to my house, on Sunday evening, to play with me at chess. She did not appear in the room; and her reproof, which from its mildness was like the manna of heaven, has operated perpetually as an injunction from above; for, several years since I detected the vanity of sublunary things, and knew that the good of man consisted in Christianity alone. I have often hinted a wish that we had instituted a course of family prayer for the benefit of our children, on whose minds, when most pliant, the habit might be fixed. But I know not why the plan was not enforced until during her last illness, when she and I frequently joined in prayer. She always thanked me when it was finished; and it grieves me to think that she should suppose that this enlivening inducement was necessary in order to excite me to this duty."

This exposition of his religious sentiment was designed for his children only; but its beautiful simplicity and genuine piety make it justly a part of his history. It is the halo of Christianity, ornamenting the brow of this distinguished governor and Grand Master of Virginia.

BENJAMIN FRANKLIN,

MASTER OF THE FIRST WARRANTED LODGE IN PENNSYLVANIA, AND PROVINCIAL GRAND MASTER OF THAT PROVINCE.

THE name of BENJAMIN FRANKLIN illumines the history of Masonry, and of our country, for more than one-half of the last century. Its diamond light is not confined to the city, the province, or the country that gave him birth. The orient borrows a ray from it, and wherever the evening twilight lingers, or the polar-star guides, or the southern-cross gleams, there the torch which he lighted from the clouds above him, irradiates the pathway still of every civilized nation. Of his humble birth in Boston, on the 17th of January, 1706; of his early employment in an occupation unsuited to his genius; of his being indentured to his brother as a printer's apprentice, and fleeing from his petty tyranny to Philadelphia; of his amusing introduction to that city, and his boyhood success there; of his leaving it for a voyage to London while he was yet in his minority, and of his first London life;—every step from tottering infancy to bold reliant manhood, has been often told, and we need not repeat them in our sketch of his Masonic life.

Leaving the youth of FRANKLIN with all its romantic incidents and instructive lessons behind us, we find him on his return from England in the autumn of 1726, in his twenty-first year, recommencing his citizenship in Philadelphia, with a body strong and vigorous, a mind active and well cultivated, and with a knowledge of his art, and an experience gained in the school of the world, which well fitted him to step boldly on to the platform of active life. His intentions at this period were to fit himself for a mercantile life, but the death of his employer soon induced him to engage again as a printer, and his industry, integrity, and studious habits soon gained him friends, competence, and distinction.

His social qualities and intelligence at first drew around him a few congenial spirits, and a literary club was formed for mental improvement. While in London he had become familiar with the existence of the various clubs and other social societies that existed there, and the organization of Freemasonry had no doubt come under his observation. This institution there was then just emerging from a situation which the common observer might have regarded as a system of voluntary social clubs, and its pretentions to antiquity, its moral and scientific basis, and its written rules and regulations, had lately been given to the public in a quarto volume called "Anderson's Constitutions." These had been accepted there by a part of the Fraternity as their governing code of rules, while others still adhered to the immemorial rights and usages of Masons when convened. There can be very little doubt but that FRANKLIN brought home with him some knowledge of the Fraternity, although not an initiate into its mysteries.

As the limits of this sketch will not allow a detail of all the incidents of FRANKLIN'S private and public life, however interesting and instructive they may be, we shall pass over many of them, and confine our consideration more to those which show his character as a Mason, and the influence which his connection with this fraternity may have had on his after-life. This we do more especially from believing that all which concerns the personal history of our representative men, should be fairly considered as a part of our national character, and from a belief that the Masonic character and connection of our public men of the last century, has been unwarrantably lost sight of, in the history of our country. Perhaps this has arisen from an undue prejudice which writers may have had against the institution of Freemasonry, or from an ignorance of its principles and influence.

With FRANKLIN, whatever induced scientific research, and strengthened the fraternal bonds that thus bound society together, had especial value; and when he found that Freemasonry embraced in its teachings the highest moral rectitude, founded on the Fatherhood of God as a common parent, and the brotherhood of man as His offspring, and that it inculcated a study of His perfections as revealed in the works of nature as well as in His written word, he at once became a devotee at its altar. No record has come down to us of the time and place where he first received Masonic light. It was not the custom of the Fraternity in the early part of the last century to preserve written records of its meetings when convened for work; besides, when warranted lodges were first established in America, they little knew how much interest would in time be felt in their early history. The brief records they may have written, have in many cases, too, been destroyed or lost. It is not known how or when the first lodge of Freemasons was instituted in Philadelphia. A few brethren who had been made Masons in the old country, may have met and opened lodges from time to time, and initiated others, without keeping any record. The earliest notices we find of Masonic lodges in that city, are in the public newspapers of that day, which show the meetings of the Fraternity there in 1732, where they give the name of WILLIAM ALLEN, the Recorder of the city, as their Grand Master. They met at that time at the "Tun Tavern;" and one of the oldest lodges in Philadelphia was formerly called *Tun Lodge,* in allusion to the place of its early meetings.

There is no known record of FRANKLIN'S being a member of the Fraternity previous to this; but in 1732 he was Senior Warden under WILLIAM ALLEN. In his own personal narrative he gives his written observations, in May, 1731, in which he says:

"There seems to me at present to be great occasion for raising a *United Party for Virtue,* by forming the virtuous and good men of all nations into a regular body, to be governed by suitable, good, and wise rules, which good and wise men may probably be more unanimous in their obedience to, than common people are to common laws. I at present think, that whoever attempts this aright, and is well qualified, cannot fail of pleasing God, and of meeting with success."

He has also left us a record of what he believed should be the fundamental principles of such a union or society, which he reduced to six heads—viz.:

"That there is one God, who made all things.

"That He governs the world by His providence.

"That He ought to be worshipped by adoration, prayer, and thanksgiving.

"But that the most acceptable service to God is doing good to man.

"That the soul is immortal.

"And that God will certainly reward virtue and punish vice, either here or hereafter."

It is a matter of curious speculation rather than of

certainty, whether FRANKLIN drew this epitome of the great moral governing principles of Freemasonry from his own reflections, or had been taught them in a lodge of the craft. If the former, he was certainly prepared *in his heart* to be a Mason: if the latter, he either believed that to be a Mason, required in addition to these, a greater attention to the arts and sciences than all good men were disposed to give; or he believed that an organization, semi-masonic, might be beneficial, in which the initiates might first be schooled in the moral principles of Masonry, before they were admitted to its mysteries; for he proposed at that time to form a secret club, to be called THE SOCIETY OF THE FREE AND EASY. This, he says, he communicated in part to two of his companions, who adopted it with some enthusiasm; but his multifarious public and private engagements so occupied his time, that it was postponed, and finally abandoned.

We pass over three years more of FRANKLIN's life, during which he was engaged as a printer and stationer —and in which he commenced the publication of his *Poor Richard's Almanac**—and find him receiving a written warrant from HENRY PRICE, Provincial Grand Master of Massachusetts, constituting him Master of the Lodge, and probably of all the Masons in Philadelphia. The exact date of this authority from PRICE cannot be given. Massachusetts authorities say it was June 24th, 1734, while Pennsylvania authorities say that on that day the brethren in Philadelphia celebra-

* This almanac was commenced in 1732, and continued until 1757. It was exceedingly popular, and he sold about ten thousand copies of it annually.

ted the festival of St. John the Baptist, under their old organization, and having accepted the authority of St. John's Grand Lodge at Boston, they ratified the choice of FRANKLIN as their Master (or *Grand Master*, as they chose to term him). This apparent discrepancy in the date of FRANKLIN's authority from PRICE, and his commencing his official duties under it in Philadelphia, both being given as the same day, probably arose from PRICE having granted to FRANKLIN a deputation previous to the 24th of June, and that at the festival which was held simultaneously in Boston and Philadelphia on that day, the act of PRICE was ratified by the Grand Lodge at Boston, and FRANKLIN's commission accepted by the brethren assembled in Philadelphia.

The Masonic Fraternity was not so novel at this time in Philadelphia, nor its members so obscure as to be unknown or unnoticed; for at the festival of St. John the Baptist, in 1734, when FRANKLIN's commission was accepted, and at the one which had been held on the same day the year before, the governor of the province, the mayor of the city, and many other distinguished citizens were present as members or guests. FRANKLIN on this occasion appointed JOHN CARP his Deputy, and JAMES HAMILTON and THOMAS HOPKINSON his Wardens. There is no doubt but that for some years previous to this the Masons in Philadelphia had been organized as a body, holding annually their festivals and electing their Grand Master without written authority from the ruling Grand Lodge of England or any of its dependencies, but by virtue of what had been deemed the immemorial right of Masons. Through

FRANKLIN they may have learned of the new regulations of the Order, and they perhaps instructed him to take such measures as would justify them before the world in the regularity of their organization. They had virtually existed as a Grand Lodge previous to FRANKLIN'S commission, and under it they no doubt exercised all the prerogatives, and assumed the dignity of a Grand Body. The claim, therefore, that FRANKLIN was the first Master, or the first Grand Master in Pennsylvania, can only mean that he was so by authority derived from the Grand Lodge at London, which had, in 1721, assumed authority over all lodges of Masons.

From the correspondence which took place between FRANKLIN and the Grand Master and the brethren in Boston, soon after he became connected with their authority, we give the following letters of his which have been preserved:

"RIGHT WORSHIPFUL GRAND MASTER, AND MOST WORTHY AND DEAR BRETHREN—We acknowledge your favor of the 23d of October past, and rejoice that the Grand Master (whom God bless) hath so happily recovered from his late indisposition, and we now (glass in hand) drink to the establishment of his health, and the prosperity of your whole Lodge.

"We have seen in the Boston prints an article of news from London, importing, that at a Grand Lodge held there in August last, Mr. PRICE'S deputation and power was extended over all America, which advice we hope is true, and we heartily congratulate him thereupon. And though this has not as yet been regularly signified to us by you, yet, giving credit thereto, we think it our duty to lay before your

Lodge what we apprehend needful to be done for us, in order to promote and strengthen the interests of Masonry in this province (which seems to want the sanction of some authority derived from home, to give the proceedings and determinations of our Lodge their due weight); to wit: a Deputation or Charter, granted by the Right Worshipful Mr. PRICE, by virtue of his commission from Britain, confirming the brethren of Pennsylvania in the privileges they at present enjoy, of holding annually their Grand Lodge, choosing their Grand Master, Wardens, and other officers who may manage all affairs relating to the brethren here, with full power and authority according to the customs and usages of Masons, the said Grand Master of Pennsylvania only yielding his chair when the Grand Master of all America shall be in place. This, if it seem good and reasonable to you to grant, will not only be extremely agreeable to us, but will also, we are confident, conduce much to the welfare, establishment, and reputation of Masonry in these parts. We therefore submit it to your consideration; and as we hope our request will be complied with, we desire that it may be done as soon as possible, and also accompanied with a copy of the Right Worshipful Grand Master's first Deputation, and of the instrument by which it appears to be enlarged, as above mentioned, witnessed by your Wardens, and signed by the secretary, for which favor this Lodge doubt not of being able to behave as not to be thought ungrateful.

"We are, Right Worshipful Grand Master, and Most Worthy Brethren, your affectionate brethren and obliged humble servants,

"B. FRANKLIN, G. M.

"Signed at the request of the Lodge.

"PHILADELPHIA, November 28, 1734."

FRANKLIN sent with this letter to the Grand Lodge of Massachusetts, the following private note to Mr. PRICE the Grand Master:

"DEAR BROTHER PRICE—I am heartily glad to hear of your recovery. I hoped to have seen you here this fall, agreeable to the expectation you were so good as to give me; but, since sickness has prevented your coming while the weather was moderate, I have no room to flatter myself with a visit from you before spring, when a deputation from the Brethren here will have an opportunity of showing how much they esteem you. I beg leave to recommend their request to you, and to inform you that some false and rebel brethren, who are foreigners, being about to set up a distinct Lodge, in opposition to the old and true brethren here, pretending to make Masons for a bowl of punch; and the Craft is like to come into disesteem among us, unless the true brethren are countenanced and distinguished by some such special authority as herein desired. I entreat, therefore, that whatever you shall think proper to do therein, may be sent by the next post, if possible, or the next following.

"I am your affectionate brother and humble servant,

"B. FRANKLIN, G. M. of Pennsylvania.

"P. S.—If more of the Constitutions are wanted among you, please hint it to me."

The *Constitutions* here alluded to, were a reprint of the English Constitutions of Masonry, which had been collated and published in London in 1723. An American edition of this work was printed by FRANKLIN in Philadelphia, in 1734, and it was the first Masonic book ever published in America. It was a small quarto volume, and a few copies still exist in antiquarian collections.*

FRANKLIN was at this time twenty-eight years of age; and while he diligently pursued his business as a printer and stationer, he also devoted his spare moments to the acquisition of useful knowledge. He was not a recluse, and he associated with him in his literary pursuits a few young men of studious habits and congenial tastes, who formed a club they called the *Junto.* The governing rules of this club have been incorporated into the Philosophical Society of Philadelphia; and the collection of books they formed, was the nucleus of the present magnificent library of that city.

In 1735, FRANKLIN was superseded in his position as Master, or Grand Master as it was termed, by JAMES HAMILTON his Senior Warden, who was elected in his stead. Freemasonry in Philadelphia, although it appears to have been popular at this time, was soon after under the ban of public suspicion there, and FRANKLIN's connection with it was much commented on by the public press of that city. It appears from the civil records and public journals of that day, that in 1737 a few thoughtless individuals attempted to impose on an ignorant young man and persuade him that by submitting to some ridiculous ceremonies he might become a Mason. He submitted to all they required, and was by them invested with sundry pretended Ma-

* It is worthy of note by the Masonic student, that the first *written* warrant granted in America by Provincial authority was to FRANKLIN; the first American Masonic book was printed by him; and the oldest American Masonic letters that have been preserved, were written by him.

sonic signs, and told he had taken the first degree. The principal perpetrators of the farce appear not to have been Masons, but they soon after communicated to FRANKLIN and others an account of their practical joke, and told him they might expect to be saluted with the signs they had given to the young man when they met him. FRANKLIN did not approve of their imposition, but laughed heartily at the ridiculous farce they had played, and thought no more of it. Not so with the active parties in it; for they determined to farther dupe the young man, and for this purpose induced him to take a second degree, in which they blindfolded and conducted him into a dark cellar, where one of the party was to exhibit himself to him disguised in a bull's hide, the head and horns of which were intended to represent the devil; while the others were to play a game they called *snap-dragon*, which consisted of picking raisins from a dish of burning fluid. When the bandage was taken from the young man's eyes, and he had gazed for a moment on the scene before him, one of the party thoughtlessly threw upon him the pan of burning fluid, which set fire to his clothes, and so burned him that he lingered for but three days and then died. This occurrence caused great excitement in Philadelphia, and the guilty parties were arrested and punished for manslaughter.

As it appeared at the judicial investigation, that FRANKLIN had been made acquainted with the first outrage on the young man after its perpetration, although he had no knowledge that a second attempt was to be made, and disapproved of the first, many ignorant or excited citizens, knowing his Masonic position, sought to cast odium on him and the Fraternity of which he was a leading member. A personal attack was also made on the character of FRANKLIN by a newspaper in Philadelphia, accusing him of conniving at the outrage. This was promptly denied by him, and the denial was verified by the oaths of those who were acquainted with the whole affair. The Grand Lodge also deemed it its duty to express its disapprobation of such proceedings, and the Grand Officers appeared before the authorities in Philadelphia and signed the following declaration :

" *Pennsylvania, ss.*—Whereas some ill-disposed persons in this city, assuming the names of Freemasons, have, for some years past, imposed upon several well-meaning people who were desirous of becoming true brethren, persuading them, after they had performed certain ridiculous ceremonies, that they had really become Freemasons ; and have lately, under the pretence of making a young man a Mason, caused his death by purging, vomiting, burning, and the terror of certain diabolical, horrid rites ; it is therefore thought proper, for preventing such impositions for the future, and to avoid any unjust aspersions that may be thrown on this ancient and honorable Fraternity on this account, either in this city or any other part of the world, to publish this advertisement declaring the abhorrence of all true brethren of such practices in general, and their ignorance of this fact in particular, and that the persons concerned in this wicked action are not of our society, nor of any society of Free and Accepted Masons, to our knowledge or belief.

"Signed in behalf of all the members of St. John's Lodge in Philadelphia, 10th day of June, 1737.

"Thos. Hopkinson, G. Master.
"Wm. Plumsted, D. G. Master.
"Jos. Shippen, } Wardens."
"Henry Pratt, }

The knowledge of the outrage that had been perpetrated in Philadelphia in the name of Freemasonry, and the attack on Franklin's character, soon came to his parents in Boston, and his mother, with true maternal feelings, induced his father to write to him on the subject, and make inquiries respecting the society which was then agitating the public mind. To these inquiries Franklin replied under date of April 13th, 1738:

"As to the Freemasons, I know of no way of giving my mother a better account of them than she seems to have at present; since it is not allowed that women should be admitted into that secret society. She has, I must confess, on that account, some reason to be displeased with it; but for any thing else, I must entreat her to suspend her judgment till she is better informed, unless she will believe me when I assure her, that they are in general a very harmless sort of people, and have no principles or practices that are inconsistent with religion and good manners."

Although the excitement had run so high in Philadelphia, that during the trial of those who had been engaged in duping the young man with pretended Masonic degrees, every Mason was challenged from the jury-box, yet FRANKLIN's popularity did not suffer. He was then postmaster of the city, and clerk of the Provincial Assembly, and he continued to hold these offices for many years. In 1747 he was elected a member of the Assembly, and held the office by re-election for ten years. In 1749 the old authority from HENRY PRICE to FRANKLIN in 1734 was superseded by a new warrant to him from THOMAS OXNARD, Provincial Grand Master of all North America, constituting him Provincial Grand Master of Pennsylvania, with power to charter new Lodges. On the 5th of September of this year, FRANKLIN accordingly convened the brethren by virtue of his new authority, and appointed Dr. THOMAS BOND Deputy Grand Master; JOSEPH SHIPPEN and PHILIP SYNG, Grand Wardens; WILLIAM PLUMSTED, Grand Treasurer; and DANIEL BYLES, Grand Secretary. The following year FRANKLIN was succeeded as Grand Master by WILLIAM ALLEN, the Recorder of the city of Philadelphia, who was commissioned direct by the Grand Master of England.

FRANKLIN at this time was deeply absorbed in philosophical investigations, and soon after was able to verify his belief that the lightnings and thunder of the summer cloud were but electrical phenomena. The story of his drawing down the lightning with his kite is well known; and the discovery he thereby made has rendered his name immortal in the annals of science. He was well known at this period as the friend and patron of popular education and every useful art. It was not apathy and indifference on the part of the community respecting education that he had to contend with alone; but there was an element in the population of Philadelphia and its vicinity that regarded all measures for the greater diffusion of knowledge, as dangerous innovations on the established customs of society. There still exists a correspondence between one CHRISTOPHER SOWRS, a German printer in Germantown, and CONRAD WEISER, in which the former complains bitterly of the efforts of FRANKLIN and the Freemasons generally to establish free-schools. He says:

"The people who are the promoters of the *free* schools, are *Grand Masters* and *Wardens* among the Freemasons, their very pillars."

The loss of old Masonic records makes it impossible to determine the lodge membership in Philadelphia at this time, but enough remains to show that it embraced the first men in the city.

At the middle of the last century, FRANKLIN had reached the meridian of his life, being forty-four years of age; but the sun of his fame was still in the ascendant, and from that period onward until it passed from our sight in a glowing west, its blaze seemed brighter and fuller. From the time when he was first seen a forlorn boy in the streets of Philadelphia, he had been steadily gaining strength of mind and public confidence, until his services were almost exclusively claimed by his fellow-citizens. In 1753 he was appointed deputy postmaster of all the British colonies in America, and the same year a commissioner to negotiate a treaty with the Indians. In 1754 he was a delegate to the Congress that met at Albany to devise means of defence against the French; and in this body his wisdom and sagacity were seen in the recommendation which he made of a Union of the colonies. He rendered important aid to the British commanders in the early part of the old French war, but was soon after sent to England as the agent of Pennsylvania and other colonies. There he was greatly caressed and distinguished, and found his situation widely different from what it was when he entered London a few years before, a poor journeyman printer: for now he was admitted into the presence of kings; and the Universities of Edinburg and Oxford conferred on him the degree of Doctor of Laws as a mark of their appreciation of his scientific attainments. This literary degree was not the first he had received; for the college at Cambridge, in Massachusetts, had before conferred on him the degree of Master of Arts. He also, while in London, visited the Grand Lodge of England; and its records show that he was honored with the rank of Provincial Grand Master on his visit to that body.

He returned to America in 1762, and resumed his seat in the Provincial Assembly of Pennsylvania, but two years afterwards he was sent again as their agent to England. He remained there until 1775. It was during this period that the disputes between the colonies and the mother country assumed their utmost seriousness, and his task was a difficult and delicate one; but so faithfully did he perform it, that on his return, he was elected a delegate from Pennsylvania to the Continental Congress, and the following year had the honor of signing the Declaration of Independence. During the whole period of the Revolution he was continually active in some civil capacity, either at home or abroad. Congress sent him in 1776 a commissioner to the court of France, and no diplomatist at Versailles was able to perform his duties with greater ability. He was well known in France at that time for his varied scientific attainments, and his plain republican manners rendered him a dignitary of a new light.

His residence was continued in France until 1785, and during this time he held intimate Masonic intercourse with the Masons of that country, and became affiliated, either as a special or honorary member, with the Grand Orient of France. He was also presented by his French brethren with a medal, of which the following description is given:

> "Diameter one inch and three-fifths. Obverse—Fine bust of FRANKLIN. Legend—'BENJAMINIS FRANKLIN.' Reverse—Masonic emblems, the serpent's ring, carpenter's square and compass; in the centre a triangle and the sacred Name in Hebrew, &c. Legend—Leo. Mac. Fran. a Franklin. M: de la L— des 9 Soeurs O. de Paris, 5778."

When in 1785 he had fulfilled all the public duties which his country required of him in Europe, and was about to return to America, his Masonic brethren in France bade him a tender adieu, particularly the lodge at Rouen. When he arrived in Philadelphia he was received by his fellow-citizens with public testimonials of their gratitude and respect, and was soon afterwards elected to the chief executive office in Pennsylvania. He was then in his eightieth year, and might well have claimed a rest from his public labors; but he still continued for three years to give all his strength of body and mind to secure the fabric of liberty he had helped to erect. For this purpose, in

1787 he permitted himself to be elected a member of the convention that framed the Federal Constitution, and his master hand gave to that instrument many of its provisions.

FRANKLIN's official life closed in 1788, for his great age and infirmities rendered him unable to longer serve his country in a public capacity; but amid much suffering he survived for two more years, and died at Philadelphia on the 17th of April, 1790, in the eighty-fifth year of his age. He was buried on the 21st, in Christ Church yard in that city, and more than twenty thousand persons, it was said, attended the funeral. The highest dignitaries of the State were present on the occasion, and both the State and National Government decreed that badges should be worn in token of the loss all had sustained in the death of so great a man. It has been asked why so distinguished a Mason as FRANKLIN was not interred with Masonic rites. The reader will remember that his Masonic connection in Philadelphia had been with the so-called Moderns, whose organization there had been superseded, during the absence of FRANKLIN in Europe, by another denomination of Masons, called Ancients; and at his death, the Grand Lodge of which he had been the Grand Master was extinct. His name, however, and his virtues, have ever been kept in high veneration by Masons throughout the world, and with that of WASHINGTON are household words wherever the Craft is found.

WILLIAM FRANKLIN,

THE LAST OF THE ROYAL GOVERNORS OF NEW JERSEY, AND GRAND SECRETARY OF THE PROVINCIAL GRAND LODGE OF PENNSYLVANIA.

WILLIAM FRANKLIN, the last colonial governor of New Jersey, was born at Philadelphia in 1731. He was the son of Dr. BENJAMIN FRANKLIN, the most eminent statesman, philosopher, and Mason of Pennsylvania, of the last century. WILLIAM was his first-born and only son, and his father doubtless reared him with paternal care, and felt a strong desire to see him win for himself distinction.

Of his youth but little is now known. He is said to have inherited from his father an early fondness for books, but no accounts of remarkable attainments in literature have been handed down to us. His father says of him, in 1750: "WILL. is now nineteen years of age—a tall, proper youth, and much of a beau." He had a desire, in his youth, to connect himself with a privateer that was fitting out in Philadelphia; but in this he was opposed by his father, who soon after obtained for him a situation in the provincial troops, in one of their campaigns to the northern frontier, and in it he rose to the rank of a captain.

On his return, his father's social and political position was such as to secure for him the appointment of clerk in the Colonial Assembly and postmaster of the city of Philadelphia. He had now come to years of manhood, and was his father's companion and assistant in his scientific pursuits. He also became a Mason about this time in the old Lodge in Philadelphia, and was soon after elected its Master. In 1754 he was one of the Trustees in behalf of the Fraternity to hold the title to the lot and building in that city which was used for Masonic purposes. This was located on the lot since occupied by the Pennsylvania Bank; and from the circumstance of the Masons' Hall having been there, the alley retains the name of Lodge Alley to the present time.

The Masonic Fraternity in Philadelphia at that time were in a prosperous condition; and the banqueting-room of the hall they had erected was of great service to the citizens, aside from its Masonic purposes. Public meetings were often held in it, and the belles and beaux of the city frequently met there for balls and other amusements. There were three Lodges at that time in Philadelphia, presided over by WILLIAM ALLEN, the Recorder of the city and chief-justice of the province, as Grand Master. On the completion of their Hall, they determined to celebrate the Feast of St. John the Baptist, in 1755, with great pomp and display.

They accordingly assembled on that day in their new Hall on Lodge Alley, and clothed themselves for a public procession. There were no doubt quaint looks cast by some of the old inhabitants of the Quaker City, as this assembly of the Brethren gravely passed through their streets, with their singular dress, emblems, and implements. The number of the Brethren present has been given us by the chroniclers of those times as one hundred and twenty-seven. There were wealth and dignity in the procession; for the governor of the province and the governor of New Providence were in it as Masons, as well as many officers of the city government. These, with their cocked hats, must have contrasted strongly with the broad brims and plain coats of some backsliding Quaker Masons who were also in the line. In the usual assemblages in Philadelphia, the Quaker element generally had the preponderance; but cocked hats, royal wigs, velvet breeches, embroidered coats, silver and gold knee and shoe buckles, were evidences of the social position of a majority of the members that day.

To make the procession more imposing, it was followed by the *empty* carriages of the Grand Master, of the governor, and other distinguished Brethren—their owners being in the line as Masons. There was also a band of music in attendance, which belonged to a British regiment then stationed in the city. It was a great novelty at that day to see such a gorgeous parade of Masons; and as they passed up Second-street, on their way to the church, when opposite Market, a salute from some cannon in a vessel on the river must have awakened from his reveries the drowsiest Quaker in the city. At the church, Dr. JENNEY, the rector of Christ Church, offered prayers, and the Rev. Brother Dr. WILLIAM SMITH, the provost of the college, preached a sermon from the text, "Love the Brotherhood, fear God, and honor the king." It was a goodly custom of our Brethren of that day to thus repair to the church to testify their respect for religion and enjoy its teachings. WASHINGTON in after-years often did the same, and with his Masonic brethren publicly bent the knee at the religious altars of our country, clothed in his Masonic costume.

After the services of the church were closed, the procession was re-formed, and returned to the Lodge-room. As it passed through the streets, the cannon again fired their salute, and the populace again gazed on the drawn swords of the Tylers and the strange badges and mystic implements of the Fraternity, as, with measured steps to the band's playing the tune of the "Entered Apprentice Song," they marched to their Hall. It was befitting the occasion that the ceremonies should be crowned with a feast; and accordingly, at one o'clock, they repaired to their banqueting room. Merry things were there said, and entertaining songs sung; for such were the Masonic customs of those good old days. There were pledges, too, of lasting friendship drank, and friendly interchanges of sentiment made, between cocked hats and broad brims, while seated there. The regular toasts on the occasion were:

"1st. The King and the Craft.

"2d. The Grand Master of England.

"3d. Our Brother FRANCIS, Emperor of Germany.

"4th. The Grand Master of Pennsylvania.

"5th. Our Brother, his Honor the Governor of Pennsylvania.

"6th. Our Brother, his Excellency JOHN TINKER, Esq., Governor of Providence, returning him thanks for his kind visit.

"7th. The Grand Master of Scotland.

"8th. The Grand Master of Ireland.

"9th. The several Provincial Grand Masters of North America and the West India Islands.

"10th. All charitable Masons.

"11th. All true and faithful Masons, wheresoever dispersed or distressed, throughout the globe.

"12th. The Arts and Sciences.

"13th. General BRADDOCK, and success to his Majesty's forces.

"14th. Prosperity to Pennsylvania, and a happy union of his Majesty's colonies."

The ceremonies of the day closed at five o'clock in

the afternoon, and the Fraternity returned to their homes, no doubt well pleased with the inauguration of their new Hall. From the position held in the Fraternity at that time by WILLIAM FRANKLIN, he was doubtless present on the occasion, and one of the participants in the ceremonies. During the same year he accompanied his father, with some troops under his command, to build some forts on the frontiers of Pennsylvania.

In 1757, his father was appointed by the colony its agent in London, and he sailed with him for England. He seems to have made a pleasing impression upon his new acquaintances in London; for one of them, Mr. STRAHAN, who was a man of talent and discernment, and a friend of his father's, thus wrote to his mother soon after his arrival in England:

"Your son I really think one of the prettiest young gentlemen I ever knew from America. He seems to me to have a solidity of judgment not very often to be met with in one of his years. This, with the daily opportunity he has of improving himself in the company of his father—who is at the same time his friend, his *brother*, his intimate and easy companion—affords an agreeable prospect that your husband's virtues and usefulness to his country may be prolonged beyond the date of his own life."

While in England young FRANKLIN studied law in the Middle Temple, and was admitted to the bar. Both father and son were treated with much distinction by those of the highest rank in civil and social life. The flame of Dr. FRANKLIN's genius as a philosopher had cast its light across the Atlantic; and his fame as a statesman was even then being built by the wise counsels he gave to the ministerial powers concerning the government of their colonial dependencies. Both father and son, too, were treated with marked distinction by the Masonic Fraternity in England, and on visiting the Grand Lodge in London in November, 1760, both were honored according to their rank in Pennsylvania, —the Doctor as Provincial Grand Master, and WILLIAM as Grand Secretary,—an office which he had held in the Grand Lodge at Philadelphia; and their names as visitors stand duly recorded as such on the Grand Lodge records in London. He also travelled with his father through England, Scotland, Flanders, and Holland, and enjoyed the literary and scientific society that sought in all places intercourse with the distinguished philosopher from the new world. He seems, too, to have profited by such advantages; for when the University at Oxford conferred on his father in 1762 the degree of Doctor of Laws, it also thought the son worthy of that of Master of Arts, and consequently conferred it upon him. During the same year, after undergoing a close examination by Lord HALIFAX, the minister of American affairs, more close perhaps on account of his colonial birth and youth, he was appointed by the king his representative as royal governor of New Jersey. It was an honor rarely, if ever, before conferred on a native-born American, and more complimentary from its having been conferred without any request from his father. He also married about this time a Miss ELIZABETH DOWNS, and brought her with him to America, where he arrived in February, 1763.

Governor FRANKLIN was at that time thirty-two years

of age. No native-born citizen in America held a better position. Of WASHINGTON he was about one year the senior; had served like him in the provincial wars, and like him had enrolled himself with the Masonic brotherhood as soon as he came to manhood. But the similitude did not extend farther. WASHINGTON had been from his boyhood an orphan—a *widow's son;* while WILLIAM FRANKLIN had grown under his father's shadow. WASHINGTON had retired from the army to his farm on the return of peace; while FRANKLIN had gained the smiles of royalty in London, and had borne back to America a commission as royal governor of New Jersey, and was honored as the representative of his sovereign in that province.

Governor FRANKLIN reached Philadelphia on the 19th of February, 1763, and he started for Perth Amboy, in New Jersey, on the 24th, and arrived there at the end of the second day. It was midwinter, and he was escorted to the seat of the colonial government by a troop of horse, and by the citizens in sleighs, and there received by the former governor and the members of his council. The weather was intensely cold; but a chronicler of that day says, he was inducted into his office "with as much decency and good decorum as the severity of the season could possibly admit of." A day or two afterwards he went to Burlington from Amboy, and published his commission there also, according to the custom of the province, these having been the early seats of government in East and West Jersey.

It had been the custom of the royal governors to reside at Amboy, but FRANKLIN fixed his residence in Burlington—perhaps from its being nearer Philadelphia, the residence of his friends. He resided in this West Jersey capital until 1774, a period of eleven years, when he removed to the old East Jersey seat of colonial government at Amboy. On his leaving Burlington, the corporation of that city gave him a public entertainment, and presented him a farewell address, expressing their regard for him, regretting his departure, and thanking him for his courtesy and kind deportment during his residence with them.

Governor FRANKLIN was at this time popular with the people of New Jersey; but the vexatious measures of the British ministry began to excite that abhorrence in all the colonies, which soon led to their separation from the mother government. In his administration FRANKLIN appears to have been mild and conciliatory with the people, yet firm in his maintenance of the royal right of the king to govern his colonies. Dr. FRANKLIN was then in England as the colonial agent, and he wrote to his son endeavoring to persuade him to take the American side of the controversy, and withdraw from his advocacy of the royal cause. He also visited Amboy on his return to America in 1775 to urge him to unite his fortunes with the patriot cause; but Governor FRANKLIN was firm, and each failed to convince the other of the impropriety of his course. Their conversations were perhaps too warm for continued harmonious intercourse, and both father and son became so alienated in their feelings, that when they separated, it was not to meet again till the impending American conflict was over, and the last royal governor of New Jersey was a fugitive from his people, and a pensioner in a foreign land.

It is curious, sometimes, to take a retrospect of the past, and retrace the pathway of individuals on the ground-floor of human life. Half a century before, Dr. FRANKLIN, then a poor unknown boy in search of a place where he might earn his daily bread, had passed a lonely and feverish night in the same ancient city. He had left it on foot to pursue his journey through a province where he was to all a friendless stranger, and subjected to injurious suspicions of vagrancy. Now, again, he had come from his sojourn in a foreign land, where he had been honored by the most distinguished statesmen and men of science as a luminary of the age, to confer with his son, who was the royal representative in the very land where, when a boy, his own footsore pathway had been taken.

The tide of popular sentiment in New Jersey was now fast setting in the channel of Liberty; and although no open resistance was at first made to Governor FRANKLIN'S authority, yet when he refused to call the Colonial Assembly together to appoint delegates to the Continental Congress in Philadelphia in 1774, the people of the colony met by convention and chose representatives themselves to that body. In November of 1775 he convened the old Colonial Assembly for the last time; and although he prorogued it on the 6th of December, to meet again on the 3d of January, 1776, it never reassembled; but an independent legislature met a few months later, and resolved that the authority of Governor FRANKLIN should no longer be obeyed, and as he had showed himself an enemy to his country, his person should be secured. This was accordingly done, and under an order from the Continental Congress at Philadelphia, the deposed governor was, about midsummer in 1776, sent under guard to Governor TRUMBULL in Connecticut, by whom he was kept a prisoner until 1778, when he was exchanged for an American officer (Brigadier-General THOMPSON) then in possession of the British, and FRANKLIN sought protection under the wing of the British army in the city of New York.

When he left New Jersey a prisoner in 1776, his wife remained in Amboy, and he never saw her more. She was allowed to seek British protection in New York, where she died on the 28th of July, 1778, while he was yet in Connecticut. He loved her tenderly; and ten years later, when the war was over, he caused a tablet to be placed to her memory in the chancel of St. Paul's Church in New York where she was buried, with a mournfully elegant inscription, which closed by saying that it was erected " by him who knew her worth, and still laments her loss."

Governor FRANKLIN remained in New York nearly four years, where he was the president of a band of associated loyalists who were the most virulent enemies of all Americans who took part against the British authority; but in August, 1782, he sailed for England, and never more visited his native land. He received from the British government eighteen hundred pounds in consideration of his personal losses in support of the crown, and an annual pension of eight hundred pounds for life. After leaving America he married again; the lady being a native of Ireland. He had one son, WM. TEMPLE FRANKLIN, and died November 17, 1813, aged eighty-two years.

During the whole of the Revolutionary War there was no intercourse between Dr. FRANKLIN and his son, and their mutual estrangement continued long afterwards, and probably was never forgotten; for the Doctor left him but a small part of his estate, saying in his will:

"The part he acted against me in the late war, which is of public notoriety, will account for my leaving him no more of an estate he endeavored to deprive me of."

He had, however, called upon his son in England on his return from France in 1785, and some correspondence took place between them after the war. But the Doctor seems to have still regarded him not only as an alien to his country, but to himself; for in a letter written to the Rev. Dr. BYLES, of Boston, January 1, 1788, he thus speaks of him, after adverting to his daughter, who continued with him in Philadelphia:

"My son is estranged from me by the part he took in the late war, and keeps aloof, residing in England, whose cause he *espoused*, whereby the old proverb is exemplified:

"'My son is my son till he gets him a wife,
But my daughter is my daughter all the days of her life.'"

David Wooster

GENERAL DAVID WOOSTER,

AN OFFICER OF THE REVOLUTION, AND MASTER OF THE FIRST LODGE IN CONNECTICUT.

General David Wooster, whose name is familiar to every American citizen as a martyr to liberty in the war of the Revolution, was born in Stratford, Connecticut, March 2, 1710–11 (old style), and was the youngest of six children. He was educated in the Puritan principles of New England, and after he came to manhood entered Yale College, where he graduated in 1738, in the twenty-eighth year of his age.

In 1741 the first war-vessel of Connecticut was fitted out at Middletown, to guard the coasts of New England against the Spanish and other hostile vessels that were preying upon the infant commerce of the colonies, and DAVID WOOSTER was its first-lieutenant, and the following year its captain. His service in the first naval office in Connecticut was not of long continuance; for soon after, war commenced between France and England, and in 1745 he went as captain of a company of Connecticut militia, under Colonel PEPPERELL, in the New England expedition against Louisburg.

He had previously settled in New Haven, where he married a Miss MARY CLAP, the daughter of President CLAP of Yale College, and in a quiet home he had purchased, was enjoying his honeymoon when called to go on this Louisburg expedition. The spirit of New England, at this period, had in it as much religious fanaticism as patriotic regard for justice and national honor, and military ardor was much warmed by sectarian zeal in this expedition. Banners were borne with religious mottoes, and a hatchet, which had been consecrated for the occasion, was carried on a Chaplain's shoulder to hew down the images in the Papal churches of the devoted city against which the expedition was undertaken. The incidents of the expedition are well known in history, and give a romance to many of its pages. One of them is connected with the name of Captain WOOSTER, which serves well to illustrate the spirit of the times, and shows with what care he watched the well-being of those under his command. A British captain had ventured to strike with his rattan one of WOOSTER'S men, who was *a freeholder and a church member.* WOOSTER was indignant that a soldier of such claims to consideration should receive a blow, and remonstrated with the British officer for thus abusing his man. The foreign captain resented his interference, and drew his sword upon him. But he at once disarmed him, and compelled him to ask pardon of the Connecticut soldier, and promise never again to disgrace with a blow a soldier in the service. This act endeared Captain WOOSTER to his men, and gained him the applause of the provincial army.

At the close of this expedition he was sent in charge of a cartel ship to France, but was not permitted to land in that kingdom, and went with his ship to London. He was received there with marked distinction, and honored with a captain's commission in the regular service. He returned soon afterwards to America, and at this period our earliest records of his Masonic life commence. It is probable that he was made a Mason while in England. Lord CRANSTON was at that time Grand Master in England, and upon the acquisition of Louisburg by the British crown, he granted a Deputation to Captain CUMMINS to establish a Provincial Grand Lodge there.

Soon after Captain WOOSTER returned to New Haven he received a warrant from THOMAS OXNARD, Provincial Grand Master of Massachusetts, to establish a Lodge in that city. It bore date November 12, 1750. It was the first Warranted Lodge in Connecticut, and the seventh in New England; four having previously been organized in Boston, one in Portsmouth, New Hampshire, and one in Newport, Rhode Island. A warrant was also granted for a Lodge in Annapolis, Maryland, by THOMAS OXNARD, about the same date as that in New Haven. The Lodge organized by DAVID WOOSTER had at first but six members—viz.: DAVID WOOSTER, Master; SAMUEL MANSFIELD and JOHN ELIOT, Wardens; and NATHAN WHITING, ELIHU LYMAN, and JEHIEL TUTTLE, members. Its first meeting was in December, 1750. The Lodge was called Hiram Lodge, and still exists by that name as Lodge No. 1 of Connecticut.

The hollow peace between France and England was of short duration, and in 1756 WOOSTER was again called to take the command of Connecticut militia, with the rank of colonel. This contest is known in history as the old French and Indian war, and he served each year in its campaigns, from 1756 to 1760, and rose to the rank of a brigadier-general. On retiring again from military service, he returned to New Haven as a half-pay officer of the regular British army, and was appointed revenue collector of the port of his city. He also engaged successfully in mercantile pursuits, and led a life of domestic felicity.

Again the war of the Revolution found him as ready to draw his sword in defence of the colonies against the usurpations of England, as he had been to repel the invasions of Spain or France. His commission and his half-pay in the British army were at once relinquished, his collectorship of the port resigned, and when the troops of the colony were organized, he was invested with their command, with his former rank as brigadier-general. It is related of him that when his regiment was prepared to leave New Haven for the headquarters of the army, he marched it to the church-yard green, where his men stood in their ranks with their knapsacks on their backs, and their muskets in their hands, while he sent for his pastor, the Rev. JONATHAN EDWARDS, to come and pray with them, and give them a parting blessing. He then conducted his men into the church to await his pastor's coming. He was absent from home, and when this became known to General WOOSTER, he stepped into the deacon's seat in front of the pulpit, and calling on his men to join him in prayer, led their devotions with the fervent zeal of an apostle. So pathetically and so eloquently did he plead for his beloved country, for himself and the men under his command, and for the families they left behind them, that it affected all, and drew tears from many eyes. How true to the first sublime lesson in Masonry, which teaches us at the commencement of all laudable undertakings to implore the aid and blessing of God, was his act on this occasion!

The first military service of General WOOSTER during the Revolution, was in guarding New York. In the spring of 1776, he was sent in the expedition to Canada; and during the following winter and spring he was in command in his own State, guarding it from the attacks of the British, who lay at New York. When, in April of 1777, Governor TRYON made an incursion on Danbury, he led a body of militia in an attack on the invaders at Ridgefield, and fell mortally wounded at the head of his forces, on the 27th of that month. His wound was by a musket-ball in his spine, and he was borne to Danbury, where he expired on the 2d of May, at the age of sixty-seven years, and was interred in the public burial-ground of that town. Upon learning of his death, Congress voted that a monument should be erected to his memory, but it was not done, and for nearly fourscore years no permanent memorial marked his grave. The legislature of his native State, in whose defence he died, however, resolved to perform this long neglected duty, in which they were joined by the Grand Lodge of Connecticut, and the corner-stone of a befitting monument over his grave was laid by the Grand Master of the State, on the 27th of April, 1854, according to the ancient ceremonies of the Fraternity. Among the deposits under this stone was the identical bullet by which General WOOSTER was slain. Above this stone, a monument, beautifully wrought with civic and Masonic emblems and inscriptions, now rises. It was well thus to mark his grave; but his deeds are his true monument,—lasting as the granite hills of New England, from which the craftsmen wrought the towering shaft that rises over his dust.

THOMAS WOOSTER, the only son of General WOOSTER, was also a Mason. He was initiated in Hiram Lodge, April 14, 1777, a few days previous to his father's death. He was then about twenty-five years of age. Before the close of the Revolutionary War, the Masonic brethren in Colchester, Connecticut, obtained a warrant from the Massachusetts Grand Lodge for a Lodge in that town, which they denominated Wooster Lodge. It bore date January 12, 1781. A second Lodge, bearing that name, was also chartered by the Grand Lodge of Connecticut, a few years ago, in New Haven. The names of WARREN, MONTGOMERY, and WOOSTER became a standing Masonic toast during the war, commemorative of their virtues as patriot Masons, who fell early in their country's defence.

PIERPONT EDWARDS,

THE FIRST GRAND MASTER OF CONNECTICUT.

PIERPONT EDWARDS, the first Grand Master of Masons in Connecticut, was born in Northampton, Massachusetts, in 1750. His father was the Rev. JONATHAN EDWARDS, who afterwards became president of the college in Princeton, New Jersey, and his mother was a daughter of the Rev. JAMES PIERPONT of New Haven. The memory of both has been preserved for their piety and talents. A few weeks after the birth of their son PIERPONT, who is the subject of this sketch, Mr. EDWARDS was dismissed from his pastoral charge of the church in Northampton, and soon after removed to Stockbridge, in the same State, as a missionary to the Stockbridge Indians. He remained there for six years; and the only school in the vicinity was composed of both Indian children and those of white parentage. The constant association of these young urchins together in their studies and their sports, rendered many of them equally fluent in the native language of each other. The elder brother of PIERPONT, who was six years his senior, was said by the natives to "speak as plain as an Indian." Surrounded by such circumstances, young PIERPONT learned to lisp his early wants as readily in Indian as in his mother tongue, but we know not whether he retained a knowledge of that dialect when he came to manhood. His brother afterwards went to reside with one of the Western tribes in New York, to improve in his knowledge of their language and customs, with a view on his father's part of his becoming a missionary among them when of suitable age. He, however, chose a different field of usefulness for himself, and became afterwards president of Union College in Schenectady.

When PIERPONT was about six years of age, his father left his residence in Stockbridge and removed to Princeton, New Jersey, where he had been elected president of the college. His labors there, however, were short, for in less than a year he died; and his amiable widow's death soon followed, and the future Grand Master of Connecticut was left a full orphan before he was eight years old. Though thus early bereft of his parents, he received the fostering care of kind friends; was educated, we believe, at Yale, and settled in New Haven as an attorney at law. In that city, at the age of twenty-five years, he was made a Mason in old Hiram Lodge. His initiation was on the 28th day of December, 1775. It was the oldest Lodge in the State, and he was subsequently elected its Master.

About the close of the Revolution in 1783, thirteen of the old Lodges in Connecticut met in Convention in New Haven to establish some general regulations for the good of Masonry in that State, and of this Convention PIERPONT EDWARDS was a member from Hiram Lodge in that city, and was appointed Secretary of the body. He was also chosen by it as one of a committee of four to act as general guardians of Masonry in that State. All the Lodges in Connecticut at this time were held under authority that had been granted by pre-revolutionary Provincial Grand Masters on this continent, and as their authority was now at an end, the Lodges in the State met again in convention by delegates in Hartford on the 14th of May, 1789, to consider the propriety of forming a Grand Lodge for that jurisdiction.

PIERPONT EDWARDS was a delegate also to this Convention, and was appointed chairman of a committee to prepare a plan for forming a Grand Lodge, to submit to a convention of delegates to be held at New Haven on the 8th of July following. When the Convention met, Mr. EDWARDS presented the plan he had formed for a Grand Lodge, together with a constitution for its government, which were adopted; and upon a ballot being taken for its Grand Master, he was elected to that office, and held it for two successive years, when he was succeeded by WILLIAM JUDD.

Mr. EDWARDS was distinguished in civil as well as Masonic life. He was a member of Congress under the old confederation, but of the particulars of his public history we have not the records before us. He died on the 14th of April, 1826, at the age of seventy-six years. His son, HENRY W. EDWARDS, who afterwards became governor of that State, was also a Mason, having been initiated in Hiram Lodge, February 2, 1809. He was also a member of Franklin Royal Arch Chapter in New Haven, having been exalted June 14, 1810. On the 16th of October, 1818, Governor EDWARDS also became a member of Harmony Council of Royal and Select Masters in that city.

JABEZ BOWEN, LL.D.,

LIEUTENANT-GOVERNOR OF RHODE ISLAND, AND GRAND MASTER OF MASONS IN THAT STATE.

JABEZ BOWEN was born in Providence, Rhode Island, about the year 1740. Of his youth and parentage we have no account. He graduated at Yale College in 1757, while yet in his minority, and afterwards became chancellor of the college in Providence as the successor of Governor HOPKINS. He held the chancellorship for thirty years. During the Revolutionary War he was devoted to the cause of his country, was a member of the Board of War, judge of the Supreme Court, and lieutenant-governor of his State. He was also a member of the State convention to take into consideration the constitution of the General Government when it was formed. During the administration of WASHINGTON, after Rhode Island had accepted of the constitution, he was the Commissioner of loans for his State. With a great capacity for public business, and of unquestionable integrity, he gained an elevated character and great influence in society.

Governor BOWEN was a Mason, and rose to the highest rank in the Fraternity. We are unable to give the date of his initiation, but in 1762 he was the Junior Warden of St. John's Lodge in Providence. He also held the same office from 1765 to 1769, when the labors of his Lodge were for a few years suspended. St. John's Lodge had been organized in 1757, and at the close of 1769 it had so declined that at its meetings no more than eight were usually present.

> "Thus discouraged, without numbers, without funds, and without accommodations, they closed the Lodge, shut up the books, and sealed up their jewels."

JABEZ BOWEN was at this time its Junior Warden. We may imagine the Genius of Masonry weeping over that deserted Lodge, and saying, as she departed—

> "Those walls are tott'ring to decay;
> There's dampness on the stair;
> But well I mind me of the day,
> When twoscore men met there—
> When twoscore brothers met at night,
> The full round moon above,
> To weave the mystic chain of light,
> With holy links of love."

Upon the 15th of July, 1778, JABEZ BOWEN received a commission from JOHN ROWE, Provincial Grand Master of Massachusetts, to reopen this Lodge and act as its Master. It was during the midst of the Revolutionary War, and they met by permission of the State authorities in the council-chamber. The genius of Masonry returned; the Lodge was reorganized under its new Master, and upon St. John the Evangelist's day, in December of that year, held a public celebration which was largely attended by brethren of the army who were stationed in that State. The address on the occasion was delivered by General VARNUM. It was the first Masonic celebration ever held in Providence, and seventy-one members of the Fraternity were present.

JABEZ BOWEN continued to preside over St. John's Lodge as Master until the close of 1790, a period of nearly thirteen years. In 1791 a Grand Lodge was formed in Rhode Island, and he was elected its first Deputy Grand Master. He continued to hold this office for three years, and in 1794 was elected Grand Master. He held this office until the close of 1798.

The official labors of Mr. BOWEN in Masonry covered a period of twenty years after the revival of his Lodge, and during the same time he was constantly engaged in public employments. In the religious improvement of society he also took a deep interest. He was a member of the Congregational church in Providence, and president of the Bible Society of Rhode Island. He lived a life of usefulness, and died lamented, on the 7th day of May, 1815, at the age of seventy-five years.

COLONEL WILLIAM BARTON,

THE RHODE ISLAND MASON WHO CAPTURED THE BRITISH GENERAL PRESCOTT.

AMONG the names of Masonic brethren which the revolutionary annals of our country introduce on the pages of history, and distinguished by one bold act, stands that of Colonel WILLIAM BARTON, who successfully planned and effected the capture of the British General PRESCOTT. He was born in Providence, Rhode Island, in 1750; but of his parentage and early life we have no account. He took up arms in defence of his colony soon after the Revolution commenced, and in 1777 we find him holding a commission as lieutenant-colonel in the Rhode Island troops, and active in defending his State against the British forces under General PRESCOTT.

PRESCOTT was an arrogant and tyrannical officer, and he made himself particularly obnoxious to the citizens of Rhode Island; for his persecutions extended not only to prisoners taken in war, but to private unarmed citizens, and even women and children. All classes were alike made objects of his cruelty. His headquarters were at the house of a Quaker by the name of OVERTON, about five miles from Newport. Incensed at the daily reports of his tyranny and insolence to citizens, Colonel BARTON determined, if possible, to effect his capture. For this purpose he engaged a few trusty men, and on a sultry night in July of 1777, he embarked with them in whaleboats, and crossed Narraganset Bay from Warwick Point, passing through the British fleet, and landing in a sheltered cove near PRESCOTT's headquarters.

In the darkness of that night, they had passed the guard-boats of the British with muffled oars, and had heard the sentinel's cry of "All's well," without being discovered. Colonel BARTON now divided his comrades into two bands, and approached the house where the British commander slept. As they came to the gate, a sentinel hailed them and demanded the countersign. "We have no countersign to give," boldly replied Colonel BARTON. "Have you seen any deserters here to-night?" continued he in the same cool and collected voice. Deceived by their manner, the sentinel supposed them friends; nor did he suspect the truth, until his musket was seized and he was secured and threatened with instant death if he made any noise.

Colonel BARTON then entered the house boldly, and found the Quaker host reading, while all the other inmates were in bed. He inquired for General PRESCOTT's room, and the Quaker pointed him to the chamber. With five men he then ascended the stairs, and tried the general's door; but it was locked. No time was to be lost, and a negro who was in the party, drew back a few steps, and with a blow like a battering-ram, burst the door in with his head. PRESCOTT supposed he was in the hands of robbers, and seized his gold watch to secure it; but Colonel BARTON quickly undeceived him by telling him he was his prisoner, and that his safety lay only in his perfect silence. He begged time to dress; but as it was a hot July night, his captors compelled him to delay his toilet until they could afford him more time; and he was taken in his night-clothes to their boat, and safely conveyed to Warwick Point, undiscovered by the sentinels of the fleet. The captive was kept silent during this midnight boat-ride, by a pistol at each ear; and when he landed, he first broke the silence by saying:

"Sir, you have made a bold push to-night."

"We have been fortunate," coolly replied Colonel BARTON.

General PRESCOTT was conveyed that night in a coach to Providence, and was subsequently sent to WASHINGTON's headquarters in New Jersey. On his way there he stopped with his escort to dine at the tavern of Captain ALDEN, in Lebanon, Connecticut. The landlady set before them a bowl of *succotash*, a well-known Yankee dish composed of corn and beans. The haughty British captive supposed it an intentional insult, and indignantly exclaimed, "What! do you feed me with the food of hogs?" at the same time strewing the contents of the dish upon the floor. Captain ALDEN was soon informed of the outrage, and at once gave the British general a horsewhipping. PRESCOTT, for the second time a captive, was exchanged for General LEE, and returned to his command in Rhode Island; but that he did not soon forget his castigation by the Connecticut landlord, is seen by his afterwards excusing himself for some discourtesy to an American gentleman, by saying: "He looked so much like a d—d Connecticut man that horsewhipped me, that I could not endure his presence."

Colonel BARTON was rewarded for his gallant services in capturing General PRESCOTT, by a vote of thanks from Congress, accompanied by an elegant sword; and also by a grant of land in Vermont. He was also promoted to the rank and pay of colonel in the Continental army. He did not, however, long remain in active service; for in an action at Butt's Hill, near Bristol Ferry, in August of 1778, he was so badly wounded as to be disabled for the remainder of the war.

In 1779, Colonel BARTON was made a Mason in St. John's Lodge in Providence, Rhode Island. Of his subsequent Masonic history we have no record.

The lands Congress gave him in Vermont, proved in after-years an unfortunate gift; for in some transaction growing out of the sale of them, he became entangled in the meshes of the law, and under the code of that State, he was imprisoned in his old age for many years in the debtor's cell.

When General La Fayette visited this country in 1825, hearing of the imprisonment of the revolutionary veteran and its cause, he paid the claim and restored his venerable fellow-soldier and Masonic brother to liberty. Though kindly intended, it was a national rebuke, as well as a rebuke to the "Shylock who held the patriot in bondage, and clamored for *the pound of flesh.*" It was this circumstance which drew from the poet Whittier his touching lines on *The Prisoner for Debt:*

> "What has the gray-haired prisoner done?
> Has murder stain'd his hands with gore?
> Not so; his crime's a fouler one:
> *God made the old man poor!*
> For this he shares a felon's cell,
> The fittest earthly type of hell!
> For this, the boon for which he pour'd
> His young blood on the invader's sword,—
> And counted light the fearful cost!—
> His blood-gain'd liberty is lost."

Colonel Barton lived to the age of eighty-four years, and died at Providence in 1831, venerated and beloved by all who knew him.

JOHN SULLIVAN, LL. D.,

A MAJOR-GENERAL OF THE REVOLUTION; FIRST GRAND MASTER OF THE GRAND LODGE OF NEW HAMPSHIRE, AND GOVERNOR OF THAT STATE.

JOHN SULLIVAN, the first Grand Master of Masons in New Hampshire, was of Irish descent. His father emigrated from Ireland to this country and settled in Berwick, in Maine, a few years before his birth. There, on the 17th of February, 1740, the subject of our sketch was born. He was his father's oldest son, and his early years were spent in assisting him upon his farm. When he came to manhood he studied law, and was regularly admitted by the court as an attorney. He established himself in his profession in Durham, New Hampshire, and soon rose to distinction as an attorney and politician. In 1774 he was sent as a delegate from New Hampshire to the Continental Congress. On his return home, he was engaged with some other distinguished patriots of his State in taking possession of the British fort in the harbor of Portsmouth. It was a bold act, and one hundred barrels of powder and a quantity of cannon and small-arms were secured for the future use of the colonists by the transaction.

He was re-elected to Congress the following year, and remained in it until his services were required in his own State, when he returned home with a commission as one of the eight brigadier-generals which Congress appointed, and soon after repaired to WASHINGTON'S headquarters at Cambridge. When the Continental army was organized in 1776, he was promoted to the rank of major-general, and was sent to take the command of troops in Canada. He was not successful in this expedition; was superseded in command of the northern division by General GATES, and joined the army of WASHINGTON at New York. Here the illness of General GREENE placed him in command of his division at the battle of Brooklyn, in which he was taken prisoner. Being soon after exchanged for General PRESCOTT, he again joined the army, and was placed in command of one of its four divisions. He was with WASHINGTON at the battles of Brandywine and Germantown, but while the army was quartered the following winter at Valley Forge, he was sent to Rhode Island to take command of the troops stationed in that State. In the summer of 1778 he besieged the British force at Newport; but the want of the desired co-operation of the French fleet prevented his full success.

While in command in Rhode Island in the autumn of 1778, our first Masonic record relating to General SULLIVAN as a Mason appears. It was the permission granted by him to the Brethren under his command to join in the Masonic Festival of St. John, on the 28th of December of that year, in Providence. General VARNUM, who was also stationed in Rhode Island, delivered the Masonic address that day.

General SULLIVAN had doubtless been made a Mason previous to the Revolution, but we have seen no record of the time or place. In the spring of 1779 he was called into a new field of operations, being sent in command of the expedition against the Indians and Tories of New York. In this service he was accompanied by General CLINTON, and Colonel PROCTOR with his regiment of Pennsylvania artillery, in which a Military Lodge had recently been organized under Colonel PROCTOR as Master.

This expedition, successful in its designs but tragic in its events, was a distinct feature in the war of the Revolution; and the pages of our country's history have invested with a kind of romance the details of its progress and consummation. From the commencement of the war, the loyalists of the north had been joined with the Indians of the Six Nations in New York in cruel and destructive warfare on our northwestern borders. In Canada and along the mighty lakes and rivers of the north were British fortresses, in whose strongholds the loyalists found safe retreat and shelter from danger; and between these and the settlements and towns of the States which were in arms against the king, were the hunting-grounds and the war-paths of the Iroquois. Here, for years which they numbered by the leaves of their forest-trees, their old men and their women had rudely cultivated rich interval lands along the streams, and in many favorite places their cone-like cabins had clustered into villages. Around these the fruit-trees of their distant civilized neighbors had been planted and grown to maturity, and abundant cornfields supplied their wants when the fortunes of the chase failed them.

From these British fortresses upon the lakes, and the intervening wilderness fastnesses between them and the American settlements, the loyalists and Indians commingled together, and fell in predatory bands on many defenceless towns and villages, whose natural defenders were absent in the general defence of the country under WASHINGTON. Like arrows from an unseen bow, or fire-bolts from a mantling summer-cloud, they often came when and where they were least expected, and retired so quickly that no trace was left of them except the work of the firebrand and the hatchet, or the blood-stained footsteps of their captives in their hurried return to the wilderness of the Iroquois or the forts at Niagara. The forest domains of New York were a hiding-place for loyalists, and a storehouse and home to the Indians. The leaders of the loyalists were Sir JOHN JOHNSON, Colonel GUY JOHNSON, and

Colonels BUTLER and CLAUS, all relatives, and all formerly distinguished Masons of the Mohawk Valley, and members of St. Patrick's Lodge. Their Indian ally, BRANT, the war-chief, was also a Mason. To him history has sometimes paid a tribute of respect for a remembrance of his Masonic vows during the bloody scenes of war, but to JOHNSON and BUTLER never. Their eyes had become blind to the Mason's sign, their ears deaf to the Mason's word. In the Masonic traditions of the Revolution, they have since stood as Ishmaelites in Israel. But let the mantle we seek to draw over our own faults, in part cover theirs. History is not always impartial.

The expedition of General SULLIVAN in 1779 against these loyalists and Indians was a war measure, planned and approved by WASHINGTON as a punishment for the unjustifiable warfare of the allied loyalists and Indians; and by breaking up their strongholds and destroying their means of subsistence, to prevent their future depredations on our unprotected settlements. Sternly he gave what he deemed a necessary command, and most faithfully and severely did General SULLIVAN execute it. History has told it on its pages, and we have only space for some of its incidents.

Having no previous military road to use, General SULLIVAN was obliged to cut his pathway from Easton on the Delaware across a mountainous wilderness to Wyoming on the Susquehanna. As he approached the latter place, he sent a small advance company ahead under Captain DAVIS and Lieutenant JONES. They were met by a party of Indians, defeated, and the captain and lieutenant both slain and scalped.

They were left by the Indians on the ground where they fell, and after their departure were hastily buried by their surviving comrades. Captain DAVIS and Lieutenant JONES were both Masons, and when General SULLIVAN reached the Valley, he had their bodies taken up and reinterred at Wyoming with Masonic ceremonies. It was the first Masonic meeting ever held in that valley, and the procession of Brethren that bore the bodies of their slain companions from their first resting-place in the forest, for a more decent interment at Wyoming, was attended by the regimental band, which played Roslin Castle on their march. This Military Lodge, on that occasion, met at the marquee of Colonel PROCTOR. Neither history nor tradition has given us the names of Brethren present, but it is well known that a large number of the officers in that expedition were Masons, all of whom, whose duty permitted it, it is presumed, were present. The old town at Wyoming had, at that time, a few permanent inhabitants, whose descendants still reside there; and traditions of these events have the most positive verity. Fifteen years later (1794) a Lodge was chartered in the same place by the Grand Lodge of Pennsylvania, which still exists as No. 61, at Wilkesbarre.

General SULLIVAN proceeded soon after on his expedition, following up the Susquehanna to its junction with the Tioga. Here, while awaiting the arrival of General CLINTON who was to meet him with additional forces at this point, a Masonic funeral sermon on the death of Captain DAVIS and Lieutenant JONES was preached by Dr. RODGERS, one of the chaplains of the expedition. This service was held on the 18th of August, and the text was from the seventh verse of the seventh chapter of Job, "Remember that my life is wind." The progress of Masonry was thus following the footsteps of war in its advancement into the American wilderness. The sound of its gavel was renewed at old Tioga Point under a warrant granted by the Grand Lodge of Pennsylvania in 1796, for Lodge No. 70, which is still working but a few rods from where this Masonic sermon was preached in Fort Sullivan in 1779.

From the commencement of General SULLIVAN'S wilderness march, the scouts of BRANT and his Tory associates JOHNSON and BUTLER had watched his progress. They no doubt knew his design was to penetrate the heart of the Indian country, and perhaps proceed to Niagara. His superior numbers had now gained him an admission to their *House*, as they termed their country, the south-door of which they said was at "Tioga Point." There General SULLIVAN had been joined by two thousand men under General CLINTON, making his number then five thousand.

With this strong force BRANT, JOHNSON, and BUTLER saw General SULLIVAN enter the *south-door* of the Iroquois, and proceed up the Tioga. When near what was afterwards called Newtown (now Elmira), they laid an ambuscade and prepared to give him battle. His strength overcame their cunning and bravery, and defeated and disheartened they fell back before his victorious army, and saw him destroy their cornfields, cut down their orchards, and burn their towns without again offering a united resistance. One of the incidents of this devastating march is painfully interesting, and of a character entitling it to a place in Masonic narrative.

After General SULLIVAN had passed into the heart of the Indian country, and was near the Genesee River, he sent Lieutenant BOYD with a guide and twenty-six men to reconnoitre an Indian town six miles ahead. His guide mistook the way, and on the return of the party, they were drawn into an ambuscade by BRANT and BUTLER with several hundred Indians and rangers, as the loyalists were called, and nearly all his men were killed. BOYD was wounded, and with one of his party taken prisoner. He had been captured once before at the storming of Quebec, but then was exchanged. From the private ranks he had risen to that of lieutenant of a rifle company of the Pennsylvania division, and was about twenty-two years of age. He was the largest and most muscular man in his company, but having been wounded, he was now in the power of the enemy. Lieutenant BOYD was a Mason, and knowing the ferocity of the Indians after seeing their towns burned, he gave to BRANT, who was also a Mason, a sign of the Fraternity, claiming protection. The dusky chief recognized it and at once promised him his life. But being called away soon after, BOYD was left in the care of General BUTLER, who, as before stated, had formerly been a member of St. Patrick's Lodge on the Mohawk. BUTLER demanded of the captive information which his fidelity to his own commander would not allow him to give. The scene became one of tragic interest. Enraged at the silence of BOYD, BUTLER had him placed before him kneeling upon one knee, with an Indian on each side holding his arms, and another standing behind him with a tomahawk raised over his head. BUTLER inquired the number of SULLIVAN's men. "I cannot answer you," was BOYD's reply. He then inquired how his army was divided and disposed. "I cannot give you any information, sir," again replied the heroic captive. Again, for the third time, BUTLER harshly addressed him:

"BOYD, life is sweet; you had better answer me."

"Duty forbids," was the reply; "I would not, if life depended on the word."

Reader, contemplate the scene. Both were Masons; the one haughty, imperious, and forgetful of his vows; the other a captive in his hands, with fortitude undaunted and fidelity unshaken, thrice refusing to betray his trust. His last refusal cost him his life; for before BRANT returned to his captive, and unknown to him, BUTLER delivered him into the hands of the infuriated Indians about him, and, amidst tortures too horrid to describe, he fell a martyr to his trust. Thus fell Lieutenant BOYD on the 13th of September, 1779. His remains were found on the following day, and buried by order of General SULLIVAN on the borders of a small stream, where they lay undisturbed until 1841, sixty-two years after the event, when they were identified, collected in an urn, and reinterred with much ceremony in Mount Hope Cemetery at Rochester.

General SULLIVAN proceeded no further on this expedition than the Indian towns on the Genesee, and returned to Tioga, still burning wigwams, and destroying every means for subsistence within his reach. So dreadful and widespread was the devastation he made, that he was afterwards called by the

Indians "The Town Destroyer." General SULLIVAN was absent from the headquarters of the army in this expedition about five months, and on his return received the thanks of Congress for his services; but he was dissatisfied with the action of the Board of War, pleaded ill-health, and resigned his commission in the army. He then retired to private life, and resumed his former profession. He was, however, immediately elected by the State of New Hampshire a delegate to Congress, and took his seat in that body in 1780. He left Congress after one year's service, and again returned to his profession. In 1783 he was appointed attorney-general of his State, helped to form its constitution, and was chosen a member of its council. In 1786 he was elected governor of New Hampshire, and held the office for three successive years.

During the last year that General SULLIVAN occupied the gubernatorial chair of his State, an independent Grand Lodge was formed in that jurisdiction, and he was elected its first Grand Master. Masonic lodges were not numerous in New Hampshire at that time; but five having then been organized in the State, and but one of these (St. John's at Portsmouth) preceding the Revolution. During the same year that General SULLIVAN was Grand Master of the State, he was also Master of this old lodge at Portsmouth. In October of 1790, at a meeting of this Grand Lodge, General SULLIVAN communicated to that body by letter the fact, that the alarming state of his health would no longer permit him to serve as Grand Master, at the same time expressing his grateful acknowledgments for the honor they had conferred upon him.

Dr. HALL JACKSON was therefore elected Grand Master in his stead.

General SULLIVAN soon after received an appointment as Federal judge of his district, and held that office till the close of his life. He died on the 23d of January, 1795, in the fifty-sixth year of his age. Twenty years of his life had been spent in public service, but still he had found time to acquire a fund of general literature, and had been honored by the university at Dartmouth with the degree of Doctor of Laws. He led a life of usefulness, and his death was felt as a public loss.

GENERAL JAMES JACKSON,

GOVERNOR, AND GRAND MASTER OF GEORGIA.

THE incidents of human life are sometimes so strange, that a faithful narrative of them seems a work of romance rather than reality. Many a protraiture of heroes of the Revolution is rich with such incidents; and of names thus characterized, stands that of JAMES JACKSON, of Georgia.

He was born in Devonshire, in England, on the 21st of September, 1757. His father emigrated to America in 1772, and settled in Georgia, and young JACKSON, then fifteen years of age, became a student of law in Savannah. He loved his adopted country, and when its liberties were threatened by the English government he shouldered his musket to defend them. Previous to the Revolution, Savannah had been a military station of the British troops; and in 1774, when the controversy between the colonies and the English government began to be serious and threatening, the royal grenadiers proudly marched the streets of that city. This did not, however, deter the patriotic inhabitants from organizing as "Sons of Liberty" in common with the patriots of other colonies; and early in 1776, the royal governor of Georgia found his authority there at an end.

It was at this period that young JACKSON left his studies, took up his musket, and became a soldier. He was active in repelling the invading force that threatened Savannah, and so well did he perform his duties, that in 1778, when but twenty-one years of age, he was appointed brigade-major of the Georgia militia. In this capacity he saw active service, and was wounded in the skirmish on the Ogeechee, in which General SCRIVEN was killed.

At the close of that year, the British made an attack on Savannah, and it fell into their hands. Major JACKSON fought in its defence, but when compelled to yield to a superior force, he was among those who fled to South Carolina, and joined General MOULTRIE's brigade. The account of that dismal flight is full of romantic incidents. Hunger and fatigue had rendered his appearance wretched and suspicious, and his foreign accent induced some of the Whigs to suspect that he was a British spy. He was accordingly arrested, summarily tried, and condemned to be hung. He was taken to the fatal tree; a rope was prepared, when a gentleman of reputation from Georgia recognized him and saved his life.

Major JACKSON was soon after active in the terrible, but unfortunate siege of Savannah by the American and French forces in October of 1779; and in August, 1780, he joined Colonel CLARK'S command, and was at the battle of Blackstocks. In 1781, General PICKENS made him his brigade-major, and his zeal and patriotism infused new spirit into that corps. He was at the siege of Augusta in June of that year, and when the American forces took possession of it, he was left in command of its garrison. After this he was in command of a legionary corps, and well sustained his reputation as a skilful officer. Afterwards he joined General WAYNE at Ebenezer on the Savannah, and was the right-arm of his force until the evacuation of the Georgia capital by the British in 1782.

Major JACKSON retired on the return of peace to Savannah, and his patriotic services during the war were so highly appreciated, that the legislature of Georgia gave him a house and lot in that city. He was married in 1785. It was at this period of his life that we find our first records of his Masonic history. King Solomon's Lodge at Savannah, which had commenced its work under an old oak-tree in 1733 when the first settlement in Georgia began, had belonged to the branch of Masons denominated *Moderns;* but in February, 1785, it was proposed by Major JACKSON, who was then one of its members, that they form themselves into a lodge of *Ancients.* The proposition was referred to a committee, and was subsequently agreed to, and the brethren were duly constituted by the usual ceremonies a Lodge of Ancient York Masons.

In 1786 an independent Grand Lodge was formed in Georgia by the former Provincial Grand Master, Governor SAMUEL ELBERT'S relinquishing all authority as such; and of the new Grand Lodge thus formed, General WILLIAM STEPHENS was Grand Master, and General JAMES JACKSON (who had the same year been promoted to the rank of a brigadier-general), was his Deputy. The following year he was elected Grand Master, and held the office by re-election until the close of 1789. During the first year that he served as Grand Master he was elected governor of his State; but he declined the honor on account of his youth and inexperience, being then less than thirty years of age—a rare instance of genuine modesty that perhaps has no parallel in the history of our country. He was, however, elected soon after to a seat in the Federal Congress, and from 1792 to 1795 was a member of the United States Senate. In the mean time he received the appointment of major-general.

In 1798 he was a member of the convention that framed the constitution of the State of Georgia; and it is said that that instrument was the work of his hand and brain. He was elected the first governor under it, and held the office until 1801, when he was again elected to the Senate of the United States, and held that position until his death, which occurred in the City of Washington on the 19th of March, 1806, in the forty-ninth year of his age. His remains were at first buried a few miles from the city, but were subsequently removed and deposited in the congressional burial-ground at Washington. Upon the stone which marks the spot is an inscription by his friend and admirer, JOHN RANDOLPH, of Roanoke.

The record of his life is deeply engraven on the Masonic, as well as general history of our country. It was during his Grand Mastership, and under his direction, that the Grand Lodge of Georgia made strong efforts to unite all the Grand Lodges in America under one general head; and his correspondence on this subject is still to be found in the archives and on the record-books of most of the then existing Grand Lodges. The project, however, failed, and though at various times during the present century it has been publicly recommended by distinguished Masons, it has never yet been accomplished.

There have been other distinguished American Masons by the name of JACKSON, whose identity has sometimes been confounded with his, where the name has been found in old lodge-records and documents. One of these was Dr. JAMES JACKSON, of Massachusetts, who was Junior Grand Warden of the Grand Lodge of Ancients in that State in 1780. Another was General ANDREW JACKSON, late President of the United States, who was in 1822–3 Grand Master of Masons in Tennessee. Dr. HALL JACKSON was the second Grand Master of New Hampshire.

WILLIAM RICHARDSON DAVIE,

GOVERNOR OF NORTH CAROLINA, AND GRAND MASTER OF MASONS IN THAT STATE.

William Richardson Davie, governor of North Carolina, and Grand Master of Masons in that State, was of English birth, having been born at Egremont, near White Haven, in England, on the 20th of June, 1756. His father brought him to America when he was but five years of age, and left him to the care of a maternal uncle, the Rev. WILLIAM RICHARDSON of South Carolina, by whom he was adopted as a son. There in the old Palmetto State he was reared and educated until he was fitted for college, when he was sent to Princeton, New Jersey, where he graduated in the fall of 1776, in the twenty-first year of his age.

During his senior year in college, the storm-cloud of war burst on our land; and when the British army was advancing upon the city of New York, he left his class, and became for a time a volunteer soldier; but after the battle of Long Island, and the capture of the city, he returned to Princeton and completed his studies. His concluding lessons were taken within the roar of the British cannon, and he left Princeton just before WASHINGTON and his broken army passed through that town in their flight towards the Delaware.

The young graduate then returned to his Southern home; but he carried with him the remembrance of scenes he had witnessed at the North, and resolved to enter the field in defence of his adopted country, and resist the aggressions of his fatherland, as soon as an honorable post could be found. No position worthy of his talent at once offering itself, he engaged in the study of law at Salisbury, in North Carolina. But the fire of patriotism still burned in his breast, and as the war-clouds thickened, he joined a corps of dragoons as lieutenant, and marched towards Charleston, in South Carolina, to join the legion of PULASKI. In the battle of Stono Ferry, a few miles from Charleston, he was wounded in the thigh, and confined with his wound in the hospital for five months.

When he recovered, he returned to Salisbury, and

resumed the study of law. In 1780 a regiment of cavalry was raised by the State of North Carolina, and he received in it a commission as major. In the equipment of this troop, he is said to have expended the last shilling of his own private means, and as he mounted his war-horse, he had nothing but that mettled steed and his own good blade that he could call his own. He nobly aided SUMTER in his operations on the Catawba, and was at the battles of Hanging Rock, Ramsour's Mills, and at Wahab's Plantation. For his services in that campaign, he was rewarded with the office of colonel.

When General GREENE took command of the Southern army in 1781, he appointed Colonel DAVIE his commissary-general, and he was with that officer in his celebrated retreat, and at the battles of Guilford, Hobkirk's Hill, and Ninety-six. It was at this trying hour, when the fate of the Southern army seemed to hang upon a brittle thread, when its numbers were reduced, its ammunition nearly exhausted, and its commissariat empty, that General GREENE sent DAVIE to represent his condition to the government of North Carolina, charging him to give "no sleep to his eyes, nor slumber to his eyelids," until relief could be obtained. But the dark days of Southern despondency soon passed away, and when the peace of 1783 smiled on the land, the heroes who had won American liberty returned to their former homes and peaceful avocations.

Colonel DAVIE left the army in the autumn of 1783, married a daughter of General ALLEN JONES, and commenced the practice of law in Halifax, North Carolina. In this profession he soon became eminent, and was chosen a delegate to the convention that framed the Federal constitution. He was also commissioned in 1797 a major-general of the militia of the State, and in 1798, he was appointed under WASHINGTON a brigadier-general in the army of the United States. In the same year he was also elected governor of the State of North Carolina, and was soon after appointed by President ADAMS an associate envoy extraordinary to France, with ELSWORTH and MURRAY.

Governor DAVIE was a Mason, but we are unable to state at what time, or in what lodge, he became a member of that Fraternity. He was twenty-seven years of age when he settled as a lawyer in Halifax. An old lodge had existed since 1767 in that town, but the sound of its gavel had ceased during the Revolution. When peace was established, the old lodges of North Carolina resumed their labors, and in 1787 they all united to form an Independent Grand Lodge for that State. Of this Grand Lodge, Governor DAVIE became the third Grand Master, a position which he held for many years, and until he was sent as ambassador to France in 1799. It is presumed he was made a Mason in the "Royal White Hart" Lodge at Halifax.

Governor DAVIE took a deep interest in the educational interests of his State, and was one of the founders of the "North Carolina University," at Chapel Hill, the corner-stone of which he laid, as Grand Master of the State, on the 14th of April, 1798, in presence of all the civil and Masonic dignitaries of North Carolina.

This stone, Masonic records state, was laid at the *southeast* corner of the edifice, according to Masonic usage at that day.

The procession was composed of the—

"Architect,
Mechanics and Peasants,
Grand Music,
Teacher and Students of Chatham Academy,
Students of the University,
The Faculty of the University,
The Gentlemen of the Bar,
The Honorable the Judges,
The Honorable the Council of State,
His Excellency the Governor,
The Trustees of the University,
The Masonic Craft, with
The Grand Master."

It was the most important public Masonic ceremony in North Carolina during the last century, and the Rev. Dr. CALDWELL, a member of the Faculty of the University, delivered an oration on the occasion.

When Governor DAVIE returned from France, he was engaged by President ADAMS in some Indian treaties; but upon the death of his wife, in 1803, he withdrew from public life, and died at Tivoli (some authorities say Camden), in South Carolina, in December of 1820, in the sixty-fourth year of his age. On his retirement from the office of Grand Master, a lodge was chartered in Lexington, bearing the name of "William R. Davie" lodge. It is still in existence. Another lodge called "Davie" was soon after chartered in Bertie County, but it has since ceased to exist.

RICHARD CASWELL,

GOVERNOR OF NORTH CAROLINA, AND GRAND MASTER OF MASONS IN THAT STATE.

RICHARD CASWELL, governor of North Carolina, and Grand Master of the Masons in that State, was born in Maryland, on the 2d of August, 1729. His father was a merchant, and having met with some reverses in business, his son, RICHARD, left the parental roof to seek his fortune in the new colony of North Carolina. His education and social standing must have been good, for he bore letters of commendation from the governor of Maryland to Governor JOHNSTON, of North Carolina, and received employment in one of the public offices. He was appointed deputy surveyor of the colony, and also clerk of the court of Orange in 1753. He was then twenty-four years of age.

He soon afterwards married, and settled in Dobbs (now Lenoir) County. His first wife bore him one son, WILLIAM, and died. He married a second wife, who was SARAH, the daughter of WILLIAM HERRITAGE, an eminent attorney, and under him he studied law, and was licensed to practise in the courts of that colony. In 1754 he had been chosen a delegate to represent the county of Johnston in the Colonial Assembly, and was honored with a continuance of that appointment for sixteen successive years, the ten last of which he was speaker of the Lower House. He also bore a commission as colonel of the militia of his county, and as such, was joined with Governor TRYON in suppressing an uprising of the people in the first stages of colonial discontent at their taxations by the English government.

CASWELL was then in the meridian of life, his education and position were such as to give him influence in the colony, and he no doubt looked with disfavor on the first opposition that was shown in North Carolina to the powers of the royal government. He could not, however, have long remained an advocate of the royal pretensions; for in 1774 he was one of the delegates from his State to the General Congress at Philadelphia, and was continued in this office in 1775. In September of that year he resigned his seat in Congress, to fill the office of treasurer of North Carolina.

The old colonial government under Governor MARTIN, the last of the royal governors of North Carolina, had lost all its power after the second meeting of the General Congress at Philadelphia, and a body, calling itself the Provincial Congress of North Carolina, assumed the powers of government in that commonwealth. A declaration of rights, and a constitution, were adopted in 1776, and RICHARD CASWELL was elected the first governor under it. He had been a member of the Provincial Congress that framed this constitution, had presided over that body as its president, and had also received from it the appointment of brigadier-general of the militia of the district of Newbern. He was continued as governor of North Carolina through the years of 1777, '78, and '79, and refused to receive any compensation for his services beyond his expenses.

In 1779 he took the field as brigadier-general, led the troops of North Carolina under General GATES, and was engaged at the disastrous battle of Camden. He afterwards was a member of the Senate of his State, was chosen its speaker, and held other offices of public trust, until 1784, when he was again elected governor of his State, and again held the office for two successive years, at the close of which, by the provisions of the constitution, he became ineligible. In 1787 he was elected by the Assembly a delegate to the convention that framed the Federal Constitution in the city of Philadelphia, with power to appoint a substitute if he could not attend. WILLIAM BLOUNT was selected by him as his substitute, and his name stands on the national records as a delegate from North Carolina, instead of that of RICHARD CASWELL. In 1789 he was again elected to the Senate of his State, and also a member of the convention that finally ratified for North Carolina the Federal constitution.

When the legislature of his State met in 1789, he was again speaker of the Senate:

"But his course was run. His second son, RICHARD, had been lost on his passage by sea from Charleston to Newbern, and the father certainly entertained the opinion that he had been taken by pirates, and carried to Algiers, or murdered. This, and other events, threw a cloud over his mind from which he never recovered. While presiding in the Senate, on the 5th of November, he was struck with a paralysis, and after lingering speechless till the 10th, he expired in the sixtieth year of his age. His body was, after the usual honors, conveyed to his family burial-place in Lenoir, and there interred with Masonic honors."

His funeral oration was delivered by FRANCIS XAVIER MARTIN, of which the following is a copy:

"WORSHIPFUL SIRS AND WORTHY BRETHREN—Bereft of him who conducted our works, we are met to discharge the tribute of a tear due to his memory. How deeply the rest of the community sympathizes with us, on this melancholy occasion, the attendance of a respectable number of our fellow-citizens fully testifies.

"Shall our griefs terminate in sterile tears? Shall this discourse, sacred to the memory of the Most Worshipful and Honorable Major-General RICHARD CASWELL, Grand Master of the Masons of North Carolina, be, like the song of the untutored savage, the mere rehearsal of a warrior's achievements? No. In admiring the virtues that have rendered his death, like JOSIAH'S lamented in Judea and Jerusalem, let us, as Christians and Masons, be stimulated, not to offer idle adulation to his manes, but to imitate, in the practise of every virtue, so bright a pattern.

"Nothing excites more powerfully to virtuous deeds, than the examples of those whom they have rendered conspicuous. Man generally desires what he finds applauded in others. And, either because virtue appears more noble when he hears it praised, or less difficult when he sees it practised, he is stimulated thereto — as the labor is not without reward, and remissness would be without excuse.

"The examples of the dead are no less powerful than those of the living. We look upon the virtues of the former with a greater degree of veneration, as we view those of the latter with a greater degree of envy; perhaps, because, death having crowned them, we are willing to believe that *posterity praises without flattery*, as it praises without interest—or rather (for why should the real reason be concealed in this temple of truth?) because our pride will not suffer us to acknowledge them.

"To convene the people when some illustrious popular character has terminated his career, and to improve the opportunity of exciting them to patriotic virtues, is an ancient custom, frequent instances of which occurred in sacred and profane history. The heart of man, however obdurate, when operated upon by grief, or the idea of a future state, is prepared to receive such favorable impressions; as the stiff and close-grained stone becomes pliant and ductile when heated by the fire of the furnace.

"Thus we read that the corpse of Cæsar, having been brought into the Forum of the then metropolis of the world, Antony, holding up that Dictator's garment, addressed the Roman people: 'You well know,' said he, 'this mantle. I remember the first time Cæsar put it on. It was on the day he overcame the Nervii. If you have tears to shed, prepare to shed them now.'

"With as much propriety can I rise to-day, and addressing you, say:

"You well know these badges. They are the insignia of Masonry—of a society which, for its antiquity and utility, acknowledges no equal among the institutions of the sons of man. Behold the white apron that was girded on him, the loss of whom we bemoan, on the day he became a Mason! He has left it to you unsullied. He has left it to you, decorated with those marks of dignity to which merit alone gives title.

"If you have tears to shed, prepare to shed them now.

"He is no more. No longer shall he, *like the eastern sun*, illuminate our lodges ; no longer shall he plan or direct our works.

"You well know, fellow-citizens, that sword, emblematical of Supreme Executive Authority. I remember the first time it was delivered to him. It was on the day we shook off the British domination and became a People.

"If you have tears to shed, prepare to shed them now.

"He is no more. No longer shall he wield the sword of justice attempered by mercy. No longer shall he preside in your councils, or lead you to the hostile field.

"To enter here into a minute detail of the services he rendered you, would be to premise that they may be obliterated from your memory—you remember them. Brethren and fellow-citizens, they cannot have been forgotten.

"It was he who headed you on the day you broke down the superior phalanx of Scotch troops, at Moor's Creek ; and thereby preserved the cause of freedom from the deadly blow this re-enforcement would have enabled our enemies to strike.

"It was he who presided in the Assembly of Patriots, who framed that instrument, which defined your rights and the authority of your rulers, and has secured your liberties to this day.

"It was he whom your united voices twice called to the supreme magistracy of this State—and it was he who, but a few days ago, still filled the chair of your Senate.

"If his public character affords a vast field to the panegyrist's fancy, his private one deserves no less attention and praise. In it we shall always find an example worthy of imitation.

"Public virtue may procure a more shining reputation, but domestic virtue gives a more solid merit. The former, when unsupported by the latter, is, in the warrior, a thirst of glory—in the civil ruler, a thirst of power.

"A single instance of momentary intrepidity may make a name to the chieftain; but a continued spirit of moderation alone characterizes the virtuous individual.

"Valor is a noble passion, which evinces a greatness of soul. But too oft it is a vain generosity excited by ambition, and which has for its aim the mere gratification of a selfish pride; an inconsiderate boldness justified by success; a blind ferocity which stifles the voice of humanity, and by the tears it causes to flow, and the blood of its victims, tarnishes the laurels of the vanquisher.

"Domestic virtue, on the contrary, is so perfect, that it is laudable even in its excesses. It is peaceable and constant, and springs from a meekness and tenderness which regulate desire; and giving the virtuous individual the command of his own, causes him to reign over the hearts of others. The one excites astonishment and fear; the other commands reverence and love.

"The Swede *boasts* of the name of CHARLES XII., but *blesses* that of GUSTAVUS VASA.

"In him, of whom the hand of death has bereft us, public and domestic virtues were ever united. Not satisfied in watching with unremitted attention over the welfare of the community, he anxiously endeavored to promote the felicity of its members. Blest with a complacency of disposition and equanimity of temper which peculiarly endeared him to his friends, he commanded respect even from his enemies. The tender sensibility of his heart was such, that he needed but to see distress, to feel it and contribute to its relief. Deaf to the voice of interest, even in the line of his profession, whenever oppressed indigence called for his assistance, he appeared at the bar without even the hope of any other reward than the consciousness of having so far promoted the happiness of a fellow-man.

"Such is, Worshipful Sirs and worthy brethren, the character of one whose lessons shall no longer instruct us, but the remembrance of whose virtues will long continue to edify us.

"Such is, fellow-citizens, the character of one who bore so great a share in the Revolution by which you became a nation; who, during his life, was ever honored with some marks of your approbation, and whose memory will, I doubt not, be embalmed in your affections.

"Shades of WARREN, MONTGOMERY, and MERCER! and ye shades of those other Columbian chiefs who bore away the palm of political martyrdom! attend, receive, and welcome, into *the happy mansions of the just*, a soul congenial with those of your departed heroes, and meriting alike our esteem, our gratitude, and our tears."

Governor CASWELL was a Mason, and as such had received the highest honors of the Fraternity in his State, being the second Grand Master of North Carolina after its Independent Grand Lodge was formed in 1787, and holding the office at the time of his death. He had been preceded, as Grand Master, by SAMUEL JOHNSTON, who was governor of North Carolina at the death of Governor CASWELL; and his successor, as Grand Master, was WILLIAM RICHARDSON DAVIE, who held the office for nine years, during the last of which, he was also governor of the State. Thus from the independence of that State, until the last year of the century, each of her three governors was also the Grand Master of the Masons of North Carolina. To commemorate the Masonic virtues of its first two Grand Masters, a lodge was chartered at Warrenton with the name of "Johnston-Caswell Lodge;" and another in Caswell County, was called "Caswell Brotherhood," both of which are now extinct.

DR. JAMES MILNOR,

GRAND MASTER OF PENNSYLVANIA.

DR. JAMES MILNOR was the son of WILLIAM MILNOR of Philadelphia. He was born in that city on the 20th of June, 1773, and was by birthright a Quaker. His education was received at the public-schools in Philadelphia and in the university of Pennsylvania. At the age of sixteen he left the university and commenced the study of law, and before he was twenty years-one of age was admitted to the bar. This was in 1794, and he settled in the practice of his profession in Norristown, a few miles from Philadelphia. Norristown was then a small village but ten years old. It was in a German district, and the inhabitants there, when JAMES MILNOR settled in it as a lawyer, mostly spoke the German language. He had acquired a knowledge of that dialect in the schools of his native city, and was thus enabled to accommodate himself to the wants of a community where the common business was transacted in German. He soon rose to distinction in his profession, and had the confidence of his fellow-citizens as an able and honest lawyer. While thus engaged at Norristown, he was made a Mason in old Lodge No. 31, of that place. His initiation took place in August, 1795. He was then twenty-two years of age. He was soon after elected Master of this Lodge; but on removing the following year to Philadelphia, he became a member of Lodge No. 3, in that city. His affiliation with this Lodge was on the 6th of September, 1796, and he was afterwards its Treasurer.

When Mr. MILNOR returned to Philadelphia, he engaged in the practice of his profession in that city. In 1799 he married a lady who was by education an Episcopalian; and as the marriage ceremony was performed by a clergyman of that denomination, it gave offence to his Quaker brethren that he should be married by a "hireling priest," and this being contrary to their established "*discipline*," he was "*disowned*," and his membership with the Quakers ceased forever.

In 1805, Mr. MILNOR was chosen a member of the city council, and held the position from 1805 until 1809, during the latter year being its president. He was very popular with the people, and in 1810 yielded to the earnest wishes of his political friends, and reluctantly consented to become a candidate for Congress. He was elected, and his great popularity is shown by his being the only Federal candidate on the city ticket that succeeded. He remained in Congress until 1813, and was a steady opponent of the war and the belligerent measures of the administration. HENRY CLAY was then speaker of the House; and taking great offence at some remark of Mr. MILNOR, he challenged him to a duel. Mr. MILNOR declined the proffered combat; for he would not consent that any one should presume to call him to account for words spoken in debate, and he also deemed duelling a cowardly practice. Mr. CLAY did not press the matter further; and in after-years they met on the most friendly terms.

On becoming Master of Lodge No. 31, Mr. MILNOR became a member of the Grand Lodge of Pennsylvania; and although he had at the time been a member of the Order but about two years, he was put upon a committee to revise the "Rules and Regulations" of the Grand Lodge of that State. In 1798 he was elected Senior Grand Warden; in 1799 and 1800 he was re-elected to the same office; in 1801 and 1803 he was Deputy Grand Master; and in 1805 he was elected Grand Master of Pennsylvania, and continued to hold that office by annual re-election, until the close of 1813. During his Grand Mastership he was also, *ex-officio*, Grand High Priest of the Grand Chapter of Pennsylvania.

No Grand Master of Pennsylvania ever took a

deeper interest in the welfare of the Grand Lodge and the good of Masonry than JAMES MILNOR. His charges and addresses were full of instruction, and his constant theme was the inculcation of charity and brotherly love. During his Grand Mastership the old Masonic Hall in Chestnut-street was erected; and on its dedication on the 24th of June, 1811, he delivered, at St. John's Church, a public oration. At its close, a distinguished friend and Brother said to him, as they were leaving the church: "Why, Right Worshipful, you are cut out for a clergyman." Little did that Brother then dream that the thought would one day be realized.

In December, 1811, Mr. MILNOR was invited, as Grand Master of Pennsylvania, to visit the Lodge at Alexandria, Virginia, of which WASHINGTON was formerly Master. On this occasion Colonel DENEALE, the Master of the Alexandria Lodge, welcomed its distinguished visitor with an address, from which we give the following extract:

"Lost in amazement must be that brother, when reflecting on his own imperfection, upon finding he has been called, by the partiality of his brethren, to a station where once presided the ornament, and in whom centred the universal love of Masons; who condescended to level himself down from his exalted and towering eminence, and square himself here with his brethren in Masonry, laboring with them till midday, and, when called from labor to refreshment, entering into all the festive gayety, and innocent amusement of the Craft, even in his latter days; and although that fell destroyer, Time, has mowed down and removed from us, and, we hope, exalted to the high degree of companions with him in the Grand Lodge above, most of the brethren and companions of his juvenile days, yet they have left us an example worthy of imitation. The few survivors, by whom the sacred charge of this charter was committed to our care, have been rendered by age incapable of laboring with us in the meridian sun. They have retired to the shade, rich in the affection of their younger brethren, and ornaments to that society in which they move. These will undoubtedly prove ample incentives to the officers who shall ever preside here, to respect religion; walk in obedience to the precepts of the great book of the law given us as the rule of our faith; to preside with parental care; admonish with temperance; check vicious propensities; extend the hand of charity in silence; and induce the brethren to labor justly."

To this Grand Master MILNOR replied:

"WORSHIPFUL MASTER AND BRETHREN—The associations connected with the present meeting, are of the very opposite kinds. To receive and to reciprocate the friendly attentions of my brethren; to recognize in that portion of them, whose respected call has brought me amongst them, the neighbors, the friends, the associates of our sainted WASHINGTON; to enjoy communion with the body over which his mild virtues and dignified, yet fraternal manners, have so often shed a lustre; and to add to these causes of gratulation, the pleasing recollection of your having originally emanated from the Grand Lodge with whose honor and interests my feelings are so nearly allied, furnish causes of exultation and delight, which can be felt better than described.*

* The Lodge at Alexandria first worked under a charter granted by the Grand Lodge of Pennsylvania in 1783; in 1788 it took a new charter from the Grand Lodge of Virginia.

"Yet how is this combination of enlivening circumstances clouded by the sad remembrance that the great man, whose labors in the field and in the cabinet purchased independence and all its blessings for his country, and unfading renown for himself, while the benevolent graces of his personal demeanor in the bosom of the Lodge secured the fond attachment of his brethren, no longer adorns the East of this sacred temple! Ah! my brethren, your loss is not a common one. In the revolutions of the political scene, the mind, is lost amongst the confused whirl of many objects, and the departure of even a mighty orb appears but little to derange the general system. Even WASHINGTON seems almost forgotten by his country. Not so in the Lodge. Your hearts will find around you a thousand mementoes of the singular honor and happiness you have enjoyed in working as fellow-laborers with a man who, whilst the admiring eyes of a universe were upon him, could, with the most amiable condescension, descend from his exalted and towering eminence, and level himself with his brethren in Masonry, sharing with them in their toils, and entering with them, at the close of their labors, into all the festive gayety and innocent amusements of the Craft.

"Permit me, worshipful sir, to congratulate this Lodge on the pre-eminent honor it has enjoyed, in being so nearly allied to this illustrious hero, patriot, and statesman; to pray that all his virtues may descend upon his successors here; and that your consequent prosperity may be lasting and imperishable, as upon the bright roll of Masonic fame will ever stand emblazoned the name of WASHINGTON!"

During his congressional life, his thoughts had been much occupied upon religious subjects, and at the close of his term he determined to relinquish the profession of law, and devote himself to the Christian ministry. This involved a great sacrifice of pecuniary interests and worldly aspirations, for he was on the flood-tide of success, and political fame and fortune seemed to be within his reach. He hesitated not, however, at what seemed to him the call of duty, and turned his bark into a gentler channel, and cheerfully looked for a haven of rest and peace.

He was accordingly ordained a deacon in the Episcopal Church in 1814; in 1815 he was ordained a presbyter, and labored for a year as assistant minister in the Associated Churches in Philadelphia; and in 1816, he was called to the rectorship of St. George's Church, in New York City. Here, in his new field of labor, he devoted himself to the promotion of Christian benevolence. The Bible Society, the American Tract Society, the Institution for the Deaf and Dumb, the Orphan Asylum, the Home for aged indigent Females, and many kindred associations, felt his fostering care.

In 1830, he visited England as a delegate to the British Bible Society, and while in Europe, he visited also France, Wales, Ireland, and Scotland, and was everywhere received as a distinguished American philanthropist. He felt that his mission on earth was to do good, and few labored more zealously, or more successfully for that purpose.

During the long period that he was Grand Master of Pennsylvania, his whole soul had been absorbed in the inculcation of the moral precepts of Masonry. When called by his divine Master to fill a higher post of duty as a Christian minister, he but labored to perfect and adorn a temple upon whose foundation walls he had wrought in the lodge-room. To other hands he committed the bands of workmen who still wrought in the Masonic temple, that he might devote his whole time to a higher calling. He did not, however, forget his former associations with his Masonic brethren. After he resigned the chair of the Grand Lodge of Pennsylvania, he was elected Grand Chaplain of that Body, and continued to perform the duties of that office while he remained in Philadelphia, and a costly and appropriate jewel was voted him by the Grand Lodge, as a testimony of respect and attachment. After he removed to New York to assume the rectorship of St. George's Church, he was appointed Grand Chaplain of the Grand Lodge of the State of New York, and continued to hold the office for some years.

During the anti-Masonic excitement a few years after, he was importuned to renounce his connection with the Fraternity, but he stood firm. A brother clergyman from the country called on him one day to consult him on the propriety of withdrawing from the Order. He stated that his congregation were all anti-Masons, and he was fearful, even if he did not lose his situation, that his usefulness would be destroyed.

"Do you wish to renounce Masonry?" asked Dr. MILNOR.

"No," was the reply, "I love Masonry too well!"

"Then do as I do," was the rejoinder. "Put down your foot firmly, and say, 'I am a Mason, and am proud of it!' and if any one asks you what Masonry consists in, tell them, 'love to God, and good-will to man!'"

The advice was followed, and the country clergyman kept his place undisturbed.

Such is a brief sketch of the life of Dr. JAMES MILNOR. He labored zealously in his Master's work until 1845, when he died on the 8th of April, in the seventy-third year of his age. After his death, a testimony of respect was sent to the vestry of St. George's Church by his old Lodge No. 3, at Philadelphia, of which he had been a member nearly fifty years before. A son of his, Dr. WILLIAM MILNOR, afterwards became Grand Master of New York.

Samuel Seabury. D.D.

DR. SAMUEL SEABURY,

THE FIRST EPISCOPAL BISHOP IN AMERICA.

Rev. Samuel Seabury, D. D., first bishop of Connecticut and Rhode Island, and also the first consecrated bishop in America, was born near New London, Connecticut, in 1728, and graduated at Yale College in 1751. His father had been a Congregational minister, but changed his ecclesiastical connection and became the rector of the Episcopal church at Hempstead, on Long Island. Here his son Samuel was appointed his assistant and catechist as early as 1748, with a salary of ten pounds a year.

At this period the contest between Puritanism and Prelacy was so bitter and virulent, in the Anglo-American colonies, that it became the key-note to political liberty. A "society for propagating the Gospel in foreign parts" had been established in England in 1701, which was believed by the Puritans of New England to be a mere disguise for the introduction into America of lords spiritual, with hated tithes and oppressive hierarchy.

After young SEABURY had graduated at Yale, he was recommended as rector for a vacant church in New Brunswick, New Jersey, and in 1753 he proceeded to England to receive orders from the Episcopal authorities there. He returned to America in the following year, as rector of the church at New Brunswick; but in 1757 he was removed to the church at Jamaica, Long Island, and in December, 1766, was instituted, at his own request, rector of St. Peter's church in Westchester, New York.

As the religious and political controversies of that period were closely interwoven, many of the Episcopal clergy in America, and among them Dr. SEABURY, entered strongly into the field of polemic warfare. He wrote political pamphlets, under the *nom de plume* of "A Farmer." These were widely circulated, and gave great offence to the liberals, or "Sons of Liberty," as they were called, while they were much applauded by the loyalists.

This was at the commencement of the American Revolution, and a party of Whigs, from Connecticut, who were bitterly incensed against Dr. SEABURY and other loyalists, crossed over to Westchester, took them prisoners, and carried them to New Haven; but they were soon reclaimed by the provincial authorities of New York, as they deemed it an unwarrantable action in the then existing state of affairs, more especially the removal and imprisonment of Dr. SEABURY, "considering his ecclesiastic character," say they, "which, perhaps, is venerated by many friends of liberty, and the severity that has been used towards him may be subject to misconstructions prejudicial to the common cause."

Dr. SEABURY was accordingly set at liberty, and returned to his parish; but here he was subject to occasional visits from armed parties, who would offer one hundred dollars for the discovery of that "vilest of miscreants, 'A Farmer.'" Independence being declared, he considered it more prudent to close his church, as he determined there should be "neither prayers nor sermon until he could pray for the king."

This was the period during which WASHINGTON held possession of the city of New York, and nearly all the Episcopal churches in the northern colonies were closed by their rectors, as their customary prayers for the king and royal family gave great offence to the patriots of that day, who could see in them only a stubborn and servile adherence to English tyranny. That King George needed prayers they probably did not doubt, but these they evidently desired should be for his conversion rather than his confirmation.

When WASHINGTON evacuated New York, after the battle of Long Island, in 1776, Dr. SEABURY withdrew within the British lines, and was engaged by General CLINTON, in furnishing plans and maps of the roads and streams in the county of Westchester, to assist the British army in their movements. He also served as a chaplain in a regiment of loyalists, commanded by Colonel FANNING, called the "King's American Regiment." This regiment was stationed in New York, and Dr. SEABURY continued to reside there until the return of peace.

Dr. SEABURY was a Mason, but we have never learned when or where he was made one. Local and Military Lodges existed in New York while the British troops held possession of that city, and records still exist which show that they not only held their stated communications, but that the Masonic festivals of St. John were observed by them. The pre-revolutionary Provincial Grand Lodge of New York, having become extinct during the war, a new Provincial Grand Lodge was established in the city of New York in 1782, under a warrant from the Grand Lodge of *Ancients* in London, bearing date, September 5, 1781, and before this Grand Lodge Dr. SEABURY delivered an address, December 27, 1782, as seen by the following record of that body.

"*Resolved* unanimously, that the thanks of this Lodge be given to our Rev. Bro. Dr. SEABURY, for his sermon delivered this day, before this and other Lodges, convened for the celebration of St. John the Evangelist.

"That the thanks of this Lodge be presented to Rev. Dr. INGLIS, rector of New York, for the very polite and obliging manner in which he has accommodated this and other Lodges with the use of St. Paul's chapel, for the celebration of Divine services this day."

In the following June, the "Loyal American Regiment," of which Dr. SEABURY was chaplain, received a warrant for a new Military Lodge, and of this, it is probable, he was also a member.

In 1784, he went to England to obtain consecration as a bishop, but meeting with some difficulties at the hands of the English dignitaries, he proceeded to Scotland, where he was consecrated at Aberdeen, in November, by some non-juring bishops, as the first bishop of America. He returned to this country and settled in New London, near his native town, as the first bishop of Connecticut and Rhode Island, and continued to discharge his duties as such in an exemplary manner until his death. He died on the 25th of February, 1796. His monument stands in the churchyard at New London, bearing this inscription:

"Here lyeth the body of SAMUEL SEABURY, D. D., Bishop of Connecticut and Rhode Island, who departed from this transitory scene, February 25th, Anno Domini 1796, in the sixty-eighth year of his age, and the twelfth of his Episcopal consecration.

"Ingenious without pride, learned without pedantry, good without severity, he was duly qualified to discharge the duties of the Christian and the bishop. In the pulpit he enforced religion; in his conduct he exemplified it. The poor he assisted with his charity; the ignorant he blessed with his instruction. The friend of men, he ever designed their good; the enemy of vice, he ever opposed it. Christian! dost thou aspire to happiness? SEABURY has shown the way that leads to it."

Dr. SEABURY received his degree of Doctor of Divinity from the college of Oxford in England, and he became entitled to a fund of one thousand pounds, which had been left by Archbishop TENNISON in his will, in 1715, towards maintaining the first bishop who should be settled in America. This fund was afterwards increased by an equal amount, left in the same manner, for that purpose, by Archbishop SECKER; but we do not know whether Dr. SEABURY ever received or applied for it.

That he continued his support to the Masonic Fraternity, until his death, is seen from a sermon which he preached at the installation of Sumerset Lodge at Norwich, Connecticut, on the 24th of June, 1795, before a special session of the Grand Lodge of that State. This he published, with the following dedication to WASHINGTON:

"To the Most Worshipful President of the UNITED STATES OF AMERICA, the following discourse is respectfully inscribed,

"By his affectionate brother,

"And most devoted servant,

"SAMUEL SEABURY."

From the above dedication, we are induced to believe that in his later years this distinguished bishop and good brother prayed as fervently and heartily for GEORGE WASHINGTON, as in former years for the royal GEORGE of England.

Bishop SEABURY was succeeded, in 1797, by the Right Reverend ABRAHAM JARVIS, D. D., who was also a Mason. Dr. JARVIS was a native of Norwalk. He was born May 5, 1739, graduated at Yale, in 1761, and became rector of the Episcopal church in Middletown about 1764. There he remained until after he was consecrated as bishop in the place of Dr. SEABURY. In 1798 he was appointed Grand Chaplain of the Grand Lodge of Connecticut. In 1799 he left Middletown, and removed to Cheshire, and from thence to New Haven, in 1803, where he died, May 3, 1813, at the age of seventy-three years. The first Episcopal ordination by Bishop SEABURY was that of the Reverend ASHBEL BALDWIN, in 1785. It was the first Episcopal ordination in the United States. Mr. BALDWIN was also a graduate of Yale College, and a zealous Mason. He was the first Grand Chaplain of the Grand Lodge of Connecticut, and interested himself much in the prosperity of the Craft. He died at Rochester, New York, on the 8th of February, 1846, at the age of eighty-nine years.

GENERAL RUFUS PUTNAM,

FIRST GRAND MASTER OF OHIO.

FEW names on the pages of our country's history are suggestive of purer patriotism and bolder deeds than that of PUTNAM. Two who bore it have rendered it immortal in the historic annals of America. These were ISRAEL and RUFUS, both officers of the Revolution, and both Masons. RUFUS, who is the subject of this sketch, became the First Grand Master of Ohio.

He was born in the town of Sutton, Worcester County, Massachusetts, on the 9th of April, 1738. He lost his father before he was seven years old, and went to live with his maternal grandfather in Danvers, where he enjoyed the privilege of a district-school for two years. At this time his mother married again and took him home. His stepfather was an illiterate man, and desired to keep all over whom he had control in the same situation. Young PUTNAM was, therefore, denied all further opportunities for education while under his roof. Before he reached his sixteenth year his stepfather died, and his mother apprenticed him to a millwright. In his indentures no provision was made for his education, and his master was as indifferent to his mental improvement as his stepfather had been.

But although the path of science was thus hedged up to him, he sought every means to improve his mind with useful knowledge. He had tasted the Pierian spring during the time he lived with his grandfather, and had learned to read with considerable accuracy. While with his stepfather, who kept a public house, he gained much information by listening to the conversation of travellers to whose wants he was required to attend; and the little sums of money they sometimes gave him for his obliging attention to their wants, were expended by him in the purchase of books. A thirst for knowledge thus grew so strong in his mind, that during his apprenticeship every leisure hour was devoted to the elementary branches of an English education. When the toils of the day were over, he sought retirement for study; and when the morning sun arose, he resumed his labors with a mind attentive to his duties, but still free to improve itself by reflection on the lessons he had learned the evening before.

In the prosecution of his trade, a knowledge of mathematics was very serviceable to him, particularly that which was connected with geometry; and it was not long before a knowledge of circles, squares, and angles enabled him to draft plans, and comprehend the most complex machinery on which his labor was employed. While he was engaged in his apprenticeship, the old French and Indian war commenced, and the accounts he heard from time to time of the incidents of its campaigns, awoke in his mind a military ardor, and he longed to be like his brother ISRAEL, an actor in those exciting scenes.

At the age of nineteen, he therefore enlisted as a private soldier in the provincial army. His commander was Captain EBENEZER LEONARD, whose company consisted of one hundred men, many of whom had been young PUTNAM'S associates. They were soon required to rendezvous on the Hudson River a few miles below Albany; and the young soldier, who kept a daily journal, states the praiseworthy fact, that his captain prayed morning and evening with his men, and on each Sabbath read a sermon to them. The details of his military adventures during this war are far too numerous for this sketch. He was in military service four years, and shared with his comrades in all their privations and dangers.

When the term of the first enlistment of his company expired, the British commander sought to prolong their services by arbitrary measures. The men, however, left him in a manner not justifiable by military rules, although they were entitled to an honorable discharge. Mr. PUTNAM in after-life saw and condemned the mistake. In their homeward march they fled like fugitives, and as it was in the depth of winter, suffered much from hunger and cold; but at last they reached their homes. The military ardor of Mr. PUTNAM was not all expended by one campaign, and in a few months he enlisted for another, and at its close for still another; but in 1761 he left the army, married a wife, and engaged in farming, mill-building and surveying. He was now twenty-three years of age; and with a body hardened by toil, and a mind enriched by study and observation, he resumed his peaceful avocations, but at the same time devoted all his leisure moments to the acquisition of more knowledge from books.

In 1773, Mr. PUTNAM had become so proficient as a surveyor, that he received an appointment from a land company to explore and survey some lands in Florida which had been granted to troops engaged in the provincial war. He was accompanied in this expedition by his brother ISRAEL and a Captain ENOS. He was kindly treated by the governor of Florida, appointed by him deputy surveyor of that province, spent eight months there, and then returned home. The rich lands of the sunny South, which have since produced all the varied productions of that flowery clime, were then dense forests, or thick-grown cane-brakes, where no path was found except the Indian trail, or the track of the wild animals that made them their haunts. But on the report of Mr. PUTNAM of their climate, fertility, and beauty, several hundred families from New England emigrated there to form a settlement. They were doomed to disappointment, for before their arrival the land-office was closed against them.

About two years after Mr. Putnam's return from the "Yazoo country," the war of the Revolution commenced, and he left his home and rural pursuits to join the gallant bands of New England's sturdy yeomanry, who were arming in defence of their rights. He entered the army at Cambridge as a lieutenant-colonel, soon after the battle of Lexington, and was stationed at Roxbury, in General THOMAS' division. The British army had at that time possession of Boston, and Colonel PUTNAM was employed by his commander in planning and constructing lines of defence for the provincial troops who surrounded the city. He at this time professed no skill as a military engineer; but the lines were surveyed and defences erected with such good judgment, that when General WASHINGTON took command of the army a few weeks afterwards, and he and General LEE viewed the works of the amateur engineer, they received their highest commendation.

General WASHINGTON at once employed PUTNAM to draw a map of the enemy's fortifications at Boston, and all the American defences around it, and from this he arranged his plans for future action. So great was WASHINGTON'S confidence in the good judgment of this self-taught engineer, that he often consulted him before he determined on changes in the position of his forces.

He received from Congress, in August, 1776, a commission as engineer, with his previous rank as colonel, and was the chief-engineer until 1778. He was then succeeded by KOSCIUSKO, the brave Polander, whc frequently consulted him in planning works of defence. It was to PUTNAM's engineering skill that the military works at West Point owed much of their efficiency, for he changed the plan of construction that had been adopted by foreign engineers. He was principally engaged as an engineer during the war, but at one time, in 1778, was in command as colonel of troops in the northern division of the army. By both WASHINGTON and LAFAYETTE he was highly esteemed as an officer and a man. With both he became connected in the fraternal bonds of Masonic fellowship. He was not a Mason when he entered the army of the Revolution, but he became one in the summer of 1779.

The festival of St. John the Baptist was celebrated by the Masonic brethren in the army that year upon the Hudson, near West Point, and WASHINGTON joined, as was his custom, with the Military Lodge there on that occasion. Many other distinguished officers of the American army were present as Masons, and the ceremonies were highly impressive. Two days after this, Colonel PUTNAM applied to the lodge under whose charter these proceedings were held, to be made a Mason. It was the "American Union Lodge," which was instituted in the Connecticut line of the army at Roxbury, in 1776. Colonel PUTNAM's application was favorably received, and, at the same meeting of the lodge at which it was presented, he was made a Mason. It was the 26th of July, 1779. On the 26th of August he was made a Fellow Craft, and on the 6th of September a Master Mason. The place of meeting of the lodge when he received his degrees, was at the "Robinson House," on the east bank of the Hudson, about two miles below West Point. The fortunes of this lodge during the Revolution, and after its close, have a highly romantic interest, and are worthy of a place in the history of our country. Colonel PUTNAM'S connection with it was continued to the close of the war, and we afterwards find him cherishing its privileges and maintaining its chartered rights on the banks of the Ohio, as the pioneer of Christianity and civilization.

As the dangers of the country lessened, in a like degree were lessened the exertions of the different States to pay their troops, and early in 1783, Colonel PUTNAM contemplated a retirement from the army in consequence of a delinquency by the State of Massachusetts in providing funds for this purpose. General WASHINGTON sympathized with his distressed officers and soldiers, but used every means to persuade them to continue in the field till peace should be confirmed. When he heard of the contemplated retirement of Colonel PUTNAM, he wrote him an affectionate letter, proffering him promotion in the army, and he soon after received a commission as brigadier-general. This office he accepted, more on account of his personal regard for WASHINGTON than for its honors or emoluments, and he honored it with devotion to his country till the army was disbanded. After this, he was consulted by WASHINGTON as to the best manner of arranging a military peace establishment for the United States. He was also a prominent member of the Society of the Cincinnati.

From the close of 1783 to the commencement of

1788, General PUTNAM was engaged in organizing a company to settle on the far off but fertile banks of the Ohio, and in the spring of 1788 he went there as general agent of a New England company, accompanied by about forty settlers. They pitched their tents at the mouth of the Muskingum River, formed a settlement there, and called it Marietta. Here suspecting hostility from the neighboring Indians, they built a fort, and called it *Campus Martius*. They also planted that year one hundred and thirty acres of corn. This was the beginning of that tide of emigration to the Ohio which soon spread over all its rich valleys; and General PUTNAM may justly be regarded as the father of its pioneers.

Soon after the first settlement of Marietta, the old charter of the "American Union Lodge," which General PUTNAM had joined in 1779, was used to convene a Lodge in that place. JONATHAN HART, the last Master of the Lodge during the Revolution, and many of its members, had removed since the war to the new settlements on the Ohio, and here they reopened their Lodge. Of this Lodge at Marietta, General PUTNAM became the first Junior Warden. In 1789, President WASHINGTON appointed him judge of the Supreme Court of the Northwest territory, and in 1792, he was appointed a brigadier-general under General WAYNE. In 1796 he was made surveyor-general of the United States, and held that office until the accession of Mr. JEFFERSON to the presidency in 1804. He was also a member of the convention that formed a constitution for the State of Ohio in 1802. In every situation of honor or trust with which he was honored by his country, he was found capable, faithful, and true.

General PUTNAM still continued an officer or active member of the "American Union Lodge," and when, in 1808, Lodges had been multiplied in that new State, and a convention met to form a Grand Lodge there, they unanimously made choice of him as their first Grand Master. He never enjoyed the honor, however, of presiding over that body, for he was then three-score and ten years old, and the infirmities of age were upon him. At the next annual communication, therefore, he resigned the office, by the following letter to the Grand Lodge.

"TO THE GRAND LODGE OF THE MOST ANCIENT AND HONORABLE SOCIETY OF FREE AND ACCEPTED MASONS FOR THE STATE OF OHIO, YOUR BROTHER SENDETH *Greeting:*

"It was with high sensibility and gratitude I received the information that the Grand Convention of Masons at Chilicothe, in January last, elected me to the office of Grand Master of our Most Ancient and Honorable Fraternity. But however sensibly I feel the high honor done me by the Convention, and am disposed to promote the interests of the Craft in general, and in this State in particular, I must decline the appointment. My sun is far past its meridian, and is almost set. A few sands only remain in my glass. I am unable to undergo the necessary labors of that high and important office. I am unable to make you a visit at this time, without a sacrifice and hazard of health which prudence forbids.

"May the great Architect, under whose all-seeing eye all Masons profess to labor, have you in his holy keeping, that when our labors here are finished, we may, through the merits of Him that was dead but is now alive and lives forevermore, be admitted into that temple, not made with hands, eternal in the heavens. Amen. So prays your friend and brother,

"RUFUS PUTNAM.

"MARIETTA, December 26, 1808."

With this letter, so full of touching tenderness, we close our Masonic record of General PUTNAM. He survived for many years, and when, upon the first day of May, 1824, he died, all said a good man had gone to his rest. With him it was indeed a rest to which he had long looked forward, confidently believing, that when death divested him of his earthly robes, his Saviour, in whom he trusted, would stand by him to reinvest him with the robes of immortality.

AARON OGDEN,

GOVERNOR OF NEW JERSEY.

AMONG the gallant sons of New Jersey whose patriotism was thoroughly tried during the Revolution, and who were rewarded with high civil office by that State after its close, stands the name of AARON OGDEN. He was born at Elizabethtown on the 3d of December, 1756, and graduated at Princeton, in 1773, at seventeen years of age. Princeton College was at that time the nursery of patriots, and Doctor WITHERSPOON, its president, had the proud satisfaction, when the Revolution commenced, of seeing many of his pupils and graduates enrolled in the service of their country. Among these was AARON OGDEN, the subject of this sketch.

One of the early revolutionary incidents in which he bore a part, was the capture of a British vessel called the "Blue Mountain Valley," lying off Sandy Hook, and bringing her into Elizabethport in the winter of 1775–6. At what time he entered the regular army we have no records to determine. He received a commission in the spring of 1777 (then in his twenty-first year), in the First New Jersey regiment, and continued in the service during the war. He was with General SULLIVAN in the attack upon the Tory forces on Staten Island in August of 1777, at the battle of Brandywine in the following month, and at the battle of Monmouth in the summer of 1778. In this last battle he held the rank of a brigade-major, but served as assistant aid-de-camp to Lord STERLING.

In 1779 he accompanied General SULLIVAN in his expedition against the Indians of New York, in the capacity of aid-de-camp to General MAXWELL. In 1780 he was at the battle of Springfield, in New Jersey, where he had a horse shot under him while on the field as aid of General MAXWELL. When that general resigned his commission in August of that year, OGDEN was appointed to a captaincy of light infantry under LAFAYETTE. While in this capacity, he was intrusted by WASHINGTON, his commander-in-chief, with the execution of a delicate commission relating to ANDRE and ARNOLD. It was while Major ANDRE was under sentence of death as a British spy, and ARNOLD, a fugitive for his treachery, was in the British camp, that feelings of strong commiseration for ANDRE, and a greater desire to inflict a merited punishment on ARNOLD than on him, induced General WASHINGTON to desire to exchange the condemned spy for the arch-traitor. He well knew that a formal proposition to this effect would not be received by the British commander; he therefore inclosed an official account of the trial of ANDRE, together with a letter from the condemned officer, in a package, and under a flag of truce transmitted them to the British headquarters at New York. The execution of this trust was committed to Captain OGDEN. The package he carried contained no allusion to a meditated exchange of ANDRE for ARNOLD, but he was instructed to incidentally suggest to the officer to whom he might deliver the package the idea that such an exchange might perhaps be made.

Captain OGDEN proceeded to execute his trust, and, as was anticipated, while awaiting at the lines of the British army near New York for an answer to his communications, the conversation turned upon the unfortunate ANDRE.

"Is there no way to save his life?" asked the British officer.

"Perhaps it might be done," replied OGDEN, "if Sir HENRY CLINTON would give up ARNOLD."

He told the officer, however, that he had no assurance from WASHINGTON to this effect, but he believed it might be effected if desired. The British officer immediately left Captain OGDEN, and hastened to General CLINTON with the suggestion; but military honor would not permit, what, perhaps, both parties would gladly have done, had not military rules forbid. A request for a parley was, however, sent from CLINTON to WASHINGTON by Captain OGDEN, and three British officers of rank repaired under a flag of truce near the American headquarters, to confer with a corresponding deputation of American officers; but General GREENE who headed the American deputation, refused to confer with the British officers except as private gentlemen, as he assured them that the case of an acknowledged spy admitted of no military negotiation, and the conference ended. The unfortunate ANDRE paid the penalty of a spy, while his more vile accessary, was permitted to hold a military commission in the British army.

Captain OGDEN afterwards accompanied LAFAYETTE in his memorable campaign in Virginia, in 1781. At the siege of Yorktown he gallantly led his company, in storming the left redoubt of the enemy, and received from WASHINGTON his marked approbation. The military operations of the American contest were virtually closed after the capture of CORNWALLIS, but the army was not disbanded until peace was confirmed. During this interim a number of new Masonic lodges were formed in the army, and of one of them Captain OGDEN was a Warden. He had previously been made a Mason, but of the time and place we have no record. On the 2d of September, 1782, the records of the Grand Lodge of Pennsylvania state:

"A petition, signed by twenty brethren, officers in the

Jersey Line, was read, praying for a warrant to hold a travelling Military Lodge, to be attached to said line.

"The same was unanimously granted. The proposed officers were the Rev. ANDREW HUNTER, for Master; JOSEPH J. ANDERSON, Senior Warden, and Captain AARON OGDEN, Junior Warden.—To be numbered 36."

After the close of the war Captain OGDEN studied law, and rose rapidly in the legal profession. He was popular with the people, and in 1800 was one of the presidential electors; a state senator, in 1801; and, in 1812, he was elected governor of the State of New Jersey. He died in 1839, at the age of eighty-three years.

The Rev. ANDREW HUNTER, the Master of the Military Lodge of which Governor OGDEN was Warden, became after the war a chaplain in the navy, and died at Washington in February, 1823, at the age of seventy-five years.

GENERAL MORDECAI GIST,

AN OFFICER OF THE REVOLUTION AND GRAND MASTER OF SOUTH CAROLINA.

General Mordecai Gist was one of the patriots of the Revolution whose name is alike honorably connected with the annals of Masonry and with the history of our country. His ancestors emigrated from England to Maryland at an early day, and settled in Baltimore. He received a mercantile education, and was employed in that business when the war of the Revolution commenced. It is not known at what age, or in what lodge, he became a Mason. Two lodges of Ancient York Masons were chartered in the city of Baltimore, by the Grand Lodge of Pennsylvania, in 1770, and it is probable he was made in one of these, as he had risen to the rank of Worshipful Master previous to the Revolution.

When the war of the Revolution commenced, the young men of Baltimore formed an independent company, of which they elected MORDECAI GIST as captain. This was the first military organization in Maryland for the defence of American liberty. In 1776, Mr. GIST was appointed major of a battalion of Maryland regulars, and bravely led his men in the terrible conflict on Long Island in that year. For his bravery on that occasion he was commissioned as a colonel in 1777; and in 1778, while in command of his Maryland troops, at Locust Hill, near New York, he was attacked by the combined forces of Generals SIMCOE, EMERICK, and TARLETON, of the British army, but he discovered their approach in time to escape from their hands. He was engaged in the battle of Paoli, where the terrible massacre of American troops took place, and distinguished himself soon after at the battles of Germantown and Whitemarsh.

In January of 1779 he was appointed by Congress a brigadier-general in the Continental army, and was honored with the command of the second Maryland brigade. In the winter of 1779–80 he was encamped with his command at the general headquarters of the American army at Morristown in New Jersey.

While in their winter-quarters here, the Masonic Brethren in the army celebrated the festival of St. John the Evangelist. The meeting was held under the charter of the American Union Lodge, and WASHINGTON and a large number of distinguished officers of the American army, who were Masons, attended on the occasion. The Masonic Lodges of America had formerly all owed their existence to, and been dependent upon, the Grand Lodges of Great Britain; but the misfortunes of war had caused all intercourse to cease between them and their parent head; and although some provincial Grand Lodges still existed in this country, they were regarded but as the subordinates of the Masonic powers in Great Britain by whom they were created.

At this army festival of the Masonic Brethren in 1779, a petition was presented, setting forth the condition of Masonry in the new political state of the country, and expressing a desire that a general union of American Masons might take place under one general Grand Master of America. A committee was appointed to take the subject into consideration, consisting of distinguished Masons from each division of the army.

The Committee met in convention on the 7th of January, 1780, and chose General MORDECAI GIST as their President, and General OTHO HOLLAND WILLIAMS as their Secretary. An address to the different Grand Masters of the United States was drawn, considered, and adopted on the occasion, setting forth the same general views as those embraced in the petition they were called on to consider, and asking that measures might be taken to secure a union of all the Lodges of the country under one American head. Copies of this address were sent to the different Grand Masters in the United States; and although the Convention had delicately forborne to mention the name of WASHINGTON as their choice for General Grand Master, yet it was well understood that such was their wish.

In the following spring, General GIST was sent with his command to assist General GATES in South Carolina. While at the North, he and the Brethren in his troops had enjoyed Masonic privileges in the different Masonic Lodges in the army. No Military Lodges existed in the Southern army, and he therefore applied to the Grand Lodge of Pennsylvania for a warrant to hold one in the line under his command, and a warrant was granted, constituting him its Master. This Lodge was numbered 27 on the Pennsylvania Grand Lodge registry. Its warrant bore date, April 4, 1780.

During the same year the battle of Camden, in South Carolina, occurred, in which, although the Americans were defeated by CORNWALLIS, General GIST won for himself an imperishable renown. Even after the battle was irretrievably lost, it is said that he rode from point to point, amidst a storm of fire, and by his own enthusiasm and bravery preserved his broken troops from annihilation. He was afterwards engaged in the conflict at Yorktown, in 1781, and had the proud satisfaction of seeing the haughty CORNWALLIS become a captive to American bravery.

After the capture of CORNWALLIS, General GIST joined the southern division of the army under General

GREENE; and when the army was remodelled in 1782, General GREENE gave him the command of the "light corps." It was a part of his command, under General LAURENS, that dealt one of the last blows to the enemy in an engagement on the banks of the Combahee. Thus was it the fortune of General GIST to fight gallantly for his country from the commencement to the close of the war. He had heard its first clarion notes and its last battle-shout; and when it was closed, he retired to a plantation which he had purchased near Charleston, in South Carolina, and, like WASHINGTON, engaged in agricultural pursuits.

The warrant from the Grand Lodge of Pennsylvania to General GIST, empowering him to hold Lodges in the Maryland line of the army, was, by resolution of that Grand Lodge, vacated at the close of the war; but in 1786 another was granted to him to hold a Local Lodge, with the same registry number (27), at Charleston, South Carolina, by the same Grand Body. This warrant constituted General MORDECAI GIST, Master, and THOMAS B. BOWEN and EPHRAIM MITCHELL, Wardens. In 1787 the Lodges of Ancient York Masons in South Carolina united to form an Independent Grand Lodge for that State; and of this Grand Body General GIST became the first Deputy Grand Master.

The Hon. WILLIAM DRAYTON, chief-justice of the State, was at the same time Grand Master. He was the first Grand Master of Ancient York Masons in that jurisdiction. General GIST was his Deputy in 1787–88–89, and succeeded him as Grand Master in 1790, and held the office for two years, when he was succeeded by Major THOMAS B. BOWEN, who had been his first Senior Warden under his Pennsylvania local Lodge warrant.

It was while General GIST was Grand Master, in 1791, that WASHINGTON visited, as President, the Southern States, on which occasion the Masonic correspondence between these two distinguished Brothers took place which we have given in our sketch of WASHINGTON. It was the last official act of General GIST which we have seen. He died in the following year, in September (1792), leaving two sons, one of whom he named INDEPENDENT, and the other, STATES. He was, at the time of his death, fifty years of age.

INDEX.

B.

C.

K.

L.

O.

P.

Q.

R.

Y.

Z.

ABOUT THE AUTHOR

Sidney Hayden (1813-1890), an active Mason and bookseller, was born in Colesbrook City. On 23 March 1836 he married Florilla E. Miller (1814 - ca. 1869). On 20 March 1840, Hayden, his wife, and their son Julius moved to Athens, Greece where he and his wife had five other children: Algernon Sidney (1843), Albert (1844), Charles (1846), Ruth (1848), and Sidney (1857).

While residing in Athens, Hayden engaged in a variety of activities. He owned and operated a farm during the 1840s and 1850s in order to support his young family.

There is evidence that he may have also dabbled in railroads and real estate during this time. As a member and eventual master, 1863, of the Rural Amity Lodge of Free and Accepted Masons, No. 70, Hayden was very involved in lodge affairs, attending Grand Lodge encampments and collecting Masonic literature. In the early 1860s, Hayden also began to write pieces for Masonic works. He contributed a sketch to a work entitled *Leaflets of Masonic Biography or Sketches of Eminent Free Masons*, which was edited and published by Cornelius Moore, Hayden's close friend and business associate.

Soon after his book was published, Hayden began the research for his own work entitled, *George Washington and his Masonic Compeers.* Throughout the 1860s and 1870s, Hayden travelled through the Mid-Atlantic States as a dealer for both the *Leaflets* and his own *Compeers.* His trips took him through Ohio, Michigan, New York, New Jersey, and Pennsylvania where he introduced his Masonic works at various lodge meetings. Although these ventures as a bookseller were profitable for Hayden, he often expressed regret over his extensive absences from home.

While Hayden travelled, his son Albert kept track of the book sales and also maintained the farm for his father. During the later years of his life, Sidney Hayden retired to his farm in Athens, which was then still managed by Bert, where he died on 4 April 1890.

www.ingramcontent.com/pod-product-compliance
Lightning Source LLC
LaVergne TN
LVHW050916080826
845145LV00001B/102

* 9 7 8 1 7 8 1 0 7 0 7 2 7 *